Inyo-Mono SUV Trails

A guide to forty interesting and scenic four-wheeling excursions in California's Inyo and Mono Counties

Roger Mitchell

Two roads diverged in the woods, and I-
I took the one less traveled by,
And that has made all the difference.

Robert Frost

Inyo-Mono SUV Trails

A guide to forty interesting and scenic four-wheeling excursions in California's Inyo and Mono Counties

Roger Mitchell

All photos by the author except where noted

Track & Trail Publications
Oakhurst California

Published by Track & Trail Publications
P.O. Box 1247
Oakhurst CA 93644

© 2003 Roger Mitchell
All rights reserved
Printed in the United States of America

First Edition 2003

Cover photo: Laurel Canyon

Other current Track & Trail Publications:
 Death Valley SUV Trails
 High Sierra SUV Trails Volume I - The East Side
 High Sierra SUV Trails Volume II - The Western Slope

Other titles currently in preparation:
 Great Basin SUV Trails Volume I - Southwestern Nevada
 Great Basin SUV Trails Volume II - Northwestern Nevada
 High Sierra SUV Trails Volume III – The Far North Country
 Southern California SUV Trails Volume I – The Mojave Desert
 Grand Canyon SUV Trails

Maps, book design and layout by Track & Trail Publications

Library of Congress Cataloging-in-Publication data:

Mitchell, Roger, 1938-
  Inyo-Mono SUV Trails, 1st ed.
  Bibliographic references (p.) and index
  Includes ISBN Number 0-9707115-3-0
  (1) Guidebook – Inyo and Mono Counties (Calif.) – (2) History–Mines and mining

This book is dedicated to Jim Roberts, a friend, a companion of many campfires, and a fellow four-wheeler of the 1950s.

The author and publisher of this guide make no representations as to the condition and safety of any of the routes described in this publication. At the time of this printing, all route descriptions were reasonably up to date as far as is known to the author. Keep in mind, however, that conditions can and do change, sometimes in a matter of minutes. Backroad travelers should enter the mountains and deserts with their vehicles in good mechanical condition, carrying extra clothing, water, and food, should a breakdown or other emergency occur. It is recommended that each vehicle carry a detailed map of the area to be visited, and that drivers first inquire about road conditions at the office of the appropriate land management agency before attempting any of these routes.

It should also be noted that administrative actions by the U.S. Forest Service, the Bureau of Land Management, the Bureau of Indian Affairs, the State Department of Fish & Game, and the City of Los Angeles Department of Water & Power can limit and otherwise impact the visitor's use of roads without any prior notice. Roads that are open one day may be closed the next.

Finally, unknown to the author, some of the routes described herein may cross unposted private property. Please respect the owner's rights, and obey any NO TRESPASSING signs that may be lawfully posted.

Contents

Acknowledgments

As usual, I am indebted to my long-suffering wife, Loris, who has been my traveling companion, my scribe, my research assistant, my indispensable proofreader, and my literary critic. Without her support and assistance, this book would not have been possible. Another key link in the production chain was Glenn Harmelin, whose computer skills also greatly contributed to the project.

Traveling companions Dan and Debbie Carter helped lengthen the campfires and thus shorten the many nights. The staff at several museums kindly gave me access to their library and research materials. My profound thanks go to Beth Sennet Porter of the Eastern California Museum, as well as Barbara Moss and Jim Sailor of the Laws Railroad Museum, for help in providing historic photographs from their extensive collections. Likewise, Rich McCutchan was very gracious in making his extensive collection of historic photos available when I was unable to obtain images from other sources. Truman Denio of CalTrans District 9 Office kindly provided background material for the flooding incident on Highway 6 below Milner Canyon. My thanks also go to botanist Anne Halford of the BLM's Bishop Field Office, who patiently assisted me with plant taxonomy. State Park Ranger and rail fan Rod Duff at Bodie State Park kindly provided details of the Bodie & Benton Railway that I was unable to obtain from other sources.

I sometimes tried the patience of county library staffs in Lone Pine, Independence, Bishop, Mammoth Lakes and Bridgeport, but they always came through with a smile. Also supportive were the very professional staffs of the USGS Library in Menlo Park, and the library staff of the California Division of Mines and Geology in Sacramento.

Introduction

The roots of this guide go back to the 1968-1973 era, when La Siesta Press published my previous works: *Death Valley Jeep Trails*, *Inyo Mono Jeep Trails*, and *Western Nevada Jeep Trails*. I have revisited all of those old jeep trails, updated the route descriptions, and added quite a few new ones. If you enjoy following this guide, you might look for our companion volumes, *Death Valley SUV Trails*, *High Sierra SUV Trails Volume I – The East Side*, and *High Sierra SUV Trails Volume II – The Western Slope,* all published by Track & Trail Publications. Other titles in this series are being prepared.

Unfortunately, off-road vehicle recreation is often associated with acts of vandalism, destruction of our natural resources, and other criminal acts. In doing this series of *SUV Trails,* it has been my hope that I could pass on a little appreciation of our western heritage, both natural and historical. You will notice that many of the routes described lead to old mining camps and other historic sites. The author fully acknowledges his fascination with the history of the west. However, I have tried to make this more than just another ghost town guide. Many of the historic sites visited are little known and seldom visited. I attempt to provide an adequate historic description without creating a doctoral dissertation. Along the way, I also try to point out interesting tidbits of natural history and geology, things not covered in most ghost town guides.

If you are a dedicated rock crawler, or simply interested in getting your motorcycle or dune buggy up some hill, then this guide is certainly not for you. But if you are truly interested in exploring the forgotten corners of Inyo and Mono Counties, not readily accessible to most, then read on and perhaps this modest guide will be of interest.

Most of the routes described are rough backroads suitable only for vehicles with high clearance. Often, but not always, four-wheel drive is needed. I have attempted to provide practical information describing the time required, miles involved, and degree of difficulty to be expected. Pay particular attention to warnings in bold face type.

In summary then, this publication is a bit different from other guidebooks you may have used. I hope you will find these outings interesting and these route descriptions helpful to your enjoyment of the land. Please remember to tread very lightly upon the land, and leave the landscape just as you found it, so that the next person can enjoy it, too.

A Word of Warning

Although most of the roads and trails described herein have been used by the author for the last forty or more years, they were, nevertheless, all re-scouted within two years prior to the printing of this book. The route descriptions were accurate at the time they were last rechecked. Conditions change, however, sometimes in a matter of minutes. Bad roads become graded, and good roads can become flooded, washed out, or buried by landslides. A section of trail that has been Class I or II for the last fifty years may deteriorate to Class V very suddenly. A single thunderstorm may make a road suddenly dangerous or impassable. **The reader must exercise great caution and use common sense when traveling any of these routes. Never drive anyplace where you cannot see ahead. When in doubt always stop and scout the route ahead on foot. If possible, have a passenger slowly guide you through difficult places. Stream crossings warrant particular attention for water depth, current, and bottom conditions. Remember, the Inyo-Mono Country is a very lonely land. If your vehicle gets stuck or breaks down, you are on your own. Help may be a very long distance away.**

The number one rule in backcountry exploration is to let someone know where you are going, when you expect to return, and then to check in when you do return. This simple procedure could save your life. Of course, two vehicles are safer than one. Either way, go prepared. Always carry plenty of extra water, food, gasoline, and a few simple mechanics' tools. Even a rudimentary knowledge of automotive mechanics may get you out of a serious jam. Every backcountry rig should be permanently equipped with a toolbox, wire, electrical tape, tire repair kit, and an assortment of nuts and bolts. Vehicles larger than a motorcycle should also carry a shovel, a tire pump, and a tow chain. Other survival essentials include matches, an adequate first aid kit, canteens of water, flashlights, and warm jackets for all (see *Appendix D*). If you should become stuck, stalled, or otherwise stranded, be calm. Analyze your situation. If somebody knows where you are and you are prepared, there will be little to worry about. You will survive! Unprepared, you will have some crucial decisions to make.

Be aware, too, that public land managing agencies such as the United States Forest Service and the Bureau of Land Management can administratively close a road or area with little or no advance notice. One must always heed the signs placed by these agencies.

In summary then, be vigilant, be cautious, and be safe. Remember: no guarantee is made that the reader will find the trail as described.

The Ten Commandments
for Four-Wheelers

Off-road driving has received a lot of bad press in recent years, occasionally with some justification. Responsible four-wheelers will follow these common sense "Ten Commandments":

1. **Do** *Tred Lightly* on the Land. Follow established roads, and don't make new ones. Make camp where others have camped before you. Pack out your own garbage. There is nobody else who is going to cleanup after you.
2. **Don't** go off without letting someone know where you are going and when you expect to return.
3. **Do** go well prepared for any contingency.
4. **Don't** go off without a proper map.
5. **Do** the necessary preventative maintenance on your vehicle before you leave home.
6. **Don't** travel alone; a caravan of two or more vehicles is always safer.
7. **Do** be very careful with fire. Be sure your campfire is dead out when you leave it.
8. **Don't** disturb archaeological sites. They may be of great value to science, but not if they are looted.
9. **Do** respect private property, and heed *No Trespassing* signs.
10. **Don't** enter old mines. Most are simply unsafe.

TREAD

LIGHTLY!

ON PUBLIC AND PRIVATE LAND

Acronyms

In order to economize in the use of words, I have resorted to the use of initials in certain frequently used word groups. Hopefully, these initials will not sound foreign to the reader, as we tend to use them this way in everyday speech.

ATV   All terrain vehicle usually not licensed for highway use.

BLM   Bureau of Land Management, a federal agency under the Department of the Interior responsible for the multiple use management of millions of acres of federal land outside of our national parks, national forests, and national wildlife preserves.

DFG   Department of Fish & Game, an agency of the State of California responsible for managing the state's wildlife.

DWP   Department of Water and Power, an agency of the City of Los Angeles and a major property owner in the Owens Valley.

INF   Inyo National Forest.

JEEP   A registered trademark of a specific auto manufacturer, but I use the term, both upper and lower case, in a generic sense, to include all four-wheel drive vehicles.

OHV   Off highway vehicle including ATVs, motorcycles and four-wheel drive vehicles.

NPS   National Park Service, a federal agency under the Department of the Interior.

SUV   Sport Utility Vehicle.

TOI   Toiyabe National Forest.

USFS   United States Forest Service, a federal agency under the Department of Agriculture responsible for the multiple use management of millions of acres of federally owned forest lands.

USGS   United States Geological Survey, a federal agency under the Department of the Interior responsible for mapping and geological studies.

The Mitchell Scale

Everything seems to have its standard of measurement. Earthquakes have their Richter Scale. Temperature has its degrees. Sound has its decibels. Thus it is that I have attempted to quantify the degree of difficulty to the various SUV trails I describe. This scale, which I modestly call *The Mitchell Scale,* was blatantly stolen from rock climbers and mountaineers, who have their own peculiar brand of madness. It goes from Class I - the easiest, to Class VI - the impossible.

CLASS I: This includes just about any kind of semi-improved, not normally maintained road over which you can safely maneuver a standard automobile. A Class I route should cause no one problems.

CLASS II: This road is a bit more rough than Class I, and may have a high center or deep potholes requiring vehicles with greater clearance. Four-wheel drive may not be absolutely necessary, but extreme care should be taken if you don't have a vehicle with high clearance.

CLASS III: Here high clearance and four-wheel drive are a necessity, perhaps low range gears and limited slip differentials, too. But the route is not so difficult that your SUV should be damaged if reasonable care is taken.

CLASS IV: The going gets rougher still. If you are not a skillful and experienced off-road driver, the body of your vehicle may suffer a little. You may wish to have a passenger outside the vehicle to act as a spotter, guiding you through the tight places. To avoid damage, drivers of SUVs should attempt these areas with extreme caution.

CLASS V: Most people will turn back before attempting a road of this severity. It is highly questionable whether the abuse your vehicle is taking is really worth the effort. Vehicle damage is always a possibility. Skid plates under everything are a must. Don't try this trail alone!

CLASS VI: This is for the foolhardy only. The route is so extreme that the use of a winch or two is often required. "Road building" and other creative feats of engineering are a likely necessity. You certainly don't want to try this trail without a second vehicle along, one equipped with a master mechanic, a welding torch, a complete set of spare parts, and a world-wide satellite communications system. No Class VI routes are described in this book.

Class I

Class II

Class III

Class IV

Class V (May require a winch)

Historic Bridgeport

Bridgeport around 1915.
(Photo courtesy of Laws Railroad Museum)

Mono County has the second oldest continuously occupied
court house in California. It was built in 1880-1881.

Learn more about Mono County history with a visit to the
Mono County Museum, in a schoolhouse built in 1880.

Chapter I

Trails Out of Bridgeport

The county seat of Mono County, Bridgeport is nestled in a valley drained by the East Walker River. To the west of this 6500' basin, the eleven and twelve thousand-foot peaks of Yosemite National Park dominate the skyline. To the north is the Sweetwater Range with 11,673' Mt. Patterson. In the summer, the weather is very pleasant in Bridgeport, but, in the winter, this enclosed basin tends to be very cold.

Bridgeport's written history started on the bitter cold night of January 25, 1844, when John C. Fremont's second expedition west camped in the valley on the way to California. In 1857 a German emigrant named Cord Norst is said to have found gold in one of the streams that flows through the valley. Two years later a large group of Mormon prospectors moved in and established Dogtown, the first settlement in "Big Meadows" as the Bridgeport Valley was then called. About this same time, gold was discovered in nearby Bodie and Aurora, and thousands of hopeful miners poured into the area. Food, lumber, hay, mining equipment, and supplies of all kinds were all needed by those camps, and Bridgeport became a supply point for the mines to the east. In 1860 Napoleon Bonaparte Hunewill came to the valley, started a ranch, and provided much of the meat, eggs, vegetables, hay and lumber for the camps. His neighbor, George Byron Day, provided the teams and freight wagons. The California legislature created Mono County on April 24, 1861, with the county seat established in Aurora, but, soon thereafter, a problem arose. In 1863 a controversial state boundary survey determined that Aurora was in Nevada! So Mono County needed a new center of local government. There were several candidates. People living in Monoville thought the courthouse should be there. The folks of Owensville (present day Bishop) thought the county seat should be there. But in the end it was the citizens of Big Meadow who prevailed, and thus the town of Bridgeport was born. Visitors with an interest in history should certainly visit the second oldest courthouse in the state, the old stone jail building behind it, and one block west, the Mono County Museum in the old schoolhouse.

On its half-mile long Main Street, Bridgeport has half a dozen motels, several places to eat, two markets, an auto parts store, and, of course, gas stations and sporting goods stores. There is even a self-service car wash. There are seven U.S. Forest Service campgrounds to the east and southeast of town in the Buckeye, Honeymoon Flat and Twin Lakes areas, plus several privately operated resorts that offer camping.

1

Searching for Fremont's Lost Cannon

Primary Attraction:	A needle in a haystack search for a cannon abandoned in 1844 by Lt. John C. Fremont's Second Expedition west to California.
Time Required:	This journey can take a few hours to a lifetime.
Miles Involved:	Variable depending on your persistence and your determination.
Degree of Difficulty:	The roads are generally no worse than Class II.

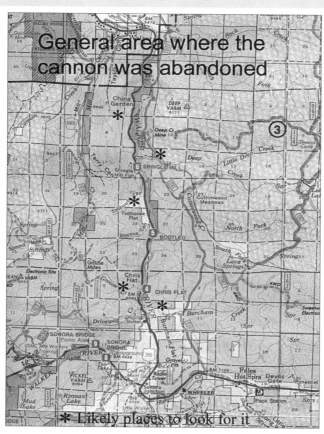

It was a bitter cold January in 1844 that found John C. Fremont and his party of forty men, including the famous scout, Kit Carson, wallowing in crotch-deep snows near Fales Hot Springs on the West Walker River. An Army officer, Fremont was married to the daughter of influential Senator Thomas Hart Benson of Missouri. He was given the responsibility to take a detachment from the Army's Corps of Topographical Engineers to scout railroad routes west across the continent. (Never mind that much of the territory he was going into belonged to Mexico. He was, in essence, on a spy mission to northwest Mexico, laying the geographical foundation for the United States' expansion westward to the Pacific Ocean.) Fremont had already made one scouting trip west in 1842. He was only a Lieutenant at the time, but thanks to his father-in-law, Fremont was given broad latitude in his mission.

Major-General John C. Fremont two decades later during the Civil War.

Fremont's second expedition west left St. Louis in May of 1843. Because of the threat posed by grizzly bears and the possibility of hostile Indians along the way, Fremont thought that his party's muzzle loading muskets might be supplemented with a small inconspicuous cannon. Obviously, one does not use a cannon against a grizzly bear, but one might use a cannon against Mexican troops defending their country.

Over the objections of some quartermaster at the Jefferson Barracks in St. Louis, Senator Benson cleared the way for his son-in-law to pick up a mountain howitzer. It was a twelve-pounder of French design. The US Army had purchased several from the French, and then several dozen more look-alikes were purchased from a Boston company between 1836 and 1841. The cannon was normally pulled on its carriage by two mules, but could easily be broken down and packed by the animals if the country became too rough. The cannon and carriage had a combined weight of 525 pounds, and had an overall length of about six feet. The powder and shot weighed twelve pounds per shot fired, and it is thought that they took enough to fire the weapon fifty times. Thus, the cannon and its ammunition added another one thousand pounds to the expedition's already heavy load.

Fremont's route to the west took him across the Oregon Trail, which he mapped to the Pacific Ocean, and then south down Western Nevada. During this incredible journey of well over 1,000 miles, Fremont's diary never once mentions the need to use the cannon to fight off a grizzly bear attack. It was once prepared to repel an attack of Sioux Indians, but was never needed. Later, however, the cannon was fired to impress some potentially troublesome Paiutes in northern Nevada. A few practice rounds were also fired from time to time. The expedition's gunner, Louis Zindel, proved he could hit a four-foot high post at a distance of a quarter of a mile. His skill arose from the fact that he had once served in the Prussian army as a sergeant of artillery.

The soldiers and mountain men in Fremont's party had wanted to abandon the cumbersome field piece months before back at South Pass, Wyoming, but Fremont insisted it be brought along. After encountering deep snows in the Bridgeport Valley on January 25th, the cry once again went out to leave the cannon behind. Fremont knew he was rapidly approaching California with its Mexican garrisons at Monterey and Benicia, and once again he refused to abandon it. The main party, weary and short of rations, camped just north of what is now Bridgeport on January 25th and 26th. On the 27th, Fremont and another man moved up the Huntoon Valley to reconnoiter the party's path. Fremont's diaries are very good up to this point. Unfortunately, the route descriptions for the next two days are confusing and ambiguous.

Fremont made camp here in Huntoon Valley on the night of January 27, 1844.

Charles Preuss, who brought the main party up the Huntoon Valley, made a map which shows their campsite on the 28th at what is now Tollhouse Flat, on the west side of the West Walker River about halfway through its canyon. This infers that the party forded the river at some point. The Preuss map shows their position on the night of the 29th in what is now the Antelope Valley. Fremont's diary, however, suggests that the group did not cross the West Walker River after passing Fales Hot Springs, but turned north to camp north of Burcham Flat on the night of the 28th. Why the two accounts differ remains a mystery. A third possibility is that the group spent the night of January 28th near Grouse Meadows, on the western side high above the river.

The author favors the second theory, as no river crossing is mentioned, and an icy event like that seems noteworthy to record in a diary. Whatever the scenario, deep drifts finally broke Fremont's will to continue on with the cannon. It was abandoned somewhere along the Walker River in northwestern Mono County. Has the "lost" cannon ever been found? This aspect of the story is just as controversial as where it was abandoned.

Some say the cannon was found during the Civil War by a Virginia City newsman, who took it back home. This cannon later went to Lake Tahoe for guest appearances, and, ultimately, in 1941 ended up at the Nevada State Museum where it is still on display. However, there are credible serious technical doubts that the cannon in Carson City could be the one dragged by Fremont's party. Most serious researchers don't believe this, and suspect this cannon came from Fort Churchill in 1861. They believe it was transferred to Captain Augustine Pray, who had organized a band of pro-Union volunteers in Glenbrook, Nevada.

A second story has the cannon found by two prospectors in the early 1860s, with it eventually being recovered and moved to Virginia City as discouragement to local Southern sympathizers, of which there were many. After the Civil War this cannon disappeared and reappeared a number of times, but was finally sold for scrap and melted down during World War I. There are credible arguments against this scenario, too.

Still a third theory is that the cannon still lies out there, hidden in a willow thicket or aspen grove, just waiting to be found. I subscribe to this possibility, and my bet is that the Fremont party did not cross the river to camp at Shingle Mill Flat or anywhere else. I particularly don't think they climbed some 2000 feet to camp at Grouse Meadows on the night of the 28th. My guess is that Fremont moved north from Burcham Flat, onto the high wide shelf above the east bank of the river. Travel here in deep snows would be easier than down in the river canyon below. However, reaching the defile of Deep Creek that stretched across their path was the final straw, and the cannon was finally abandoned there. Tireless

Fremont cannon researcher Ernest Lewis thinks the cannon is somewhere up off the saddle on an unnamed mountain identified as a highpoint labeled 8,422' on the topographic map. It is more likely in a bowl on the north face of that topographic feature. He may be right. His book, *The Fremont Cannon – High Up and Far Back,* is well researched and certainly worth reading.

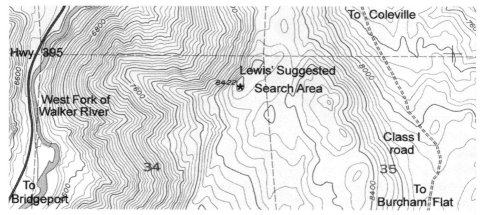

Lost cannon researcher Ernest Lewis thinks the cannon is in this area.

This is an interesting story you say, but what does all this have to do with *Inyo-Mono SUV Trails*? Well, dear reader, that cannon may still be out there somewhere just waiting for some enterprising four-wheeler to find it. If it lay on some sage-covered flat, it would have been found years ago, even though the carriage might have rotted away. But if it had been pushed over the edge of Deep Creek, for example, it could quickly be overgrown by aspen and willows and lost forever. The barrel was made of brass (or bronze if a Boston-made copy), was 37 inches long, and weighed 225 pounds. It should survive the 150 years since its abandonment, although months of tedious exploration with a metal detector might be required to find it. But where should you start looking?

If you agree with my theory, go north out of Bridgeport on Highway 395 through Huntoon Valley, through Devil's Gate and past Fales Hot Springs. Just before reaching the Forest Service Wheeler Guard Station, a good graded road turns north off the highway, doubles back to the east on the north side of the creek and then turns north again. This is Forest Road 031. It eventually rejoins Highway 395 in the Antelope Valley, but Fremont's cannon never got that far.

Proceed north across the vast expanse of Burcham Flat. Burcham Creek is crossed, and this is one place where Fremont's cannon could lie. There is a Class II road off to the left going down the creek a ways. This is the first area that should be carefully checked. Search Burcham Creek for a couple of miles on either side of Forest Road 031.

View north of the country beyond Burcham Flat.

Once this is done to your satisfaction, continue north up the graded road. At a point 4.1 miles from Highway 395, an 8066-foot high point is reached. Here a Class II road goes east to Lava Springs and on to Lobdell Lake and points to the north. Don't take this side road, but carefully check out the country on the east side of the graded road as it descends into the Deep Creek Drainage. At a point 2.4 miles beyond the summit, a side road goes east to Cottonwood Meadows at an elevation of 7200 feet. This side road provides access to Deep Creek. It is in the two or three miles above or below Cottonwood Meadows that I think Fremont's cannon lies hidden just waiting to be discovered.

In the unlikely event that you do find the old fieldpiece, the location should be promptly reported to the U.S. Forest Service at the Bridgeport Ranger Station, the agency responsible for administering this federal land. Otherwise your troubles could just be beginning. Just the act of attempting to recover the cannon could run you afoul of the law. First, the Army might want their cannon back. Do you want to face the wrath of the U.S. Army? Then there is the U.S. Forest Service, who would no doubt view the cannon as an historical resource. Tampering with it might prompt them to ask the United States Attorney to charge you with violating the *National Antiquities Act of 1906* and the *Archaeological Resources Protection Act of 1979*. Do you want to take on the Department of Justice? There is also the problem with the Attorney General of the State of California. Section 12303 of the *California Penal Code* prohibits the possession of firearms in excess of .60 caliber. Trust me folks, a twelve-pound mountain howitzer is larger than .60 caliber!

So is the search worth the effort if you cannot keep the gun? It most certainly is! Finding the old cannon would finally dispel and put to rest all of the various theories as to where the piece was abandoned and what happened to it. Those questions have been puzzling historians and researchers for over 150 years. The cannon's discovery would prove that it wasn't melted down for scrap during World War I. It would prove that it is not the Nevada State Museum cannon.

So there you are Buckaroos and Buckarettes. Put the family SUV in four-wheel drive and go out there and find that old cannon. And call me when you do (right after you call the District Ranger)!

Fremont's mountain howitzer is believed to look very similar
to this one on display at the Nevada State Museum in Carson City.

Fremont's cannon might also look like this one on display at the Ordnance
Museum at the U.S. Army's Aberdeen Proving Ground in Maryland.

Freemont's party fighting the snow.
(Drawing by Steeple Davis)

2

Silverado Canyon

Special Features:	The site of what was once a very impressive ore mill, and miles of high mountain roads to explore.
Time Required:	This outing can be coupled with Excursion #3 or #4 for a full day of exploration.
Miles Involved:	From downtown Bridgeport to the Silverado millsite, the distance is a little more than 22 miles, of which only four miles are dirt roads.
Degree of Difficulty:	The road to the millsite is generally Class II, with perhaps a little Class III in the last half mile.
Remarks:	The roads above Silverado Canyon will likely be blocked by heavy snow from November through May, and even the millsite at 7,600 feet is likely to be in snow from December through March.

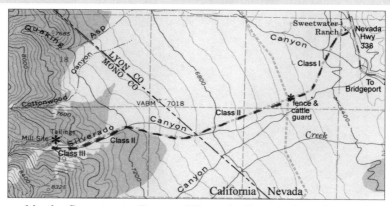

Located in the Sweetwater Range, Silverado Canyon is at the northern end of a highly mineralized band that starts to the southeast in Frying Pan Canyon and ends in Silverado Canyon some four miles to the northwest. At the southern end of this zone, the ore contained mostly gold with a little silver. As the mineralized zone went north, the gold content became less and the silver greater. The two principal mines of Silverado Canyon produced mostly silver, although gold was also recovered in the milling process. The mill originally built for the Kentuck Mine later processed ore from the Silverado Mine as well.

To find the site of the great mill in Silverado Canyon, take California State Route 182 north out of Bridgeport. After 12.5 miles the road becomes Nevada Route 338 as you cross the state line. A little over six miles into Nevada you will come to the Sweetwater Ranch on the left. Turn here, where a U.S. Forest Service sign reads *Silverado Canyon*, and note your odometer reading. The road passes corrals and seems to go through the middle of the ranch. Nevertheless, this is a public road. After 1.1 miles, the road passes through a fence and forks; take the right fork, which is Forest Road 191. The left fork, Forest Road 198, goes on to the sites of Star City, Boulder Flat and Belfort (see Excursion #4).

The road begins as Class I, but within a mile it deteriorates to Class II as you cross back into California. At a point 2.2 miles from the highway, a side road left goes to the site of Clinton (see Excursion #3). Silverado Canyon is entered three miles from State Route 338. After traveling 3.6 miles from the highway, the foundations of a once huge ore mill are seen on the canyon wall to the right.

Initially it was the Kentuck Mine whose output fed the insatiable appetite of this mill. At first the rich ores of the Kentuck Mine went by pack mule down to the relatively crude stamp mill in Clinton. Before long a wagon road was pushed up Silverado Canyon to the mine. Now, for the first time, large quantities of ore could be moved. A small mill was built in the bottom of Silverado Canyon. It was kept busy. Between 1880 until its closing in 1884, the Kentuck Mine is said to have produced a half million dollars in ore.

After the Kentuck Mine closed, activity moved across the canyon to the Silverado Mine. A half-mile long aerial tramway was built to transport the ore from the mine down to the mill. At first the mill utilized a cyanide process to separate the silver and gold from the rock. The disused power plant on Green Creek, nine miles south of Bridgeport, was pressed into service again in the 1920s when a new 32-mile long power line was brought into Silverado Canyon.

This generator, on display at the Mono County Museum in
Bridgeport, was installed on Green Creek, once provided
power to Bodie, and later ran the mill in Silverado Canyon.

With the coming of electricity into Silverado Canyon, the mill changed to a flotation system, raising its capacity from one hundred tons a day to 150 tons per day. The flotation process also recovered more of the precious metals than the cyanide method. After 90,000 tons of ore passed through its doors, the flotation mill shut down in 1938.

The mill site of the Kentuck Mine in Silverado Canyon.

From the millsite, Class III roads go up the north and south walls of Silverado Canyon. Above the mill, the road on the north side goes up to the head of Silverado Canyon to a mine at 10,000 feet. The road on the south side goes up to the north side of Ferris Canyon, where the Kentuck Mine is situated at 9800 feet. These roads are breathtaking in their beauty, geologically interesting, and fun to explore. They lead to remote cabins and old mines. **Warning: Stay out of the underground workings. They are not safe to enter.**

3

Clinton

Special Features:	This excursion visits the faint remains of a flash-in-the-pan mining camp of the 1880s. If you come in here in early October, you may be rewarded with an abundant crop of piñon nuts, as well as a spectacular display of quaking aspen in their full fall colors.
Time Required:	Couple this outing with Excursion #2 or #4 for a full day of backroad exploration.
Miles Involved:	It is nineteen miles by State Highways 182 and 338 from Bridgeport to the Silverado Canyon Road. From there it is four miles by dirt roads to the site of Clinton.
Degree of Difficulty:	Generally the dirt roads to Clinton are no worse than Class II.
Remarks:	Situated at an elevation of 7,600 feet, access to the site of Clinton may be blocked by snow during the winter months.

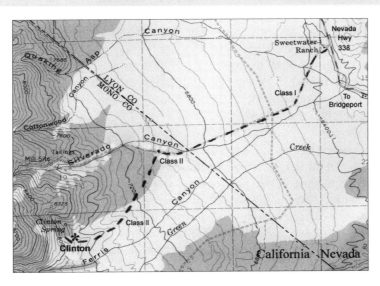

Clinton was the largest and most long-lived of the half a dozen mining camps that sprang up in the Sweetwater Range. To find this lonely and forgotten camp, take California State Route 182 north out of Bridgeport. After 12.5 miles the road becomes Nevada Route 338 as the state line is crossed. Slightly more than six miles into Nevada you will come to the historic Sweetwater Ranch on the left. Turn left here where a USFS sign reads *Silverado Canyon*. Note your odometer reading as you leave the pavement. The road passes corrals and seems to go through the middle of the ranch. After 1.1 miles, the road passes through a gate and immediately forks. Take the right fork, which is Forest Road 191. The left fork, Forest Road 198, goes on to the sites of Star City, Boulder Flat and Belfort (see Excursion #4).

Our road begins as Class I, but within a mile deteriorates to Class II as it re-enters California. A tenth of a mile beyond the state line, a Class II road goes off to the south; turn left here. You are leaving the Silverado Canyon drainage to soon enter Ferris Canyon. After winding through the piñon forest for a little more than a mile, you will come to an open meadow area that was once the eastern suburb of the mining camp of Clinton. The road goes on, passing the ruins of the old Summers Consolidated Mill on the left. Now just a set of tracks through the sage, the road swings around to the right. It passes the mute stone walls of an old structure and then abruptly ends in an aspen grove.

Clinton was one of the first of the many mining camps in the Sweetwater Range. Although you would never know it by looking around today, Clinton was also the largest of these old camps. It all began in 1881 with the discovery of the Kentuck Mine just three miles to the west by pack trail. A town was needed to support the mine and its miners, and the head of this little valley was the nearest flat spot with a reliable source of water. Thus Clinton was born by necessity. By June of 1882, Clinton could boast of some forty buildings scattered along its east-west Main Street. There were a couple saloons, of course, but also a general store, a bakery, a butcher shop, a blacksmith's shop, a livery stable, a boot maker, two assay offices and a boarding house. In May of 1883, a school opened with eighteen students.

Things were not going well with the mines, however. Almost from the very beginning, ownership of the Kentuck Mine was disputed, leading to years of litigation. Ownership of the Mineral Chief Mine was also challenged, and while the litigants were squabbling, it filled with water.

Lawsuits not withstanding, most disputes in Clinton were handled in the streets in a more expeditious manner. Indeed, the January 4, 1884, edition of the *Bridgeport Chronicle-Union* carried the following brief news item:

> *A China woman died in Clinton on Wednesday. As it was the first*
> *natural death that ever occurred there, the miners feel quite proud.*

While the mines faltered, Clinton remained a viable community until about 1891. By 1892 it had lost its status as a voting precinct. Today scarcely a trace of the town remains. One can find traces of a dozen former buildings, although sometimes that evidence consists of no more than looking at a geometric pattern in the vegetation.

Although largely overgrown with vegetation, the foundations of the Summers brothers' stamp mill can still be found at the western end of Main Street. In another area, the remains of its boiler lie rusting among the sagebrush. It seems unlikely that Clinton will ever again hear the ceaseless pounding of those stamps.

Site of the Summers brothers' stamp mill in downtown Clinton.

The rusting innards of a steam boiler lie hidden in the sage.

4

Belfort, Boulder Flat and Star City

Primary Attraction:	In this excursion you will see traces of three obscure mining camps, coupled with some outstanding high mountain scenery.
Time Required:	This is an all day outing out of Bridgeport, but one that can be combined with excursions to Clinton and Silverado for a full day of four-wheeling adventures.
Miles Involved:	It is nearly nineteen miles by highway from Bridgeport to the Sweetwater Ranch turn-off, and then another nine miles to the road's highpoint at Belfort. In addition, one can drive another 25 miles exploring the various side roads in this area.
Degree of Difficulty:	Most of the lower elevation roads are Class II, with the higher portions Class III.
Remarks:	Deep snow will cover all but the lower portions of these roads from late November well into May.

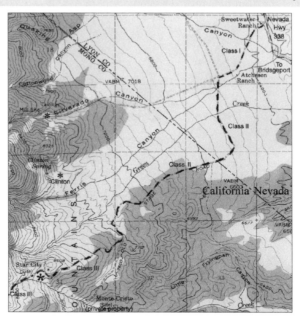

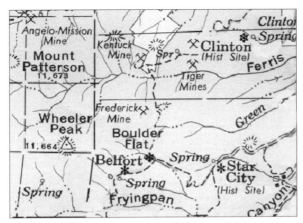

Old mining camps of the Sweetwater Range

Virginia City, Bodie, and Aurora were three of the most famous mining camps east of the High Sierra. Much has been written about them. Three of the least known of the mining camps were Belfort, Boulder Flat and Star City. Practically nothing has been written about them.

To find this forgotten trio, take California State Route 182 north out of Bridgeport. The road becomes Nevada Route 338 as the state line is crossed. Six miles into Nevada you will come to the Sweetwater Ranch on the left. The elevation here is 6,400 feet. Turn here where a USFS sign reads "Silverado Canyon". The road passes corrals and seems to go through the middle of the ranch. After a mile, the road passes through a gate and immediately forks; take the left fork. The right fork goes on to the site of Clinton (see Excursion #3) and to the mines of Silverado Canyon (see Excursion #2).

By turning left, the now Class II road follows a fence line, fords several small streams, goes through a cattle gate and re-enters California. Entering the piñon forest, it swings to the west. Several roads go off to the sides, but stay on the road showing the most signs of use. At a point 4.8 miles from Highway 338, take the right fork. After a tenth of a mile, a second fork is reached; again keep to the right. (Both of the roads to the left go to the sites of other mining camps, Monte Cristo and Cameron, but a locked gate prevents access.)

The right fork heads westward, and the road deteriorates to Class III in places, as it climbs the brushy hillside. After 1.4 miles from the last fork (6.3 miles from the highway) and at an elevation of 8,500 feet, you will come to a flat meadow area with some tailings on the slope to the north. Although little remains, this was the site of Star City.

History failed to record much about what went on here. We do know that prospectors were here during the 1860s. The camp did not amount to much until September of 1878, when J.H. Patterson and Anthony Hiatt discovered a promising outcrop containing gold and silver. Their find would become the Thorobrace Mine. By the early 1880s the little flat was covered with tents, as miners burrowed deep into the ground in search of riches. Other mines of Star City were the Rattlesnake and the Lucky Lady. All were located in the canyon to the north. One by one a few timbered buildings arose, the largest of which was a boarding house. Within ten years, however, the miners had folded their tents and the buildings had been dismantled to be used again elsewhere.

This flat was the site of Star City in the late 1870s.

From Star City, a Class III road built in the 1870s continues climbing steeply up the hillside, and, after two miles of spectacular four-wheeling, the site of Boulder Flat is reached. The elevation here is 10,200 feet. When we first visited the site in the 1960s, three old log cabins were still standing. Thirty years later, only two have survived. Boulder Flat dates back to the 1880s, although it is not known if the log cabins are that old. Their construction offers no clues. Boulder Flat was where the miners lived, because the terrain was flat here. The mines they worked in were on the nearby mountainside. By looking to the west, foot trails to a mine on the side of Wheeler Peak can still be seen.

Boulder Flat in 1968

Boulder Flat in 2000

From Boulder Flat, roads go left and right. The Class II and III right fork goes 1.3 miles north, up through a grove of Bristlecone pine trees to dead-end at the Frederick Mine, the site of the old M & M tunnel. Along the way, there are magnificent views down into Ferris Canyon. Just below the road, the tailings dump of the Frederick Mine has revealed minerals containing clusters of tiny quartz crystals. **Warning: do not enter any of the underground workings; they are not safe!**

The road to the Frederick Mine is above 10,000 feet.

If you take the left fork at Boulder Flat, the Class III road climbs up the hill 0.6 miles to a small lake and a spring. Both are fed by a long-lasting snow cornice near the ridgetop. This basin is actually a glacial cirque, a remnant of the Pleistocene Ice Age.

Here at the elevation of 10,500 feet is the site of Belfort, the last in our trio of mining camps. Only a single log cabin remains to mark the spot of this community of the 1860s.

1968   2000

The last cabin in Belfort.

The Class III road does not stop here, however. One can go on down to upper Frying Pan Creek, and then descend further to upper Murphy Creek. Technically the road goes on out to Highway 395 in upper Huntoon Valley. **Be advised, however, while this road continues on to join Highway 395, it crosses private property. There are locked gates ahead and the landowner does not view trespassers kindly. If you choose to go on, your route will eventually be blocked, and you will need to return on the road you came in on.**

5

Masonic Mountain

Special Features: This outing goes through piñon-covered hills to a century old mining camp. This is also a good place to go "nutting" in the fall.

Time Required: An excursion to Masonic and its environs makes a pleasant all day trip out of Bridgeport.

Miles Involved: The distance from Bridgeport to Masonic's "Middle Town" via the described route is about eleven miles.

Degree of Difficulty: The route is generally Class II, with only small portions of Class III.

Remarks: The higher portions of this route may be closed by snow from December well into April.

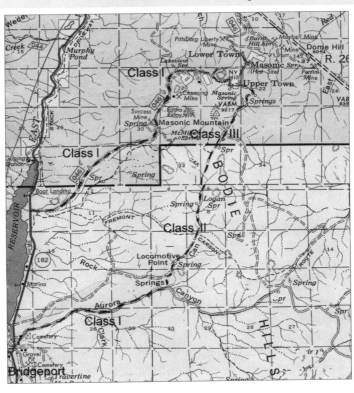

It was July of 1860 when three prospectors from Monoville were scouring the piñon-covered hills east of the East Walker River. They found float, quartz stained by iron and other metals. The men thought their find might be promising, and because they were members of the Masonic Lodge, they named the area Masonic Mountain. By chance, another even more promising find was made a few weeks later, just twelve miles to the southeast. However, in the resulting rush to Aurora, Masonic Mountain was forgotten. Forty-two years later, on Independence Day in 1902, a new trio rediscovered that same lode. Within two years their find would become the Pittsburg-Liberty Mine. Initial assay values ran anywhere from $35 to $800 per ton, certainly high enough to warrant the sinking of a shaft. For that, machinery would have to be brought in and workers hired. In the summer of 1904 roads were extended from Bridgeport and Bodie to the gulch below Masonic Mountain. Tents appeared, and it wasn't long before the first cabin was raised, built with trunks from nearby aspen trees. Soon the elongated town of Masonic was spread out along a mile of canyon bottom. There was an "Upper Town", a "Middle Town", and a "Lower Town". It was Middle Town that boasted of having the post office and general store and the Jump-Up-Joe Mine. A tramline was built in the Lower Town to bring ore from the Pittsburg-Liberty Mine down to a large mill.

The Pittsburg-Liberty Mill in Masonic's lower town circa 1905.
(Nevada Historical Society photo)

By 1910 the rich ore had played out, and people began to drift away. In the summer of 1911 only the lonely postmaster was left in Middle Town. A few months later an unusually severe snowstorm hit on the eastern side of the Sierra, and one of the few miners left in the Masonic area was killed in an avalanche.

The mines of Masonic Mountain experienced renewed interest during the Great Depression years. In 1929 the Serita Mine reopened for a while. When

State Mining Engineers R.J. Sampson and W.B. Tucker visited the area in April of 1937, they found twenty men working at the Chemung Mine. A year later that mine had closed. In 1939 it was reported that four men were working at the Lakeview Mine. In 1942 President Roosevelt ordered all gold mines be closed so that those workers might better serve the war effort. Little has happened in Masonic since, although some development work was being done in the Chemung Mine as recently at the early 1960s. Nevertheless, it seems unlikely that Masonic will ever again awaken from its deep slumber.

Still standing today, this cabin can be seen in the photo on the opposite page.

There are easy ways to get to Masonic, and there are interesting ways to get there. The author will always chose "interesting" over "easy", so our approach will be from the south via Aurora Canyon and Rock Springs Canyon. This is the road less traveled, and hence, our route of choice.

From the east end of downtown Bridgeport, leave U.S. Highway 395 taking California State Route 182 only a quarter of a mile. Turn to the right onto Aurora Canyon Road, noting your odometer reading in the process. After 0.3 miles, the road immediately makes a jog to the left, then immediately turns right again as it passes the cemetery on the right. The pavement ends 0.4 miles from Highway 182, but a county-maintained high standard dirt road continues on. After 1.2 miles the graded dirt road (also identified as Forest Road 168) will take you into the mouth of Aurora Canyon. Basalt palisades soon begin to close in on both sides of the road.

After going up the canyon 4.5 miles from Highway 182, look for little-used tracks going off to the left and passing through a gate. Please leave the gate open or closed, as you found it. Engage your four-wheel drive, and leave the Aurora Canyon Road here. The tracks ford a small stream early in the year, but it may be dry by late summer. The next half-mile is an easy Class III, as a low ridge is crossed on the way to Rock Springs Canyon, the next drainage to the north. Once you are in the bottom, stay to the right going up the canyon.

A very common plant along the roadside here is ephedra, sometimes called Squaw Tea or Mormon Tea. This is a primitive and curious non-flowering plant, more like a conifer than most other arid country shrubs. Individual plants may be male or female. There are seven species of ephedra in California, the most common being *Ephedra viridis,* with the less common but still abundant *Ephedra nevadensis.* Two species, *Ephedra funerea* and *Ephedra trifurca* are on the California Native Plant Society's list of rare and endangered plants, but they are not found here. The Indians, who had a practical use for just about any plant, boiled the tender shoots to make a tea said to cure intestinal difficulties. Early fur trappers, mountain men, and the pioneers also brewed a tea out of the hardy little shrub. The author has done this, too, but finds that a dollop of honey or several teaspoons of granular brown sugar needs to be added to counter-act the bitter tannic acid. **Warning: Ephedra contains ephedrine, a heart stimulant. Do not drink ephedra tea if you have any kind of cardiac problem! Prolonged consumption may also cause personality changes and other psychiatric disorders.**

Ephedra

Logan Spring, with its cattle trough, is passed on the left near the upper end of Rock Springs Canyon. There is then a short but easy Class III climb up onto an 8,500-foot saddle. The author's field notes indicate we were here on May 29, 1978, and could not get through due to lingering deep snowdrifts!

The road goes through a drift fence at a point 1.4 miles above Logan Spring. Here a Class III side road to the left goes up to an electronic site on top of Masonic Mountain. This road gains some 800 vertical feet in a little more than a mile. The view from the top makes this a worthwhile diversion.

Meanwhile the main road continues north. The 1904 road from Aurora comes in from the right 0.4 miles beyond the drift fence. Another ridge is topped a half-mile beyond the road from Aurora, and this time there are good views to the north. A quarter of a mile further, there is a nice campsite in the aspen grove on the left. Here, too, is a major intersection, where the graded dirt Forest Road 46 comes in from Bridgeport. We will return to here, but first let's turn right and visit the old mining camp of Masonic.

Almost immediately after making that right turn, you will enter Masonic's Upper Town. Even forty years ago when we first visited this site, no structures remained, so don't expect to see much today. An ore bunker is passed on the left after another quarter mile. A half-mile beyond Upper Town is Middle Town, once the center of culture in Masonic. The ruins of one structure are on the right. The roof no doubt collapsed a long time ago under the weight of snow.

A half-mile below Middle Town is Lower Town. Here, on the right, once stood the very impressive ten-stamp mill and cyanide plant built in 1907 by the Stall Brothers to process ores from the Pittsburg-Liberty Mine. The mine and its mill were connected by a half-mile long aerial tramway, parts of which still remain. The cabin you see still standing on the right was one of three built here which pre-date the mill. The other two cabins were torn down in 1907 to make room for the mill. Frank Wedertz's excellent book, *Mono Diggings,* has two photos of the millsite, one before and one after its construction. Both photos clearly show this only remaining structure in old Masonic.

From Masonic north, Forest Road 46 remains Class II for the next 3.5 miles, where it enters Nevada and improves to Class I for its remaining three miles to Nevada State Route 338. From here it is about fifteen miles back to Bridgeport.

Let's return to that road intersection just above Upper Town, however, where a sign announces it is twelve miles back to Bridgeport by the most direct route. Again note your odometer reading, for there are things to be seen along the way.

From the intersection, Class I Forest Road 46 steeply climbs out of the canyon. At a point 0.8 miles from the intersection, a short side road right goes over to a vista point where there are good views of the country to the north. At the second road to the right, 1.1 miles from the intersection, a Class II road climbs the low ridge known as "New York Hill". It was on the north-facing slope of this rounded hilltop that Masonic's two most important mines were located.

Practically on top of New York Hill was the Serita Mine. Old reports have its total gold production at a half a million dollars. Slightly below the Serita property were the four claims of the Pittsburg-Liberty Mine.

For years John Bryan, John Phillips, and Caleb Dorsey had sought work as miners from local mines, and, when jobs were not available, they spent their time wandering the hills in search of a mine of their own. The trio had formed a loose partnership, and was out prospecting on August 1, 1902, when the pure white "bull quartz" vein they were following suddenly became heavily iron-stained and blackened with oxidized metallic minerals. They staked their claims immediately, but development was slow. In 1907 after five men had worked all summer, seventeen tons of handpicked ore was shipped to the Selby smelter near San Francisco. The net return was an astounding $1,040 per ton, but some of the ore ran as high as $1,500 per ton. Even the poorest ore sent to the mill ran $700 per ton. With proven values like that, they were able to lease the mine to George Wingfield for $47,000. Wingfield sank a one hundred foot shaft and extracted some ore from a 47-foot crosscut. At the end of the lease, the property reverted to its original owners, who by now had sufficient capital to develop the property properly. It was then that a mill was constructed down in Lower Town, and a tramline was built to carry the ore down to there. Unfortunately, John Phillips met a premature death in July of 1909, when he fell 160 feet down a raise. By the following year the best ore had become exhausted, and the mines of New York Hill went into decline. By 1911 only one person was left in all of Masonic, but before its closure, the Pittsburg-Liberty Mine had well over a mile of underground shafts, tunnels, winzes, and raises. The total production from the Pittsburg-Liberty Mine is recorded at $700,000, a tidy sum in the early 20th Century.

The extensive workings of the Serita and Pittsburg-Liberty Mines are only 0.4 miles off Forest Road 46. If you visit these works, which are now mostly open pits, keep in mind that this is private property and act accordingly. While no *No Trespassing* signs were posted in the summer of 2002, this could change at any time. Obviously, the owners assume no liability for any injury that might occur to a visitor. To visit the tramline loading facility, a short quarter mile walk is required. **Warning: Stay out of all the underground workings; they are even more hazardous than the open pits on the surface!**

Loading facility for the aerial tramline that carried ore down to the mill.
One of the tram buckets can be seen in the photo on page 30.

Continuing on, Forest Road 46 tops another hill, and then turns to the south. Almost immediately, the several mill buildings of the Chemung Mines come into view on the left. This was one of the last operating mines in the Masonic District. Development of the Chemung Mine came along a little later, although it seems to have tapped into the same vein system as the mines of New York Hill, a little more than a mile to the northeast. From the sturdy construction of the mill structures, the developers of this mine obviously wanted to keep it in operation as much of the year as its 8,300-foot elevation would permit. A 1940 mining report says the total production from the Chemung Mine is recorded at a mere $60,000. That seems strangely low, even for the depression years of the 1930s. In looking at the capacity of the mill, it seems likely that someone was either "high-grading", "cooking the books" or, even more likely, spending much more on the development than was ever recovered in ore. **Again note that this is private property, and the underground workings are dangerous. Stay out of them!**

The Chemung Mine

Forest Road 46 continues southward from the Chemung Mine. After less than a mile the tailing dump of the Success Mine is passed on the right. In spite of its name, ore production here was only minor.

Finally, eight miles from the intersection above Upper Town, Forest Road 46 drops nearly 2,000 feet in elevation and returns to Highway 182. By turning left, it is only four miles back to downtown Bridgeport.

6

Dogtown Days

Special Features:	This easy outing goes to the site of Mono County's first mining camp.
Time Required:	Dogtown is but a ten minute drive from Bridgeport by Highway 395, but in order to walk through the site, access must be made from the west side of Green Creek over some dirt roads. That may require thirty minutes.
Distance Involved:	From downtown Bridgeport to downtown Dogtown, it is only seven miles.
Degree of Difficulty:	The road is generally no worse than Class II, although you may wish to briefly engage your four-wheel drive coming back out.

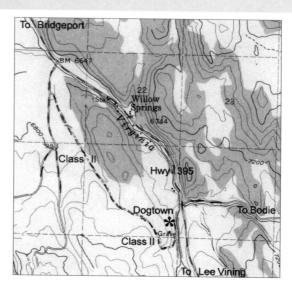

Dogtown is one of those places you can see from the paved roadway, but you cannot easily get there since Virginia Creek blocks your access. If you actually want to walk among the ruins of this old mining camp, you are going to have to take three miles of little used backroads.

From downtown Bridgeport take U.S. Highway 395 south 4.5 miles to the Green Creek Road; turn right here. After only a quarter of a mile, look for a Class II road going off to the left. This is the road to Dogtown. Follow it south 1.8 miles to a fork. If you take the left fork here, there is a short but steep Class IV descent to Virginia Creek and the site of Dogtown. If you stay to the right for a mile, it is an easier Class II route to the same place.

The road to Dogtown

Sometimes called *"Dogwood of the Desert"* because of its showy large white flower, Prickly poppy *Argemone munita* can sometimes be seen along the road into Dogtown, particularly in disturbed soils.

History is not clear on just who found placer gold in the stream gravels just below the confluence of Green and Virginia Creeks, or the year that discovery was made. The time may have been as early as 1853, and the founder may have been a man named Cord Norst, at least he bragged he was the one who first found gold here. (Those who knew him took Cord's various declarations with a grain of salt.) Whatever its origins, Dogtown was very isolated in the early 1850s, and its remoteness discouraged permanent settlement, particularly during the winter months. When the strike at Monoville became known in July of 1859 (Norst claimed to have found that, too), most of Dogtown's residents folded their tents and moved on to greener pastures just six miles to the southeast. A few years later when Dogtown's gravels were thought to have been worked out, the Chinese moved in and worked them profitably for several more years, gleaning whatever was left.

Today there is not a lot left of Dogtown; only the ruins of two stone buildings and a single grave can be seen. Nevertheless, this was the first California community on the eastern side of the Sierra Nevada.

Only stone walls mark the site of Dogtown.

One of Dogtown's original residents.

Do Your Preventative Maintenance
Before You Leave Home

...or your vehicle will end up like these!

Lee Vining's Past

LEE VINING

THE NAME OF THIS COMMUNITY HONORS LEROY
VINING. IN 1852 LT. TREDWELL MOORE AND
SOLDIERS OF THE 2nd INFANTRY PURSUED
INDIANS OF CHIEF TENAYA'S TRIBE FROM
YOSEMITE ACROSS THE SIERRA VIA BLOODY
CANYON. THEY TOOK BACK MINERAL SAMPLES
AND A PROSPECTING PARTY WAS ORGANIZED.
IN THIS GROUP WERE THE VININGS, LEE &
DICK, WHO ESTABLISHED A CAMP AT WHAT
IS NOW LEE VINING CREEK.

PLAQUE DEDICATED SEPTEMBER 8, 1979
BODIE CHAPTER OF E CLAMPUS VITUS

Downtown Lee Vining circa 1948.
(Photo from the author's collection)

The Mono Lake Historical Society has restored this old
school house and turned it into a museum.

Chapter II

Trails Out of Lee Vining

It is said that Leroy Vining took the old Indian trail over Mono Pass in 1853, searching for riches on the eastern side of the Sierra. While history doesn't record what he did for the next decade, we do know that in 1863 he was operating a small sawmill west of Mono Lake in a canyon that became known as Vining's Gulch. His timber went by wagon to the mines of Aurora, many miles to the north. The present day community gets its name from this pioneer lumberman.

Today's Lee Vining has a population of only a few hundred people who depend on tourist traffic along Highway 395 and Highway 120, Yosemite's Tioga Pass Road. The town offers half a dozen motels, several places to eat, a general store and sporting goods shop, and several service stations. Nearby in lower Lee Vining Canyon, Mono County operates several campgrounds where a modest fee is charged.

Lee Vining has been synonymous with the fight to prevent Mono Lake from drying up as the City of Los Angeles diverted the streams flowing into it. Thanks largely to the untiring efforts of a local resident David Gaines, together with supporters all over the world, an agreement was eventually reached with the city to curb water diversions. Once again the lake level is slowly rising. Anyone going through Lee Vining should certainly stop at the U.S. Forest Service's Mono Basin Visitor Center just north of town to see and hear the story of the Mono Lake country. The films and displays are excellent. Here, too, you can obtain current information about local jeep trails and other forest information. It will be an hour well spent.

The Mono Basin Visitor Center

42

7

Monoville

Special Features	This is the site of Mono County's second mining camp.
Time Required:	Allow two or three hours for this brief excursion back into history.
Distance Involved:	The total distance of this circuit is 26 miles from Lee Vining and back.
Degree of Difficulty:	Generally the roads described are Class II or better, but there are two short Class III sections.

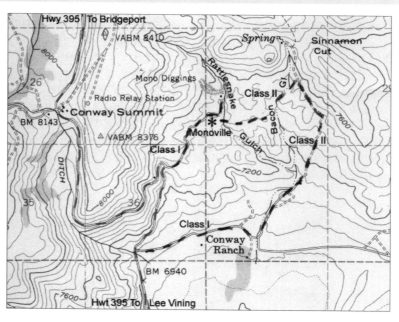

To visit Monoville, or what is left of it, head north out of Lee Vining on Highway 395. Seven miles from town, State Route 167 heads off on the right toward Hawthorne, Nevada. Continue north on Highway 395, but do note your odometer reading at this intersection. Go another 1.7 miles to the Conway Ranch Road, also on the right. This is where you will leave the pavement. Reset your trip odometer to zero here, and turn right onto this wide graded road, following it east for one mile. Just beyond the turnoff to Conway Ranch, a "T" intersection is reached. Go to the left on the Class I road that heads north.

In about 0.7 miles, mounds of gravel will begin to appear on the left. These are the course waste dumps of rocks that have had all their fine particles removed by those seeking placer gold. There will be many more such piles along the road ahead. The road forks here. Take either fork; they will soon rejoin.

Weathered granite bedrock along the road to Monoville.

At a point 2.7 miles from Highway 395, take the Class II side road that drops down into the gulch to the left. Soon more piles of worked gravel are passed. A spring and small pond are passed in Bacon Gulch, and there is a short but steep section of Class III. Three and a half miles from Highway 395, you will encounter another intersection. Stay to the left, and soon you will be in Monoville.

Cord Norst, who claimed the credit for finding the Dogtown placers on Green Creek, also claimed credit for finding gold in the hills above Mono Lake. He said he wandered over here from Dogtown on July 5, 1859, panned a small stream, and found colors in his pan. When he returned to Dogtown for beans, bacon, and bourbon, he bragged about his find. Norst had a reputation of being a talker, and was not always believed. Nevertheless, he paid for his provisions with gold dust that he had not had when he left a few days earlier. Things like that did not escape notice, and soon the tents in Dogtown were struck and many moved to the new camp of Monoville. The population of Monoville quickly swelled to anywhere from five hundred to nine hundred people that first summer. Plat maps were drawn up, and streets and lots were laid out. Lumber for the booming camp was in great demand, and several sawmills opened to fill that need. Soon tents were being replaced by more substantial structures.

The gravels of Rattlesnake and Bacon Gulch were profitably worked all summer, but by November when the cold weather set in, many of the miners packed up and left for warmer climes. Among the 150 or so who stayed and wintered over were a man and his wife. By the next spring they also had a baby. In his book *Mono Diggings,* noted Mono County historian Frank S. Wedertz says it began to snow in Monoville on November 16, 1859, and it did not stop until it was five feet deep!

I can believe that. I can recall that in late January and early February of 1969, one hundred and ten years later, CalTrans crews struggled to keep Highway 395 open to vehicles with chains. At that time, the snow depth on the downhill side of Highway 395 over 8,138' Conway Summit was over seven feet!

With the coming of spring in 1860, prospectors and would-be miners returned to Monoville by the hundreds. Any unstaked ground for miles around was claimed. By mid-summer Monoville's sober residents bragged of the camp having a population of five hundred. The more inebriated and less inhibited often claimed up to 2000. Whatever the true figure, Monoville did have some forty structures up, of which 22 were saloons and gambling halls. There were several hotels, boarding houses, restaurants, general stores, livery stables, and butcher shops. The camp had its own post office, and one saloon had a two-lane, ten pin bowling alley. Although nobody was sure if Monoville was in the State of California or the Territory of Nevada, the local citizenry was ready to make it the county seat of something.

They should have struck when the iron was hot, for by the summer of 1861 there were about fourteen hundred people living in Aurora and only seven hundred people in Monoville. Mono County was created out of lands from several other California counties, and the voters made Aurora the county seat. (Later, in 1863 when is was discovered that Aurora was actually in Nevada, the county seat was moved to Bridgeport.)

By 1863 only a couple of hundred people were left in Monoville. It is not that the gold ran out, but that new strikes were made at Aurora. Living conditions there were more attractive, because the land was more hospitable and supplies were a little closer. Those who chose to stay at Monoville continued to find gold in the gravels of Rattlesnake, Bacon, and Spring gulches.

The auriferous gravels in these ravines were about twenty feet thick before the granite bedrock was encountered. Of that twenty feet, all but about three feet were considered to be pay dirt. But water was needed to wash the gravel through sluice boxes, and there was precious little of that commodity. Ditches were dug to water sources, sometimes miles away. One hand-ditch came from the slopes of Dunderberg Peak, fourteen miles away. (Remnants can still be seen today.)

Not everyone got rich at Monoville, but those with the ability to bring the water in did well enough. One such person was James Sinnamon, whose diggings became known Sinnamon Cut. His earnings bought him the finest ranch land in the Bridgeport Valley, which was then known as Big Meadow.

Production records were scant in those days, but it is thought that a significant amount of placer gold was produced here in a relatively short period of time. Curiously, although many a prospector has hiked over these granite hills looking for the lode from which this placer gold came, no major source has ever been found. Ella Cain, a descendant of one of Mono County's pioneering families, says in her book *The Story of Mono County* that her father, M.J. Cody, worked the Rattlesnake Mine at Monoville in the early 1890s, until water flooded the shaft faster than it could be pumped out. The amount of gold recovered from underground mining seems to have been minuscule compared to that taken by sluicing the gravels for their placer gold.

The Sinnamon Cut where only piles of coarse gravel remain
after the fine sand has been washed through sluice boxes.

Follow the road down into the Rattlesnake Gulch, where there is a short, but very muddy Class III stream crossing. Check it out carefully before plunging in. Once on the other side, you will encounter another dirt road. By going to the right a quarter of a mile, you will find a couple of cabins, one of which is still in use by its owner. Please respect those private property rights.

By turning to the left after crossing the stream, the roadway now improves to Class I. After 0.4 miles it will rejoin Highway 395 on the big curve at the bottom of the Conway Summit Grade. From here it is 1.4 miles to the left back to the Conway Ranch Road, and a little over ten miles back to Lee Vining.

The stream crossing is just as treacherous
today as it was 40 years ago.

Few structures mark the site of Monoville today.

8

On Track With the Bodie & Benton Railway
Part 1: Bodie to Highway 167

Primary Attraction:	This excursion follows the old road grade of the Bodie & Benton Railway that between the years 1881 and 1917 provided timber to shore up the bottomless mines of Bodie.
Time Required:	Because of its length and required time, the journey has been broken down into two parts. Taking both excursions on the same trip makes for one very long day, but it can be done. The reader should consider breaking the total outing in half as described, allowing a day for each part.
Distance Involved:	The entire loop from Lee Vining to Bodie and then on to Mono Mills and back to Lee Vining is about 72 miles. If you opt not to do the second half on the same day as suggested, and choose to return to Lee Vining via State Route 167, the round trip distance is reduced to 53 miles.
Degree of Difficulty:	Most of the route is Class II, but the lower bypass is a rock-strewn roadway where four-wheel drive is advisable. **Also be aware that vehicle-scratching brush has overgrown portions of the railroad grade between Bodie and Lime Kiln Station. If you have a spiffy paint job, you may wish to bring some loping shears to help clear the brush off the right-of-way. Top off your fuel tank before leaving Lee Vining, as there is no fuel anywhere along this route.**
Remarks:	Down on the flatlands below the Bodie Hills, it is sometimes easy to lose the old railroad right-of-way. Rail fans and history buffs interested in the exact route of the roadbed should obtain either the current 1989 7.5-minute Kirkwood Spring quadrangle, or have the older 1958 15-minute Trench Canyon sheet. Both maps show the route of the former railroad. The Toiyabe National Forest map for the Bridgeport Ranger District also shows the railroad route, but it is much less detailed and it only shows that portion of the route north of Highway 167.

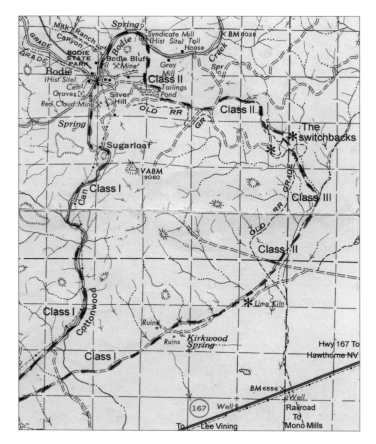

We begin our backroad excursion through history by proceeding north on Highway 395 out of Lee Vining. After seven miles turn east onto State Route 167 for another seven miles. Here you will see a sign pointing left and indicating it is ten miles to Bodie. We leave the pavement here at an elevation of 6,488 feet.

This is the Cottonwood Canyon Road, one of three high standard roads that access Bodie. The name "cottonwood" in the canyon's name is a misnomer. There are no such trees to be seen anywhere along this road. The predominate tree here, indeed the only tree, is the piñon pine *Pinus monophylla*.

Geologically the Bodie Hills are a thick sequence of volcanic rocks of Tertiary age overlying much older Cretaceous plutonic rocks. As you enter the Cottonwood Canyon, a little more than four miles off Highway 167, a narrow band of white ash is sandwiched between two masses of reddish brown basalt lava. You can follow this layer of ash for more than a mile. It is sometimes visible on both sides of the road.

About nine miles in from Highway 167, tailing dumps begin to appear on the hillsides to the right. Bodie State Historic Park is entered at nine and a half miles. The elevation here is 8,375 feet. This one thousand plus acre reserve was established in 1962 to slow, halt, and ultimately reverse the decay and neglect the ghost town of Bodie had undergone in the last one hundred years. The park is open daily from 8 a.m. to 7 p.m. during the summer months and 9 a.m. to 4 p.m. the rest of the year. A modest entry fee is charged. No food, lodging, gasoline, or any other basic services are available. Camping is not permitted within three miles of the site. **Four-wheelers should not be tempted to drive into Bodie during the winter months if there is any snow anywhere on the roadway. Many have tried, and many have gotten hopelessly stuck. The Bodie Hills are no place to be stranded in January when the sun goes down and the thermometer starts heading down towards that zero mark! If in doubt about current conditions, call the Rangers at (760) 647-6445 before setting out.**

The basic services are no longer available in Bodie.

It was one Watterman S. Bodey who accidentally discovered gold in the high hills north of Mono Lake in July of 1859. Bodey had shot and wounded a rabbit and was attempting to dig it out of its hole when he made his find. About that same time, placer gold was discovered in Rattlesnake Gulch and interest was diverted to the Mono diggings, soon to be known as Monoville. Soon similar finds at Aurora attracted all the attention. While Aurora boomed, Bodie languished. Hoping to change their luck, the city fathers changed the spelling of their community from Bodey to Bodie; that did not seem to help. In 1864 it was reported that Bodie had less than twenty buildings. The mines of Bodie continued to produce small amounts of ore for the next ten years.

Bodie Yesterday

(Historic photos from the author's collection.)

Bodie Today

Bodie State Historic Park preserves the largest ghost town in the west.

In 1874 another fortuitous event occurred. A couple of miners, who were barely eking out a living off low-grade ore, had an accidental cave-in, which exposed the rich Fortuna Ledge that seemed to go on forever. News of this discovery spread like wildfire, and people began to pour into the little valley below Potato Peak. By 1878 Bodie had a population of 3,000 and a downtown business district of one hundred substantial wooden buildings. By 1879 Bodie was the third largest city in California, with a population of 10,000, and by this time there were some 3,000 structures in the town. During Bodie's peak from 1878 to 1881, Bodie was a wide-open town whose mines, mills, saloons, gambling halls, and bawdy houses operated 24 hours a day. A decade later, however, the mines were closing and people were moving away. In 1889 the population was down to 1500.

It is interesting to note that Bodie was one of the first mining camps to have electricity. The transmission lines came eighteen miles from the Jordan powerhouse until March 7, 1911, when an avalanche raced through the facility killing seven people. (The story of that disaster is told in *High Sierra SUV Trails Volume I – The East Side*.) The Mill Creek avalanche was not the only calamity to strike Mono County. A disastrous fire swept through Bodie in 1932, burning 90% of its weathered wooden buildings. What you see today is less than 10% of what once was. In 1962 the Cain family, whose forbearers had bought up much of the town years before, sold out to the State of California, which turned it into an outdoor museum.

For a more complete history of Bodie, the author recommends that you try to find a copy of *Mining Camp Days* by Emil Billib, *Bodie 1859-1900* by Frank S. Wedertz and *The Story of Bodie* by Ella Cain.

There were miles of tunnels and shafts in the mines of Bodie, most of which had to be shored up with massive timbers. There was precious little wood in the Bodie Hills suitable for that purpose, so the mine operators had to look elsewhere. The nearby canyons in the Sierra Nevada had aspen groves, but little suitable for mine timbers. The nearest supply of timber was the Jeffrey pine forest along the southern shore of Mono Lake. Here was the right kind of wood and plenty of it. Cutting it in the woods and bringing the finished lumber to Bodie by a railroad seemed a reasonable solution. But first, sufficient capital would have to be raised, and the railroad would have to be built. On February 18, 1881, two of the principal owners of the Standard Consolidated Mine met with other entrepreneurs and formed the Bodie Railroad and Lumber Company. Bodie would get its badly needed timber.

A survey revealed that the grade from Bodie to the flatlands north of Mono Lake would involve a change in elevation of 1600 feet in a distance of only ten miles. That is a steep grade for a railroad. The line would have to be narrow gauge in order to make the tight radius on the turns, and even then, a couple of switch-backs would be needed. The line would be 31.74 miles long and would have two intermediate stations; one would be at the bottom of the grade near the Lime Kiln, the other at Warm Springs. A used Baldwin locomotive was found and purchased, and two new ones were ordered. Sufficient rail for the first ten miles was likewise purchased. Construction began in May of 1881. By July 22, miles of roadbed had been graded by two crews, one of two hundred white laborers, the other by two hundred Chinese workers. In the meanwhile a two-story sawmill was being built at what would become Mono Mills. It began operation in August, and during the month of September, the new sawmill turned out 29,000 ties. Also in September, components of the first locomotive arrived at Mono Lake by freight wagons from Hawthorne, Nevada. From here they were barged to the Warm Springs Station site for reassembly. Soon rails were being laid in each direction. Finally on November 14, 1881, the last spike was driven at the Bodie terminal. From inception to completion 32 miles of rail had been laid through inhospitable country, sometimes under very adverse weather conditions, in only seven months. The mines of Bodie could now go deeper into the mountain.

The locomotive *Tybo* was one of three in use on the line.
(Photo courtesy of Laws Railroad Museum)

As envisioned by its founders, the Bodie & Benton was a strictly a logging railroad. No passenger service was initially considered. Although no train schedule was ever published, there was a telegraph wire all along the line so that each of the four stations knew where trains were.

In January of 1882 the principal investors decided to broaden the scope of their little logging railroad to run a branch line forty miles eastward to Benton, supply center for the silver mines on Blind Spring Hill (see Excursion #13). The Bodie Railroad and Lumber Company was reorganized and renamed the Bodie & Benton Railway. The proposed extension would connect with the Carson & Colorado Railroad coming down from Mound House, Nevada, where it interfaced with the Virginia & Truckee. Bodie would be connected with the outside world, bringing freight and passenger service to the isolated, but booming community. Work began immediately. The route was surveyed nearly to Benton, and nine miles of road grade were actually prepared. In July, however, the extension to Benton was suddenly abandoned, when it occurred to someone that a connection with the Carson & Colorado Railroad might bring lumber from Lake Tahoe south, and break the Bodie & Benton's virtual monopoly on timber!

The mines of Bodie prospered for three decades, turning out $30 million in gold. All good things must come to an end, however, and a gradual decline started about 1912 as one by one the mines began to close, their ore bodies exhausted. When the largest mine on the hill, the Standard, closed in 1914, the demand for wood products was greatly reduced, and as such, the railroad had few remaining customers. The line was officially closed on September 6, 1917. Soon thereafter, the rails were pulled up and the rolling stock was dismantled.

Being somewhat of a rail fan and having had some success following old rail routes across the Rocky Mountains, I wondered if it might be possible to follow the 32-mile long rail route used to bring timber into Bodie, California. I found that the actual roadbed could not be driven on for much of the way, but that generally the old roadbed could be followed.

If you, too, want to follow the route of the tracks, reset your trip odometer or otherwise note your mileage as you leave the Bodie parking lot going eastward in the direction of Aurora. Signs announce that you are on BLM Road 270 and that it is six miles to the Nevada State line, sixteen miles to Aurora. Follow this Class I road around the base of Bodie Bluff for 2.2 miles, where a Class II road goes off to the right. Turn right here, passing the site of an old mill and follow the Bodie State Park fence line up a shallow draw. The road forks after three quarters of a mile. The right fork goes back to Bodie (locked gates ahead). Take the left fork, which immediately crosses a narrow dam holding back what once was a large mill tailings pond. A cut contouring along the hillside, a half-mile to the south, is our first glimpse of the railroad's grade.

Once over the dam, there is a half-mile of easy Class III as our road crosses rocky ground. At the half-mile point from the last fork, another road comes in from the right rear, and our road again improves to Class II as it makes its way eastward. At a point 4.2 miles from Bodie (two miles from BLM Road 270) a "T" intersection is reached. The right fork goes 0.4 miles to the old railroad grade, but it still cannot be followed at this point. Turn left, and proceed another tenth of a mile. Now you can turn right on a Class II road, and soon you will be on the railroad right-of-way heading for Mono Mills. The elevation here is about 8,200 feet.

The right-of-way contours around the south end of a hill with a rounded top, and briefly turns north. A sharp curve brings the grade south again, and then eastward through a gap. Stop along here somewhere and look back. The old stone retaining walls along the road grade can clearly be seen.

The stone retaining walls supporting the roadbed are as solid today as they were when they were built in 1881. The roadway on the right is the old railroad grade.

Once through the forested gap, the roadbed turns north again. An important road junction is ahead; three roads diverge at a point seven miles from Bodie. Do not take the road to the left. The railroad grade goes straight ahead, but it is impassible for vehicles. If you wish to walk down it a quarter of a mile, you will come to the first switchback, where an abandoned flatcar was salvaged by the Friends of the Bodie & Benton Railway. They carefully removed the pieces and painstakingly restored it. If you continue to walk along the right-of-way beyond the upper switchback, a deep cut in the rock is encountered. It is filled with debris from above.

One of the railroad's last surviving flatcars was recovered from the upper switchback and restored by the Friends of the Bodie & Benton Railway. The restoration project took four years to complete. The car is currently on display at the June Lake Marina.

The right-of-way can be seen going through the rocky cut. In the far distance are Mounts Boundary and Montgomery in the White Mountains.

At the three-way intersection, take the rocky road to the right, a bypass that steeply descends the hillside. It crosses the old railroad grade in 0.4 miles. Again the old right-of-way cannot be driven, but if you walk it a quarter of a mile to the right, you will come to the lower switchback. A half-mile walk to the left will bring you to two old trestle sites. There were only three trestles on the 32-mile line. One spanned Big Dry Creek just north of Mono Mills (see Excursion #9), and the other two were here below the rocky cut. One of the two here was 260 feet long and fifty feet high at its highest point.

We, however, must continue down our cutoff road. The right-of-way is again crossed. At a point 8.4 miles from Bodie (1.2 miles from the three-way intersection at the beginning of our shortcut road) another crossroads is reached. The road straight ahead is washed out; go to the right. The road soon drops into a rocky draw, where use of four-wheel drive is advisable in crossing it. Once on the other side, the elevation is about 7,000 feet and the ground begins to level out. The road forks at the 10.2-mile point; go to the left, heading due south. The road becomes sandy where again you may wish to engage your four-wheel drive. In 0.8 miles, turn to the right. In another tenth of a mile, you will come to a crossroads; go straight ahead. In 0.3 miles, look for a faint set of tracks to the right. These parallel the old right-of-way. (If you turn right here, you can soon see the old roadbed with the ties still in place.) Continue straight ahead on the main road. After another 0.7 miles, a road to the left goes to the remarkably well-preserved stone limekiln.

The old limekiln

I must admit that I have had great difficulty in determining who built the limekiln, when it was built, and its years of operation. The Friends of the Bodie & Benton Railway tell me there was a spur line coming over to it from Lime Kiln Station, just a mile to the northeast. However, I see no evidence of that on the ground, and author David F. Myrick makes no mention of any such spur in his book, *Railroads of Nevada and Eastern California (Volume I)*. The construction of the limekiln obviously preceded the building of the railroad, and I am inclined to think that the products of the kiln were transported to the railroad by wagon. If anyone can enlighten me on this point, I would appreciate hearing from you.

Lime Kiln Station was twelve rail miles from Bodie, 16.5 miles from Warm Springs Station, and twenty miles from Mono Mills. In spite of its importance to railroad operations, practically nothing remains of Lime Kiln Station and its rail yards. There was a siding here, because while trains ten to twelve cars long would leave Mono Mills, the steep grades going up to Bodie made it necessary to leave most of those cars here. The locomotive could pull only three or four fully laden cars for those last twelve miles into Bodie. Water for the locomotive was available at either end of the line, but not at either of the two intermediate stations. The engineer had to be prudent with his use of water. The locomotives used wood to fire the steam boilers, and a secondary supply was stockpiled here at Lime Kiln Station. The track also changed at Lime Kiln Station. Across the flatlands east of Mono Lake, thirty-foot sections of rail weighing 35 pounds per foot could be utilized. But with the steeper grades climbing 1,600 vertical feet to Bodie, forty-pound rails were needed.

From the limekiln, follow the wide Class I road westward for nearly thirteen miles. It will pass a few old ranches and will eventually return to the Cottonwood Canyon Road. There, a left turn will take you back to State Route 167, where it is only seven miles to Highway 395, and another seven miles back to Lee Vining. See Excursion #9 if you wish to continue following the railroad the rest of the way to Mono Mills.

Drawing courtesy Ken Houghton Rail Images

9

On Track With the Bodie & Benton Railway
Part 2, Highway 167 to Mono Mills

Primary Attraction:	This excursion continues to follow the old road grade of the Bodie & Benton Railway.
Time Required:	One should make this a full day's outing in order to adequately explore the country east of Mono Lake.
Distance Involved:	This entire loop trip from Lee Vining to Mono Mills via State Route 167 and back to Lee Vining again via State Route 120 involves a distance of slightly more than 46 miles. The dirt road portion is nineteen miles.
Degree of Difficulty:	Most of the route is Class II. **However, because there are some sections of very soft sand along the eastern shore of Mono Lake that can cause problems for conventional vehicles, this route should not be attempted by vehicles without four-wheel drive. Do not attempt this road in wet weather, as there are some world-class mud holes in the areas of alkali flats. Be sure to top off your fuel tank before leaving Lee Vining, as there is no fuel anywhere along the route.**
Remarks:	In the sage land east of Mono Lake, it is sometimes easy to lose the old railroad right-of-way. Rail fans and history buffs interested in the exact route of the roadbed should obtain either the current (1994) 7.5-minute Sulphur Pond and (1986) Mono Mills quadrangles, or have the older 15-minute 1958 Trench Canyon and 1962 Cowtrack Mountain sheets. Both maps show the route of the former railroad. The Inyo National Forest map does not show the railroad right-of-way.

Part two of our railroad tracking adventure begins just like part one; take Highway 395 north out of Lee Vining for seven miles, where you will then turn east on State Route 167. Note your odometer reading as you make that right turn. There are some nice views of the two islands, Negit (the dark volcanic one) and Panum (the more distant lighter colored one) in Mono Lake. At a point 13.4 miles east of Highway 395, look to the right for a rusting iron ore car resting on a pair of rails. That Noble Grand Humbug Society, E. Clampus Vitus, has mounted a brass plaque commemorating the Bodie & Benton Railway.

Since entertainment was a cherished commodity where life was hard and often brutal, this organization flourished throughout the mining camps of the West. Many fraternal organizations such as the Masons, Elks, and Oddfellows were apt to be clannish and somewhat disapproving of the rowdy miners they encountered, for they took themselves and their pomp and ceremony quite seriously. Flowery oratory, ribald songs, and practical jokes were much admired by the Clampers. To make fun of the fancy sashes and bejewelled vests the others wore, the Clampers took to cutting tin can lids into odd shapes and pinning them to their own simple vests. They called this "wearing your tin", a practice continued to this day, although badges, ribbons, and enameled pins have taken the place of the tin can lids. Dedicated to taking care of widows and orphans, particularly widows, the organization fell on hard times. It experienced a rebirth after 1900, when it counteracted the terrible influence of the Women's Christian Temperance Union. E. Clampus Vitus somehow survived the dark years during prohibition, and remains very much alive today. The largest historical organization dedicated to preserving western and mining history, the group has placed historical markers like this one all over the West.

To the left of the monument, a sandy Class II road heads south. This is the way to Mono Mills. Again, note your odometer reading as you leave the pavement. The road will be very sandy in places for the next twenty miles. It might be best to engage your four-wheel drive here, because you can find yourself needing it in soft sand very quickly. The key to getting through these sandy places is to keep your speed up in order to maintain your forward momentum. Only once, when I went far astray, have I found it necessary to lower the air pressure in my tires to fifteen pounds and dig my way out.

On one of our scouting trips, the pair of tracks we were following suddenly dead-ended in sand dunes. Being unable to continue forward, we had to stop, and then we were unable to back out.

A quarter of a mile off the pavement, a U.S. Forest Service sign announces that you are entering the Mono Basin National Forest Scenic Area. Travel off established roadways is prohibited. The area to the left is part of a BLM Wilderness Study Area.

The road skirts the eastern side of the Mono Basin National Forest Scenic Area.

A half-mile in from the highway, sun-bleached railroad ties begin to appear on the right, marking the old right-of-way. Six miles on, the old roadbed has been picked clean. Not only were the rails and spikes removed, but the ties as well. Here the route of the rails is sometimes marked only by the slightly elevated roadbed. According to Frank S. Wedertz, author of *Bodie 1859-1900*, each tie measured six by eight inches across and was seven feet long. After being exposed to the elements for more than a century, all those ties are now considerably smaller.

Old ties along the right-of-way.

There are some pleasant places to camp along here, in the shade of those widely scattered juniper trees that have not been cut down for firewood. Three quarters of a mile off the highway, our road skirts the eastern end of a sand dune, pretty much stabilized by vegetation. In the next three miles the road will pass the end of more sand dunes, all of which are still creeping eastward. At a point two and a half miles in from the highway, the moving dunes have traveled far enough in the last eighty years to completely cover the railroad right-of-way. This dune migration might not be as slow as one might think. Timothy Tierney, author of *Geology of the Mono Basin,* reports that in the spring of 1995 he found the previous winter's snow still preserved under several inches of wind blown sand. And where did all this sand come from? Why from the bottom of ancient Lake Russell, of course.

12,327' Mt. Warren dominates the skyline west of Mono Lake.

During the Plio-Pleistocene mighty rivers of melt water from glaciers in the Sierra Nevada poured into the basin containing ancestral Lake Russell, whose descendant is called Mono Lake. At that time, however, the body of water was considerably larger than the Mono Lake of today. At its peak, which it reached several times, Lake Russell extended east well into what is now Nevada. Wave-cut terraces of Lake Russell can be seen as horizontal benches on the hillsides to the south. At its highest level in the Pleistocene, Lake Russell stood at the 7,140' contour level. At that time, the lake was 750 feet deep and covered some 267 square miles. From here it drained southward into Adobe Valley, creating another lake before flowing into the Owens River and ultimately into the Gulf of California by way of the Colorado River. Compare that with the Mono Lake of today, which covers only 140 square miles. When Lake Russell all but dried up, the prevailing westerly winds picked up those fine sediments from the exposed lake bottom and concentrated them here. The lowest salt flats will eventually be covered by water once again as (by court order) the City of Los Angeles allows Lee Vining Creek, Walker Creek, Rush Creek, and Parker Creek to bring the water level up to the lake's 1941 contour level of 6,392 feet. (In 1981 the lake had dropped twenty feet to its modern day low at the 6,372' level.)

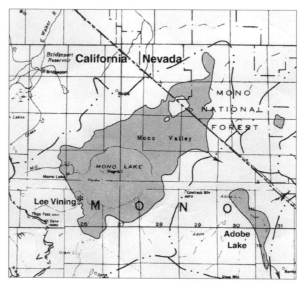

During the peak runoff times of the Plio-Pleistocene Ice Age, ancient Lake Russell was much larger than the Mono Lake of today. It apparently had an outlet to the south where water drained into Adobe Valley and eventually south to the Owens River. (Map after Snyder, Hardman, and Zdenek, 1964)

Four and a half miles south of the highway, some dusty alkali flats are crossed. These, too, are a product of the drying up of Mono Lake. During the Pleistocene, Lake Russell contained fresh water. But when the glaciers had melted, the supply of fresh water was halted, and the lake slowly dried up, concentrating the dissolved minerals into less and less water. Many of those minerals precipitated out on the lakebed, where they were eventually exposed to the air as the lake shrank. The shrubs and grasses here are very salt tolerant.

The Bodie & Benton Railway had but four stations along its 31.74-mile length, one at each end and two along the line. At a point 6.1 miles from Highway 167 is the site of what once was Warm Springs Station. It was twenty-two rail miles from Bodie and ten rail miles north of Mono Mills. Warm Springs has more historical significance than simply being a station on a logging railroad.

It was here that the first locomotive *Tybo* was barged across Mono Lake in pieces, pulled by the steamboat *Rocket*. The locomotive was brought ashore at

Warm Springs and re-assembled. Rails were then laid south on the prepared roadbed at the rate of nearly a mile a day. (About 3:00 p.m. on the afternoon of November 14, 1881, the last rail was laid in place and spiked down. The construction of the entire project, from beginning to end, had taken only eight months.)

There was a siding here at Warm Springs Station where the other two locomotives, *Inyo* and *Bodie*, were also reassembled after their barge rides. All three locomotives were wood-burning Mogul-type engines built in 1880 by Union Iron Works in San Francisco. Other rolling stock consisted of thirty flat cars, a tank car, five logging cars, two pole cars and a caboose. All were connected with "link and pin" couplers. The line had two "speedsters" for the quick movement of maintenance personnel along the line. The first was homemade using a two-cycle air-cooled engine. Just before the line closed, a second speedster was fashioned from an Oldsmobile automobile.

In 1882 it was decided to lay a branch line east to connect with the Carson & Colorado Railroad at Benton Station nearly forty miles to the east. The Bodie Railroad and Lumber Company was reorganized and renamed the Bodie & Benton Railway. The proposed extension would connect Bodie with the outside world and provide easy freight and passenger service to the isolated, but booming community. The route was surveyed nearly to Benton, with nine miles of road grade actually prepared. Nevertheless, the extension to Benton was suddenly abandoned when it dawned on the owners that connection with the Carson & Colorado Railroad might bring lumber from Lake Tahoe south to break their virtual monopoly on timber.

As important a place as Warm Springs Station once was, there is virtually nothing left to mark its presence. One must have a keen eye to discern the raised roadbed of the spur that headed east toward Benton. There is a short side road to the right here that goes through a fence and drops down to a marshy area along the old shoreline.

The road to Mono Mills continues to make its way south. A ridge of tufa rises above the roadway to the left. Soon a gate in a drift fence is encountered. Please close the gate again after you pass through. At a point two miles south of the site of Warm Springs Station (8.2 miles south of Highway 167) the old railroad grade crosses our road. This is the last time we will see the right-of-way from our car until we get to Mono Mills.

Within a mile our road again crosses alkali flats. The deeply eroded and rutted tracks remind us that this is no place to be in wet weather. While rain makes the sandy areas easier to negotiate, it turns these salt flats into a bottomless quagmire of mud. Just beyond the alkali flats, a simple one-room cabin made of railroad ties is passed on the right. While the structure's history is unclear, it appears to be a rancher's line shack. In this area several side roads to the right go down to the old shoreline.

A couple of miles south of the cabin is an area where the sagebrush grows to extraordinary size. Normally, Great Basin Sagebrush *Artemesia ranquilit* grows to heights of perhaps four to five feet. But here, I measured one giant specimen at a height of twelve feet!

The specimen of Great Basin Sagebrush, to the right
of the car, was measured at a height of twelve feet!

To the right, down by the old shoreline, some tufa towers can be seen. Common around the shores of Mono Lake, tufa is a calcium carbonate mineral that was formed where fresh water springs came up from the bottom of ancient Lake Russell.

The roadway once again becomes very sandy, so keep your speed up in order to maintain your forward momentum. This is no place for conventional vehicles!

The road forks at a point 13.0 miles south of Highway 167. The right fork continues to follow the old shoreline to eventually rejoin Highway 120 east of Panum Crater. For Mono Mills, go to the left. For the next six miles the road will gradually gain nearly nine hundred feet in elevation as it climbs up to Mono Mills. But again, in the next half-mile some areas of very soft sand are to be encountered, so don't slow down.

A severely burned area is reached at a point 14.2 miles from Highway 167. This was the northern flank of the Crater Fire, which burned through here in 2001. The fire was touched off by a lightning strike at 9:30 a.m. on the morning of August 12, 2001. Before the fire was finally controlled on August 15th, some 5,600 acres had burned. At its peak, more than three hundred firefighters were involved in the suppression effort, which cost the government $700,000 to control. Be careful with fire, folks!

The devastating effects of the 2001 Crater Fire.

A crossroads is reached at the 14.6-mile point from the pavement. Here make a 90-degree turn to the left onto Forest Road 1N21. This will take you east 0.4 miles to yet another fork; this time go to the right. The road now swings to the south again and passes a well and water tank in 0.7 miles. A half-mile beyond the cattle tank, another crossroads is reached.

Stay straight ahead for Mono Mills. The road crossing our road has all the appearance of the old railroad grade, but it is not. If you want to make a short side-trip to see the trestle site in Big Dry Creek, turn left here. It is 0.7 miles back to the arroyo carved out of the volcanic bedrock by Big Dry Creek. From the road's end at the edge of the arroyo, it is a walk of about a third of a mile upstream to the old trestle site. In his book *Mining Camp Days,* the late Emil W. Billeb (who managed the Bodie & Benton Railway from 1908 to 1917) has a photo of the Dry Creek trestle, and there are no trees to be seen anywhere near it. That trestle is gone today; not even the footings remain. The only thing to be seen is the raised roadbed on the south side of the arroyo and the cut in the bank on the north side. Prior to August of 2001, this section of Big Dry Creek was a beautiful oasis of Jeffrey pine. The Crater Fire ran through here, however, killing most of these fine trees. If there was anything good to come of that wildland fire, it was that it burned off the heavy brush, leaving the old railroad grade exposed and easy to see.

From the crossroads at 16.2 miles continue straight ahead in a southerly direction. Another water tank is passed after another mile. The next road intersection comes at the 18.6-mile point. This is where the old railroad grade comes in from the left rear. The site of Mono Mills and Highway 120 is only a third of a mile to the south.

An historical marker notes the site of Mono Mills. From the monument look down on the site and try to envision a two-story structure, with the ground floor in the ravine below and the second story on the same level as the top of the ravine. The two-story sawmill was built over a gully, so that gravity could assist in the loading of cut lumber onto the rail cars. Logs were hauled in from the forest using horse drawn "Michigan wheels". They went into the sawmill on the second floor, where they were cut to the desired dimension using one of five steam powered saws. Trees were ripped by two 54-inch saws, or a 44-inch pony saw. The rough-cut lumber was then cut to the desired length by two cutoff saws. The boiler and steam engine were on the lower level. Its concrete foundation still remains. The larger and heavier pieces of cut lumber remained on the upper floor. They were then dragged over to the lip of the ravine, where they could be lowered by skids to the flat cars waiting on the tracks in the bottom of the ravine.

At its peak, the large sawmill employed two hundred people, including not only mill workers, but also lumberjacks, teamsters, clerks, and cooks. Some workers were employed by the railroad, but most worked for a wood contractor, Gilchrist Sharp and Company. The company had machine and blacksmith shops here, as well as a boarding house and commissary. By the fall of 1882 there were some thirty log cabins surrounding the sawmill.

The sawmill looked like this when Mary DeDecker took
this picture in 1948. Today only a few timbers remain.
(County of Inyo, Eastern California Museum photo)

One of several flywheels that turned a belt.

Deep snow caused the sawmill to shut down during the winter months, January through March. In his book *Mining Camp Days,* Emil Billeb recalls that in December of 1910, it took five days to complete the 32-mile journey, because of deep snowdrifts across the track. The railroad normally did not operate during the winter months.

To return to Lee Vining, turn right onto Highway 120. Fortunately the site of Mono Mills was saved from the devastation of the Crater Fire, but the destruction along both sides of the highway are soon evident. (Highway 120 was closed for several days during the fire.) From Mono Mills, it is nine miles back to Highway 395, and from there, five miles back to your starting point in Lee Vining.

A train crew at Mono Mills.
(Laws Railroad Museum photo)

10

Pizona's Wild Mustangs

Special Features:	This lonely road leads to an old cattle camp, but along the way you are more likely to encounter free-roaming wild horses than cows.
Time Required:	This is an all day outing out of Lee Vining (or anywhere else).
Distance Involved:	From Lee Vining it is 51 miles into Pizona, the last eight being over dirt roads.
Degree of Difficulty:	Generally the road into Pizona is no worse than Class II, although there are a few areas of soft sand, and a couple of mud holes, where four-wheel drive might be helpful in getting through.
Special Features:	I cannot guarantee that you will see wild horses along the road to Pizona, but over a thirty-year period, I have always encountered them in the area.

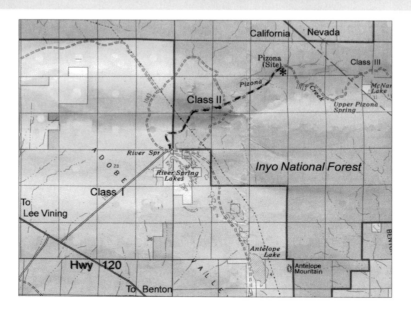

When you mention the words "wild horses", most people think of the wide-open spaces of Nevada, not California with its thirty million people. Yet tucked away in a remote corner of Mono County horses still roam free, never feeling the restraint of a halter or bridle. While I cannot guarantee you will see wild horses by going into Pizona, your chances are better here than anywhere else in the state.

It is nearly as difficult to find Pizona, as it is to find wild horses in California. From downtown Lee Vining go south on Highway 395 a distance of five miles to State Route 120. Note your odometer reading, and turn left here. Proceed eastward another 38 miles to River Springs Road (un-marked in recent years). Turn left on this graded road, again noting your odometer reading as you leave the pavement. Your watch for wild horses should begin here in Adobe Valley.

Today's wild horses and burros are the descendants of previous generations of domesticated stock which once escaped from, or were set loose by, their owners. They have been part of the western scene for perhaps two hundred years or more. In Peter Ogden's journal of 1828, he mentions seeing wild horses. In 1841 John Bidwell's California-bound party also mentions seeing wild horses. While the State of Nevada first comes to mind when wild horses are mentioned, and indeed Nevada has a little more than half of all this country's wild horses, there are nine other states, including California, which have wild horse populations, too.

Wild horses in Adobe Valley.

Prior to 1971 there was very little interest in wild horses. "Mustangers" would often capture wild horses and sell them to slaughterhouses for meat. Other animals would simply be shot for "sport". But thanks largely to the drive and compassion of one woman, Velma "Wild Horse Annie" Johnson, who lobbied Congress to protect these magnificent animals, in December of 1971 the *Wild Free-Roaming Horse and Burro Act* was passed by Congress, and the legislation was signed into law by President Richard Nixon. As a result, the Bureau of Land Management and the U.S. Forest Service are now charged with the protection and management of these animals. Those animals to be found here in Adobe Valley are part of Herd Management Area NV317, administered by the BLM

Field Office in Carson City, Nevada. **If you should see wild horses, admire them from a distance, but do not chase or otherwise harass them.**

This basin contained elongated Adobe Lake during the Plio-Pleistocene Ice Age. As pluvial lakes of the Ice Age Great Basin go, Adobe Lake was rather small. It covered a mere twenty square miles and was only seventy-five feet deep. It received its waters from an overflowing Lake Russell (Mono Lake) to the northwest, and drained its excess waters south into the Owens River.

The graded road swings to the left 3.6 miles north of the highway. Stay to the right, going through the fence at the old ranch house. The low stone walls on the left are said to be the remains of an old stage station on the Benton-Virginia City route. The wooden ranch house is the remnant of a somewhat younger cattle camp. Across the road from the structure is River Springs, a naturally occurring waterhole. Here roads take off in three directions. Keep left, with the corrals just to your left. If you are on the correct road, you will begin climbing a hill behind the ranch.

The Class II road is crossing basalt lava that is relatively recent in geologic terms. It is Pliocene in age, only some ten million years old. The lava of these mountains was important to the Paiute and earlier Indians, because it provided an inexhaustible supply of obsidian, the raw material used in the manufacture of arrowheads. The obsidian, together with salt and piñon nuts, provided the local Indians with valuable trade commodities. In the summer when the snow had melted, they would climb to the high passes of the Sierra to meet and trade with the Indians from the western side. This explains the presence of seashells and acorns in middens in the western Great Basin.

After leaving River Springs the road is either soft and sandy or rocky and rough, but always remains Class II. A mile from the old ranch house, the road crosses the power line access road and passes beneath the transmission lines. Soon the piñon forest is entered. The road crosses a low divide and descends into a small valley. This is another good place to watch for wild horses.

Today the River Springs Ranch house looks much as it did in this 1970 photo.

The lonely road to Pizona.

Eventually, four miles from River Springs and 7.5 miles from Highway 120, the first of several mud holes is encountered, just before the road enters a small canyon. Here subsurface water is forced to the surface by the twin ramparts of lava. The willows grow fifteen feet high here, and they threaten to overgrow the roadway, now reduced to twin tire tracks. Thickets of willow and wild roses give shelter to an amazing variety of wildlife. While making camp here one afternoon, we noted the presence of quail, jackrabbits, cottontails and deer. At dusk, bats came out of the cracks and crevices of the basalt cliffs towering above our campsite. They were feeding on flying insects. During the night, the distinctive odor of a skunk wafted through our camp.

Once past several more mud holes and through the willow thicket, the road comes to Pizona Meadow at a point nearly eight miles from Highway 120. In the wet meadow areas, we found two plant species that seemed very out of place in this otherwise arid land. One was the slender and seemingly leafless stems of the horsetail *Equisetum arvense*, a very primitive plant little changed from the time when they grew in great abundance during the Pennsylvanian Period some three hundred million years ago. Abrasive silica is concentrated in the *Equisetum* stems, making them useful as scouring brushes one hundred years ago.

Horsetail *Equisetum arvense*

The other plant, seemingly out of place, is the delicate and very beautiful columbine flower *Aquilegia truncata*. I would not be surprised to see it in the High Sierra, but I am here. Nevertheless, the columbines grow here in great abundance. Another pretty meadow dweller, although not found in great numbers, is the wild iris *Iris missouriensis*.

Wild iris

Columbine

At the upper end of the meadows, just beyond the canyon narrows, sits a rock-walled cabin. This is downtown Pizona, a site whose historical roots remain obscure. Many pieces of worked obsidian and a few arrowheads have been found in the Pizona area, suggesting it was a popular hunting ground for the Paiute and even earlier peoples. Look around if you wish, but remember, the looting of archaeological sites is unlawful.

Stone cabin in downtown Pizona

Upon passing the cabin the road continues across another valley 1.6 miles to Upper Pizona Spring (ten miles from Highway 120). This is another place to watch for wild horses. From here you can go on to cross the state line into Nevada, passing McBride Spring and eventually coming out onto Highway 6.

Got Gas?

Many backroad explorers feel more comfortable if they are carrying an extra five or ten gallons of gasoline. Keep in mind that gasoline carried in any container, other than the vehicle's fuel tank, poses a somewhat greater fire hazard. Extra gasoline should never under any circumstances be carried in plastic containers, and even the GI "Jerry Cans" of heavy metal are notorious for their leaking gaskets.

If you must carry extra gasoline, observe these Do's and Don'ts:

- **Do** secure the gas container so that it cannot tip over or bounce around. Utilize an appropriate external mounting bracket.
- **Don't** carry any gas can inside the passenger space of a vehicle. Not only is it an extreme fire hazard, but it is sure to leak, creating noxious fumes.
- **Do** carry an ABC fire extinguisher of adequate size.
- **Don't** fill the container while it is attached to the vehicle. Avoid static electricity by setting it on the ground when filling it.
- **Do** put the extra fuel inside your car's gas tank as soon as you can.
- **Don't** forget to bring a pouring spout, preferably with a screen filter to catch the larger rust particles that might be in the gas can.

Unless you are driving a real gas hog, the need to carry extra fuel in the Inyo-Mono country should not be necessary, providing you top off your tank before heading into the backcountry.

Always carry extra fuel outside
of the passenger compartment.

Mammoth Lakes of Old

In the late 1870s the newly formed Mammoth Mining Company built an enormous forty-stamp mill at Mill City above Mammoth Lakes. These are the mill ruins in the early1920s before the structure was intentionally burned as a fire hazard in 1929. (County of Inyo, Eastern California Museum photo)

Only stone foundations and an iron flywheel remain.

Chapter III

Trails Out of Mammoth Lakes

Mammoth Lakes is a popular resort area perhaps best known for its fine winter skiing. The community also attracts a lot of summer vacationers with its five lakes, miles of mountain trails, and other natural attractions.

Mammoth City began in 1877, when prospectors looking for the "Lost Cement Mine" found gold on what would become Mammoth Creek. In the following year the Mammoth Mine opened, as did a twenty-stamp mill just down the road in nearby Mill City. In 1879 there were 1500 people in the triple camps of Mammoth City, Mill City, and Pine City, enough to justify the opening of a post office. In that year a second bank of twenty more stamps was added to the mill, as it processed ores from the Mammoth, Headlight, Monte Cristo, and Lisbon Mines. The future seemed rosy, but it was not to be. By 1881 the Mammoth Mine had produced some $200,000 in gold; however, the expenses to obtain and process the ore were greater than the net return. It closed, as did the other mines. By 1888 there were only a handful of people left in Mammoth City. Mill City and Pine City were completely abandoned, and ceased to exist. The gold mined by today's citizenry in Mammoth Lakes comes from the tourists' pockets.

Summer visitors to Mammoth Lakes should certainly make their first stop at the U.S. Forest Service Visitor Center on Highway 203 as you enter town. There are not only attractive displays, but information can be obtained on what to see and do. The author recommends that any first time visitor walk through the earthquake fault and visit the nearby Devil's Postpile National Monument. For anglers, the possibilities are unlimited, not only in the five Mammoth Lakes, but also anywhere along the June Lake Loop just to the north, or in the creeks, rivers, and lakes just to the east along U.S. Highway 395. The outdoorsman can easily spend two weeks in the Mammoth area, doing something different each day.

Mammoth Lakes and the nearby communities offer a full range of basic services. Room accommodations are generally plentiful in the summer, and the U.S. Forest Service has nine campgrounds in the Mammoth Lakes area and a dozen more in nearby areas.

11

Glass Mountain Traverse

Primary Attraction:	This outing offers great scenic vistas, interesting volcanic geology, and some little visited country.
Time Required:	This is a full day's outing.
Miles Involved:	It is a long 39 miles from Highway 395 to Highway 120. Be sure your fuel tank is full when you leave.
Degree of Difficulty:	The roads are generally Class II and III.
Note:	Because of the labyrinth of roads in this area, it is important that you follow these directions carefully. Unfortunately, the Class III roads between Clover Patch and Sawmill Meadows do not appear on the current (1993) Inyo National Forest map.

If you are looking for a summer outing that has a little something for everyone, may I suggest the Glass Mountain country? This route can be done from either end, but it is a little easier to follow going from south to north. As you stop along the way, keep your eyes on the ground beneath your feet. Arrowheads have been found along this entire route. (Remember: The National Antiquities Act of 1906 prohibits the collecting of artifacts, including arrowheads, on public land.)

From Mammoth Lakes, take State Route 203 down to U.S. Highway 395; then turn right going towards Bishop. After 5.3 miles a paved county road heads north towards Whitmore Hot Spring and Benton Crossing. Turn left here at the little church. Glass Mountain is straight ahead on the skyline. By the end of our excursion, we will be on the other side of it.

After a little more than six miles from Highway 395, the road crosses the Owens River at Benton Crossing, and swings to the southeast following the northern shoreline of Crowley Lake. Four miles beyond Benton Crossing, look for a dirt road off to the left. This is Forest Road 3S01; turn left here. You may wish to note your odometer reading as you leave the pavement. The Class I road makes its way eastward, gently climbing the pumice-covered slope. Side roads go left after 0.4 miles and 3.3 miles from the pavement, but stay right on the main road. A spring known as Watterson Troughs is passed 4.3 miles from the pavement. Road 3S01 continues east, with two more side roads to the left

0.3 and 0.8 miles from Watterson Troughs. Again, stay right on the main road. However, at the side road 1.0 miles beyond Watterson Troughs, turn left onto Forest Road 3S49. The road now deteriorates to Class II.

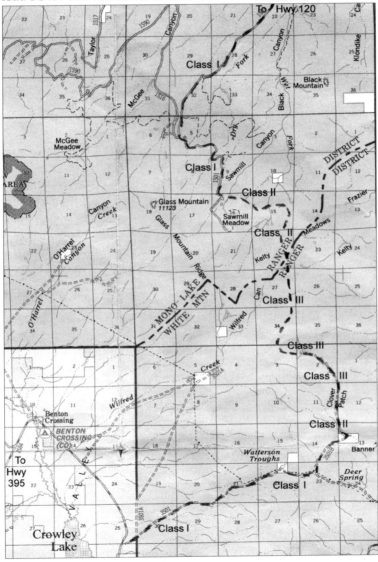

For the next 1.3 miles the road crosses a low ridge, and drops down into a meadow area known as the "Clover Patch". Keep to the left at the fork, which will turn you north going up the valley. In a mile you should see some tracks going right up a small draw; turn right here. If you have not done so already, engage your four-wheel drive here. (Note: The jeep trail you are starting on does not appear on the current Inyo National Forest map.) It is a little steep and rough Class III section for the next tenth of a mile. A quarter of a mile beyond the top of the grade is a "T" intersection; turn left.

The easy Class III road now steeply zigzags up the hillside. Once on top of this 8,600' ridge, stop and look about. To the left are great views of the Sierra skyline. To the right, Mounts Boundary and Montgomery stand out at the northern end of the White Mountains.

The road continues to climb, passing a spring and some prospect holes. It is in this area where fields of white lupine can be found in the spring. At a point 6.2 miles beyond Forest Road 3S01, a steep Class III side road goes left up the ridge. Turn left here, and soon you will be rewarded with a grand viewpoint of the entire Lake Crowley country. The elevation here is 9,900 feet.

Crowley Lake occupies the eastern end of a basin known as Long Valley. Keep in mind that this basin is known geologically as a collapsed caldera. The entire area between Mono Lake and Crowley Lake has been volcanically active for the last 3.5 million years. That activity continues today, much to the concern of the U.S. Geological Survey and state and local officials. The Long Valley Caldera has the potential to make the 1980 eruption of Mount St. Helens look minuscule.

Here on a shoulder of Glass Mountain, the volcanic rocks you are standing on came pushing up through the earth's crust one to two million years ago. The hot lava cooled so rapidly that the molecules in the minerals did not have a chance to orient themselves. Thus, instead of crystalline rocks with individual minerals showing, this rapid cooling produced a smooth glassy product known as obsidian. However, it was 700,000 years ago that a tremendous volcanic explosion occurred in Long Valley below you. A staggering 140 cubic miles of ash and lava was ejected, making it perhaps the most catastrophic volcanic eruption that North America has ever experienced. (In contrast, in May of 1980 Mt. St. Helens blew out a quarter of a cubic mile of material.) A gaseous froth of molten rock blew out from beneath the earth, with an incandescent ash cloud moving outward across the land surface at speeds of one hundred miles per hour. Part of this pyroclastic flow moved down into the Owens Valley, past the sites of today's Bishop and Big Pine. In its path it left the "Bishop Tuff", a series of volcanic rocks that underlie Highway 395 at the Sherwin Grade. To the west, this speeding cloud went up and over the Sierra crest to flow down the San Joaquin River canyon all the way to the San Joaquin Valley. This ash covered 580 square miles of Central California and Western Nevada. To the east, traces of ash from this explosive eruption can still be found as far away as central Nebraska. Glass Mountain is a remnant of that pre-explosion volcano.

This two to three foot layer of white volcanic ash from the Long Valley Caldera
can be found in fanglomerate deposits in Black Canyon southeast of Bishop.

What are the chances of this happening again? Most geologists view future
volcanic activity in the Long Valley area as inevitable, although the severity and
timing are anybody's guess. Mammoth Mountain, the 11,053' volcanic peak
just to the west, started building about 150,000 years ago, just a moment ago in
geologic time. During the last 100,000 years it has averaged a major eruption
every five thousand years. The Red Cones on Mammoth's southwest flank
are two cinder cones that erupted only ten thousand years ago. Five hundred
years ago the mountain produced a steam explosion less than a mile west of
the Mammoth Mountain Ski Lodge. Indeed, subterranean steam still warms
the waters of Hot Creek, much to the delight of locals and tourists alike. In
the twenty-year period from 1976 to 1996, the floor of Long Valley has risen
nearly two feet in elevation. This suggests that molten rock, perhaps only three
miles deep, is pushing upward. Each year thousands of earthquake swarms are
recorded in the Mammoth Lakes area. Most are quite small, but some have
reached a Richter Scale reading of 6.0, which in a big city would be disastrous.
The U.S.G.S. is actively monitoring seismic activity in the Long Valley Caldera,
but what the future will bring, nobody knows.

Continue driving along this lofty ridge. Vistas will begin to open to the
west. Soon the summit of 11,123' Glass Mountain comes into view, and then
Mounts Banner and Ritter, with the sawtooth Minarets to their left. Compare
the vegetation here at ten thousand feet with the vegetation in the Sierra Nevada

at the same elevation. While there are limited stands of Limber pine here on Glass Mountain, the predominate plant on this treeless ridge is Desert mahogany *Cercocarpus ledifolius,* an important browse plant for deer. The forest is thicker and more well developed on the northern slopes of Glass Mountain, because the volcanic soils are not as exposed to the direct rays of the sun, and thus are better able to retain moisture.

Glass Mountain

After going up this ridge for a mile, turn right to rejoin the road you were on. Once back on this main road again, turn left heading in a northerly direction. Now mostly Class II, the road swings to the west again as it descends to Kelty Meadows, a wet spot surrounded by aspen trees. This area has few visitors outside of deer season. If you examine the aspen tree trunks in the grove near the stream crossing, you will find many carvings dating from the 1930s, when Basque sheepherders often brought their flocks here for summer pasture.

The road crosses a low ridge and encounters a second meadow and aspen grove. Another small stream is forded. A quarter of a mile beyond, turn left following the drift fence uphill in a southerly direction. After a mile the road passes through the fence and turns to the west. The forest here is nearly 100% lodgepole pine. That species will change to Jeffrey pine in the next two miles.

The road soon turns to the north again, and descends into the next drainage to the west. The forest of lodgepole pine makes a transition to aspen, and then soon changes again, this time to Jeffrey pine. At a point three miles beyond the drift fence, a good graded road is suddenly encountered. To the left a half-mile is Sawmill Meadow. You will want to turn right.

Once on this graded road for a mile, the ruins of an old sawmill can be seen on the right. During the 1881 to 1914 era when the mines of Bodie were going strong, the underground workings needed enormous amounts of timber to keep the tunnels and shafts from collapsing. To fill this need the Bodie Railway & Lumber Company was organized in 1881 for the purpose of carrying lumber 34 miles from the Glass Mountain area to the mines of Bodie. The company immediately began laying its narrow gauge rails southward around the eastern edge of Mono Lake. At the same time a large sawmill, named Mono Mills, was constructed. (See Excursion #9) The rails reached the mill on November 14, 1881, just nine months after the project began. In 1897 the rails were extended four miles farther south into the forest. Those rails did not reach this particular sawmill, but lumber produced in the outlying sawmills like this one was transported by wagon to Mono Mills. If you look closely at the point where the large timbers are joined, you will see that no nails were used.

The old sawmill was built without the use of nails.

Two miles beyond the sawmill site, the McGee Canyon Road goes straight ahead, while Forest Road 1S01 turns off to the right. Either road will take you to State Route 120. By turning right it is seven miles of dusty road to State Highway 120. Once on the pavement, a left turn will take you to the site of Mono Mills in 22 miles, and Highway 395 in 31 miles. A right turn will take you to Benton Hot Springs and U.S. Highway 6.

Bishop Of Yesteryear

Horse auction in Bishop, circa 1886
(County of Inyo, Eastern California Museum photo)

Who says it never snows in Bishop. It certainly did in January
of 1933. (County of Inyo, Eastern California Museum photo)

Chapter IV

Trails Out of Bishop

Bishop sits deep in the Owens Valley astride U.S. Highway 395 connecting San Diego and Reno. Its early days were associated with farming and ranching. Then in the 1920s, the City of Los Angeles bought up most of the water rights in the Owens Valley, and built an aqueduct to send all that water south. Folks have been arguing about it ever since.

History buffs and railroad fans will certainly want to take a six-mile side trip up U.S. Highway 6 to Laws Station on the old Carson & Colorado Railroad (later the Southern Pacific). It connected with the Virginia & Truckee Railroad at Mound House, Nevada near Carson City, and went three hundred miles south to Keeler at the southern end of the Owens Valley. Laws Station serviced this narrow gauge line between 1883 and 1959. The old station and several acres of yard facilities have been preserved as part of the Laws Railroad Museum.

Bishop and its environs, with a population of 6,000, are certainly noted as a tourist center for outdoorsmen. Hunting, fishing, camping, backpacking, and photography are all pursuits that bring people through Bishop. The town has complete tourist facilities, and is the headquarters for Inyo National Forest. There are campgrounds aplenty in the Bishop area. The nearest one is at Schober Lane, a mile south of town on Highway 395. An Inyo County campground at the old millpond can be found just off Highway 395 five miles west of town. The U.S. Forest Service has seven campgrounds in the very scenic Bishop Creek Canyon just up State Highway 168 southwest of town.

The White Mountain Ranger Station on North Main Street is a good place to stop for information on current road conditions.

12

Chidago Canyon

Special Features:	Except after a rare winter snowstorm, this is an outing that can usually be done any time of the year. The outing offers a wide variety of old Indian petroglyphs, and interesting geology exposed by a canyon eroded down into a volcanic tableland.
Time Required:	This excursion can be done in a half-day out of Bishop.
Miles Involved:	From downtown Bishop to the road's end in Chidago Canyon, the distance is only twenty miles.
Degree of Difficulty:	Most of the Chidago Canyon road is Class II, except for the lower 1.5 miles of the canyon, which is an easy Class III.

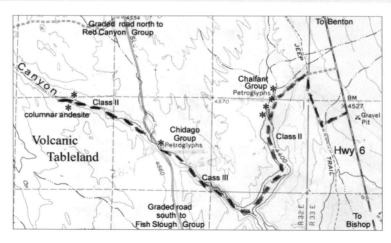

To find Chidago Canyon from downtown Bishop, go north on Main Street (U.S. Highway 395) to the far end of town. U.S. Highway 6 begins where Highway 395 makes a sweeping turn to the west next to the fairgrounds. Turn right onto Highway 6, noting your odometer as you leave Highway 395. Follow Highway 6 northward as it passes through Chalfant Valley. The highway enters Mono County after a little more than eight miles. The mile markers on the right side of the road begin at zero. Keep your eye on these paddles, for they are critical to finding the unmarked Chidago Canyon turnoff. The markers on the east side of the highway mark off every mile on the even mile. Those on the west side of the highway mark off every mile on the half mile.

Watch for mile marker 06 MNO 8^{00} on the right at a point sixteen miles from Highway 395. Again check your odometer reading. The turnoff to Chidago is 0.6 miles ahead on the left. Again set your trip odometer to zero as you turn left off of Highway 6. Go west on the wide graded road for 0.3 miles to where a "T" intersection is reached. Turn right following the high standard graded dirt road northward for another tenth of a mile. Here a Class I road starts off on the left, heading west towards the nearby bluffs. At a point 0.8 miles from Highway 6, the BLM has blocked off a large parking area, although no signs announce its purpose. Stop here and walk one hundred yards west to the base of the bluff. The Chalfant Petroglyph Site extends to the right and left for nearly a mile. (The best ones are to the right.)

Unfortunately, some of these irreplaceable cultural resources have been deliberately vandalized with firearms, while others have been damaged by attempts to steal entire blocks of the rocks containing them. That is why the BLM constructed a barrier around the parking area, so that thieves could not drive up close to the base of the cliff.

Prehistoric rock art sites come in three general types: petroglyphs where symbols, animals, and humanoid figures are pecked into the surface of the rock, pictographs where those same features are painted on the rock's surface, and geoglyphs where rocks are laid out on the ground in very specific patterns and/ or alignments. Archaeologists have been studying these sites for well over one hundred years. Yet in spite of modern technology, ancient rock art sites continue to raise more questions than answers. In spite of the claims made in some books, we really do not know why the Native Americans made rock art. We do not know what many of the various symbols represent, we do not know why the various sites were selected, and in many cases, we do not know when the rock art was created. Our Native American population of today maintains, and passes on, certain oral traditions of their culture, but they cannot interpret the meaning of these symbols any more than the most learned scientist.

Certain educated guesses can be made about some of these sites. Some rock art sites were placed at natural chock points near water sources where animals were likely to be, but that does not work for many sites. Some rock art sites were near permanent village sites, or near seasonal hunting camps, but many others seem to be remote from places of habitation.

Here at the eastern edge of the volcanic tableland, it seems that this particular group of petroglyphs was chipped in the soft rhyolite rock above a small stream.

At times, the stream might have even been a substantial river. During the last one million years great glaciers have advanced and retreated many times in the Sierra Nevada. During inter-glacial warm periods when the melt water runoff reached its peak, Lake Russell (which occupied the basin now containing Mono Lake) overflowed to the south, channeling water into Adobe Valley, where it overflowed south into the then mighty Owens River. That overflow ran down along the base of these cliffs, into lower Chidago Canyon, and on through Fish Slough to the south. There is still subsurface water in this ancient channel, as evidenced by the few scattered cottonwood trees just south of the parking area.

The petroglyphs at this site seem to be dominated by the more abstract, geometric forms that use both angular lines and circular shapes. The most striking ones are non-figurative, consisting of large circles with multiple patterns inside. Notably scarce are animals and humans, although examples of those can be found, too. When were these petroglyphs pecked into the rock? That is difficult to say, but the rhyolite rock is soft and easily weathered. BLM archaeologists guess that they were made within the last one thousand years, or more erosion would have occurred. (Other petroglyph sites in Mono and Inyo Counties pre-date the arrival of the Paiute, and they could be up to five thousand years old.) What do these creative peckings mean? That is the great, unsolved riddle.

These unusual five-foot circular forms are unique to the Chalfant site. If you visit the site in the morning, most of the petroglyphs will be in the sunshine.

As you walk along the base of the volcanic bluff, notice the native shrubs in the bottom of the sandy wash. Very common is the coyote willow *Salix eique*, a shrub that grows along dry washes and is very drought resistant. It may be recognized by its yellow catkins. Also here is the large thorny bush known as cotton thorn, sometimes called horsebush or *Tetramydia axillaries*. Like its cousin *Tetramydia canescens,* which lives higher in the White Mountains to the east, the shrub has yellow disc-like flowers that are common in the sunflower family to which it belongs. A much smaller flowering plant in the sandy wash, conspicuous by its deep purple flowers, is the indigo bush *Psorothamnus polyclenius*. Sometimes unnoticed among the sage and shadscale, is the spiny hopsage *Grayia spinosa*. The leaves (actually bracts) often display an unusual flesh to rose color. The spines notwithstanding, this little shrub is the dinner of choice for mule deer, as well as herds of domestic sheep and goats.

Coyote Willow   Indigo Bush

From the parking area, a Class II road heads south down the wash, and soon the hills begin to encroach on both sides of the wash. At a point 0.8 miles south of the petroglyph parking area, large vertically flat exposures of basalt appear on the left, yet there are no petroglyphs here. Why did the ancient ones choose to decorate one place and not another?

A mile south of the parking area, the sand starts to become soft, and it is a good idea to engage your four-wheel drive. At a point 1.6 miles from the parking area, Chidago Canyon proper is entered from the side. During peak periods of glacial runoff during the Plio-Pliestocene Ice Age, the East Fork of the ancestral Owens River flowed south along the bluffs you have been following. Here it joined what must have been a sizeable stream flowing off Glass Mountain, and together they flowed down through the last mile of Chidago Canyon, before turning south again to join the main Owens River on its way through the Owens Valley to end up in Death Valley.

Here, where the canyon forks, the roads ahead go in four different directions. A little used and very sandy Class IV road goes to the left, heading down Chidago Canyon. After a mile of brush, boulders, and sand, it leaves the Chidago Canyon to meet a Class I road that rejoins Highway 6 just north of the Brown Subdivision in Chalfant Valley. **While it is passable, I cannot recommend the trail down Chidago Canyon, particularly for stock SUVs. It should only be attempted by short wheelbase vehicles with tires aired down to 13 psi.**

There are also Class III roads to the right and left that steeply climb out of the canyon to the top of the volcanic tableland. I cannot recommend them, because once on top, the country is boring! Trust me, you will want to stay in the canyon bottom, taking the Class III road that makes its way up the wash. The route is not difficult, but for the next mile the road winds its way through an obstacle course of boulders, where the drivers of long wheelbase vehicles with running boards may want to have a passenger get out and guide them through. Short wheelbase vehicles should have no trouble weaving in and out between the rocks.

"Newspaper Rock" at the Chidago Petroglyph Site.

Since the early Pleistocene, Chidago Canyon has been eroded out of a sequence of volcanic rocks called the Bishop Tuff. It all started some 760,000 years ago, when an old and dormant volcano suddenly came to life again. Within a few days, or hours, the Long Valley Caldera blew out an estimated 140 cubic miles of rhyolite rock and dust in an enormous supercharged cloud. The prevailing winds blew the lighter material eastward as far as Nebraska, where it settled and where traces of it can still be found today. The larger more heavy particles came to rest within 25 miles on the east, southeast, and north sides of the caldera, where it accumulated to depths of many hundreds of feet. The ash was so hot that the particles fused together as they settled and compacted. The Volcanic Tableland north of Bishop reflects this great accumulation of rhyolite ash. It covers some 325 square miles! In the last 760,000 years, Chidago Canyon has been eroded down through this solidified ash.

At a point 2.5 miles from the Chalfant Petroglyph parking area, a little over three miles from Highway 6, the road suddenly improves from Class III to Class II. In another 0.4 miles is the Chidago Petroglyph Site, just off the graded dirt Fish Slough Road. Again, the threat of vandalism has caused the BLM to install a chain link fence here, but the petroglyphs can clearly be seen. If you visit this site in the morning, the petroglyphs will be in the shadows, the preferred condition by some photographers. An afternoon visit will have them exposed to the western sun.

Although this site is not as large as the previous one, the Chidago Petroglyphs seem to be concentrated in a smaller area. The patterns here seem to be somewhat different than the previous site, suggesting different ages for the two localities. BLM archaeologists say these glyphs are typical of other sites in the territory of the Northern Paiute. Local Native Americans in the Bishop area cannot interpret the various grids, checkerboards, spirals and concentric circles, because they claim they are representations of visions seen by a shaman, a tribal medicine man and religious leader. The Paiute of today do say that the rattlesnake is widely symbolized as a zigzag (from the tracks it leaves) or as a diamond chain (from the markings on its back). Likewise, lizards are another frequent representation, as they were regarded as a messenger between the natural and supernatural worlds.

From the Chidago site, one has several options. By turning to the right, you can follow the high standard dirt road north another 5.7 miles to the Red Canyon Petroglyph Site found on the left side of the road. Notable features at this site include human hands, feet, and bighorn sheep. You can also turn south on the graded road to the Fish Slough Petroglyph Site on the road opposite a large marshy area for which the site is named. Going that direction, it is 4.3 miles to the Fish Slough, and then another eleven miles back to Bishop.

Your backroad adventure need not end quite so quickly, however, as it is possible to drive on up Chidago Canyon a bit farther. Simply cross the Fish Slough Road and look for a set of Class II tracks continuing on up the wash. Soon the tracks will take you by volcanic rock on the left that has large cavities weathered out of it. Next, at a point 1.8 miles west of the Fish Slough Road, a Class II side road goes off to the right. This road will connect with other roads on the Volcanic Tableland; for Chidago Canyon, continue up the wash.

Should you be fortunate to come this way in the springtime, you may be rewarded with nature's bountiful harvest of wildflowers. Perhaps the most common is the blazing star *Mentzelia nitens*, with its pretty five-petaled yellow blossom.

Blazing Star, a common spring wildflower on the volcanic tableland.

At a point 2.5 miles west of the graded road, you will come to a waterless, but otherwise, nice campsite set amid columns of rhyolite. Notice that the columns on the south side of the canyon are leaning over to form an arch, while those on the north side of the canyon are standing straight up. This phenomenon of four, five, six and even seven-sided columns is not unusual, although it is most often seen in basalt, rather than rhyolite. In the nearby Sierra Nevada, the best examples are at Devil's Postpile National Monument on the west side of Mammoth Mountain, on the south side of the Tuolumne River above Glen Aulin High Sierra Camp, and in the bluffs on the north side the South Fork of the San Joaquin River below Mono Hot Springs.

The formation of these columns is a product of the slow cooling process of lava under particular conditions. Besides a slow rate of cooling, the molten basalt rock, or in this case rhyolite, must (1) be uniform in its consistency, (2) be fine grained, (3) be free of gas bubbles, (4) have an overall thickness of at least one hundred feet, and (5) quietly puddle in place without any flow banding. When all of these conditions are met, columns can form as the lava cools. Where these columns are leaning or bent over suggests that one side of the molten mass cooled more rapidly in its final stages of formation, thus deforming the already formed columns.

Columns of rhyolite at the road's end in Chidago Canyon.

Now Class III, the tracks continue up the canyon only another quarter of a mile to where the canyon forks. The main canyon continues west, but narrows to the point where further vehicular travel is no longer possible. From here you must proceed on foot, or turn your vehicle around and go back.

Recommended Reading For Further Information About Petroglyphs:

A Guide to Rock Art Sites by David S. Whitley, Mountain Press Publishing Co.
Rock Art of California, published by the BLM and available at BLM offices at a modest cost.

13

The Many Mines of Blind Spring Hill

Primary Attraction: This backroad excursion features old mines of the era immediately following the American Civil War.

Time Required: A basic visit to the summit of Blind Spring Hill can be done in a half-day out of Bishop. You will need a full day to explore the full myriad of roads on the hill.

Distance Involved: It is 34 miles to Benton, then four miles to Benton Hot Springs, all on paved roads. From there on, the dirt road portions are less than ten miles round trip.

Degree of Difficulty: The roads on Blind Spring Hill range from Class II to Class IV.

Remarks: The Inyo National Forest map does not show the road described.

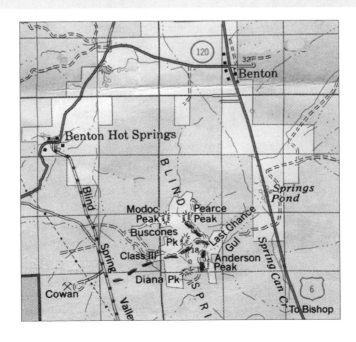

If you like to explore old forgotten mines, then a visit to Blind Spring Hill is just the trip for you. Wherever you look, you will see evidence of man's frantic search for buried riches.

To reach Blind Spring Hill, take U.S. Highway 6 north out of Bishop in the direction of Montgomery Pass. At Benton Station, 34 miles north of Bishop, turn left onto State Route 120 going west towards Lee Vining. The road will take you around the northern end of Blind Spring Hill, where it turns to the south. After four miles from Highway 6, you will come to Benton Hot Springs, the site of the original Benton.

Early in 1865, prospectors attracted by the excitement at Montgomery City (see Excursion #14) found promising silver ore on Blind Spring Hill. The Blind Springs Mining District was formed and hundred of claims were filed. Several of those first claims would be the district's biggest producers, the Diana and the Comanche. There was no water on Blind Spring Hill, so the miners tended to collect at the hot springs, just two miles to the south. In April of 1865, a mineralogist from New York by the name of Dr. A.F.W. Partz located the Elmira Mine. He laid out a town site a half-mile north of the hot springs, which he modestly named Partzwick. By December the fledgling town had a hotel, a store, and several saloons. What Partzwick did not have was water, so people continued to settle around the hot springs. With the coming of a post office in 1866, the entire town of Partzwick relocated to the hot springs, where the site was named Benton after a local, the Reverend J.E. Benton. As more people were attracted to the district, Benton grew and prospered. By late 1866, Benton had surpassed Partzwick's peak and was the largest town in Mono County.

Benton was past its prime in 1895, when Crockwell took this photo.
(Photo courtesy, County of Inyo, Eastern California Museum)

The operators of the Diana Mine raised the capital necessary to erect a four-stamp mill, with a small reduction furnace, next to the mine. They were able to ship bullion. The other less fortunate mine operators had to ship their ore by wagon 140 miles to the Central Pacific Railroad near Reno, where it was then carried by rail to the great Selby Mill in San Francisco. At a cost of $90 per ton in freight, only the richest ore could be processed. That situation continued until the early 1870s, when more and more mines developed the ability to smelt their ores on site. By 1872 the mines were in full production, and Benton was booming. By 1876 veteran desert freight hauler, Remi Nadeau, had his sixteen-mule teams plying the road from Benton all the way to the Southern Pacific Railroad's new station in Mojave, 210 miles to the south.

One of Remi Nadeau's mule trains on the way to Mojave.
(Photo courtesy of Remi Nadeau IV)

The silver wealth of Blind Springs Hill went to the railroad in Mojave.
(Historic photo from the author's collection)

In his well-researched book *The Silver Seekers,* historian and great-great grandson of Remi Nadeau, Dr. Remi Nadeau IV says:

In 1879, spurred by new mining activity, Benton had some 23 businesses, including three hotels, five saloons, two breweries, and two newspapers, the 'Bentonian' and the' Mono Messenger'. The population had grown from around 100 in the early Seventies to about 600, not counting many miners who lived by their claims on Blind Springs Hill.

A few of Benton's present buildings date back well over a century to this early period. One of those old structures was the combination store-gas station-café, which was still in use until just a few years ago. It is said to have been the Wells Fargo Office in Benton's heyday, with an estimated five million in silver bullion passing through its doors between 1866 and 1888.

The old Wells Fargo building.

In 1880, the Carson & Colorado Railroad began laying tracks southward from the Virginia & Truckee Railroad interchange in Mound House, Nevada, just east of Carson City. By January of 1883, the narrow gauge rails were extended as far south as "Benton Station", a point only six miles from the mines of Blind Spring Hill. This dramatically reduced the cost to ship bullion, and prosperity well into the future seemed assured. Alas, however, it was not to last. At a depth of 750 feet, the Comanche's four-foot wide vein was cut off by a fault. The same thing happened to the nearby Diana Mine. To compound the problem, all the silver being produced in the west caused the price to drop. One by one, the mines of Blind Spring Hill ceased operations. By 1900 Benton's population had dwindled down to only fifty.

To proceed on to Blind Spring Hill from downtown Benton, turn left off State Route 120 onto Yellow Jacket Road. Its pavement ends after a mile, but continue on. Proceed south 3.3 miles to a point where the road crosses a cattle guard on a fence line. Rather than crossing the cattle guard, turn left following the tracks leading northeasterly through the sage (but do not take the road climbing steeply east along the fence line). You might as well engage your four-wheel drive now; you will soon need it. The road ahead is Class III, as it starts the steep climb up Blind Spring Hill.

The first of the many mines will be reached within three quarters of a mile. The summit of the hill is but another mile further. Upon reaching the crest, the summit of Blind Spring Hill is level for a while. Now Class II, the tracks turn north following the ridge. Old diggings are everywhere. Massive stone walls and open holes are all that is left of many of the mines. **Warning: it has been well over a century since these diggings were excavated. They are all unsafe. Do not enter the tunnels, and stay well back from the open shafts.**

Rock ruins of a miner's cabin on top of Blind Spring Hill.

While there was never a town site up here, at times up to a thousand men may have lived or worked on Blind Spring Hill. Many were Indians and Chinese, society's lowest social strata of that time. Some of the ruins offer clues to their occupancy. Hundreds of broken crucibles near one site indicate it must have been an assay office. A pile of bones near another suggests it might have been a butcher shop.

Following the tracks steeply down the ridge (Class IV coming back up), you will pass the unmarked ruins of the Cornucopia Mine, a major producer. Keep left at the next fork, and you will come to the Diana Mine, another major producer of the hill. There are roads all over the top of Blind Spring Hill. One could spend the entire day following them all. At one time it was possible to continue down Comanche Gulch to return to Benton. That road has long ago washed out, and is impassible today. After your visit to Blind Spring Hill, you will have to retrace your route back to Benton.

14

Montgomery City

Primary Attraction:	One of Mono County's most obscure mining camps, overshadowed by the towering heights of 13,140' Boundary Peak.
Time Required:	The site can be visited in a half-day's outing from Bishop. Better yet, combine your visit with one to nearby Blind Springs Hill for a full day of early California history.
Miles Involved:	The site is only four miles off Highway 6, at a point 38 miles north of Bishop.
Degree of Difficulty:	The rocky boulder-strewn road from Benton Station is generally no worse than Class III. Except after the occasional winter snowstorm, the site of Montgomery City is usually accessible all year long.
Remarks:	The Inyo National Forest map does not show the described road.

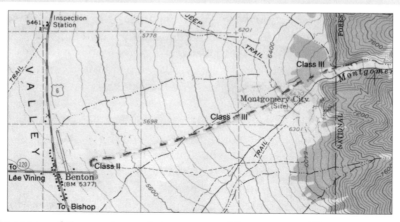

Like many of the western mining camps, Montgomery City sprang up out of nowhere overnight, and disappeared just as quickly, with hardly a note to mark its passing. Today few people have ever heard of Montgomery City, much less ever visited the camp. While the site is only three miles from a paved highway, the Class III route is rough enough to discourage all but those in appropriate vehicles.

The road into Montgomery City.

The way to Montgomery City starts in the heart of beautiful downtown Benton (it should be more properly called "Benton Station") on Highway 6, some 34 miles north of Bishop. In 1880 the Carson & Colorado Railroad began laying tracks southward from the Virginia & Truckee Railroad interchange in Mound House, Nevada, just east of Carson City. By January of 1883, the narrow gauge rails were extended this far south on their way down the Owens Valley. There was a station here to service the needs of booming Blind Spring Hill (see Excursion #13).

At the only intersection in town, opposite State Route 120, turn east on Christy Lane, passing the Mono County Road Department station on the right. After a tenth of a mile the pavement ends, but continue eastward another 0.3 miles. Turn left opposite the entrance to the landfill site. Go north a tenth of a mile, and then turn right at the "T" intersection. The road is Class II for the first mile, but the rocky surface makes for slow going. Sooner or later you will wish to engage your four-wheel drive. The road makes its way up the sage-covered alluvial fan coming out of Montgomery Canyon. Along the way, notice the great abundance of gold cholla cactus *Opuntia echinocarpa*. They obviously like this habitat.

A crossroads is reached at a point three miles from Highway 6. The fork dead ahead enters Montgomery Canyon, and after one mile ends at a hunter's camp. To find the site of Montgomery City, turn right. Within 0.2 miles you will be there. There is only one slight obstacle; the stream coming out of Montgomery Canyon has to be forded. In late summer and fall there may be no water here at all. In late spring and early summer, the snowfields of the White Mountains assure water in all of these canyons, often flowing many miles into the valley below. During the unusually wet El Niño year of 1998, a massive debris slide of mud and rock came oozing out of Montgomery Canyon to cross our road, making a minor detour necessary. Simply follow the tracks of the few vehicles that have gone before you. **If in doubt, get out and scout the way ahead on foot.** Within a quarter of a mile from the last intersection, you will be in Montgomery City. Today the site consists only of the stonewalled ruins of nearly a dozen structures, widely spread out over half a square mile. Although stone was clearly the preferred building material, the town had at least one log cabin. It had long ago collapsed when the authors first visited the site in the 1960s. The square cut nails offered the only clue to the structure's age. The dim outline of a wagon road still goes through the "town".

Montgomery City was born in October of 1863, when one E. P. Robinson found silver at the 6,800' base of the White Mountains. The word got out and within weeks prospectors began to pour in, seeking great mineral wealth. Tunnels were laboriously bored into the mountainside by hand to expose the veins. A few miners exposed ore worth mining, but the remoteness of the site and cost of transportation hindered production. At least one stamp mill was put into operation. During its heyday of 1864, Montgomery City is said to have supported two competing newspapers. By 1866 the great silver finds on nearby Blind Spring Hill (see Excursion #13) had drawn off most of Montgomery City's residents. The town was not completely dead, however. In 1869, the owners of the Diana Mine, seven miles away on Blind Spring Hill, transported their ore to Montgomery City for crushing and concentrating. By January 1883, when the slim rails of the Carson & Colorado Railroad reached Benton Station, the mines of Montgomery City had already closed, never to reopen again.

Unfortunately, in the many years since Montgomery City flowered and died, flash floods coming down out of Montgomery Canyon have devastated the town site. What was not buried in rock and sand has been overgrown by vegetation. Those stone walls that remain seem to stick up out of a sea of shrubbery. A few diggings remain up on the hillside to the east. **Warning: stay out of the underground workings; they are unsafe to enter.**

The remains of 140-year-old Montgomery City.

15

Queen Dick's Ranch

Special Features:	The century old home of one of Mono County's long time residents set in a marvelous scenic setting.
Time Required:	This is only a half-day's outing out of Bishop, but could be combined with a visit to Montgomery City or Blind Spring Hill for a full day of rough road explorations.
Miles Involved:	From downtown Bishop to Queen Dick's Ranch, the total distance is about 44 miles, of which only the last four miles are dirt roads.
Degree of Difficulty:	The first 3.5 miles are generally no worse than Class II. The last 0.6 miles are an easy Class III.
Remarks:	Except after the occasional winter snowstorm, the site of Queen Dick's Ranch is usually accessible all year long. The site of the old ranch may be private property. Please respect the owner's rights.

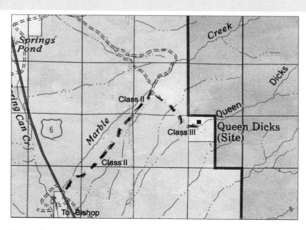

History has long forgotten Queen Dick, except to know that he was an Indian living in the mouth of a canyon below Mt. Dubois. Seemingly, he was a nobody who lived a simple life, raising goats on his small ranch, and occasionally working for white ranchers farther down the valley. But there is another side of Queen Dick's life. In 1870, it was Queen who first found mineralized quartz veins in a canyon just ten miles to the north of his ranch. The rock contained free milling gold and silver. Not having the capital, resources, or knowledge to properly develop his find, Queen sold his claims. Soon the property would become the Indian Queen Mine and go on to pay its stockholders nice dividends for a number of years. When the Carson & Colorado Railroad's narrow gauge rails were laid down through the valley late in 1882, they had a "Queen Station" at milepost 466 to service the many mines of nearby Queen Canyon. From October of 1912 to January of 1915, there was even a "Queen" post office at the station. Such is the legacy of Queen Dick.

The Indian Queen Mine just up the valley in Nevada.

Queen Station on the Carson & Colorado Railroad.
(Forbes photo from the George Turner collection, courtesy of James Saylor)

There is no particular reason to visit the site of Queen Dick's former home. Mount Vernon or Montecello, it ain't! Nevertheless, if you are looking for a pleasant outing far removed from the stress of today's living, a journey to Queen Dick's digs might be the answer.

Take U.S. Highway 6 out of Bishop, noting your odometer reading as you leave U.S. Highway 395. About 38.5 miles north of the intersection of U.S. Highways 395 and 6, start looking on the right for highway milepost MNO 20: 00. When you find it, note your odometer reading again. The turnoff to Queen Dick's ranch is but 0.4 miles farther north.

Here on the right, a dirt road goes through a gate (please close it behind you) and heads northeast, as it begins to climb the alluvial fan coming out of Marble Canyon. After 0.4 miles, stay right at the first of four coming road junctions. The second junction is 1.3 miles from Highway 6; again keep to the right, going straight ahead. The third fork comes two miles from Highway 6. Again stay right, continuing straight ahead. This Class II road generally parallels the course of Marble Creek just a few hundred yards to the north. This is cattle country, although you might not think so after looking at the unappealing sage. In the dry summer months, it takes hundreds of acres to graze a single cow for a month.

At a point 2.7 miles in from Highway 6, the fourth fork in the road is encountered. The left fork goes straight-ahead 0.8 miles to dead-end at a nice hunter's camp at the mouth of Marble Canyon. To find Queen Dick's ranch, make a sharp right turn on another Class II road heading off to the southeast. Stay to the right after 0.7 miles, but engage your four-wheel drive. The last 0.6 miles will require it. When I first saw the ranch in the 1960s, I had just returned from a yearlong stay on Bolivia's 12,000' high *Altiplano*. The many stone walls of Queen Dick's ranch reminded me very much of a Quechua Indian village set high in the Andes. The high mountain scenery was similar, too, although the elevation here is only 6,000 feet. Nevertheless, Queen Dick had a grand view. Although you cannot see it from Queen Dick's Ranch, the snow capped summit of 13,559' Mount Dubois towers over the site. The snow capped Sierra peaks stand out on the distant skyline. Clearly visible to the south are patches of white marking the location of the Palisades Glacier in the Big Pine Creek drainage. Mammoth Mountain dominates the horizon to the west.

The century old main cabin and barn were still was standing in 1967. Two years later the barn, with its shingled roof made of flattened five-gallon cans, had collapsed under the unusually heavy snows of January 1969. Today the stone walls and rafters of the cabin survive, although all of the wooden shingles have blown away. The wood stove that once heated the interior is missing, as is the solitary door.

Queen Dick's Ranch in 1967.

Queen Dick's Ranch today.

Outside everything pretty much looks as it did 35 years ago. Acres of stone walls marking the animal pens are still there, although the brush that once topped them has fallen in. The rock-lined aqueduct that diverted water from a nearby stream can still be seen. The one resource that Queen Dick had in great abundance was rocks. From the looks of it, he must have spent a lifetime moving them about.

16

The Champion Spark Plug Mine

Special Features:	High above Jeffrey Canyon on the western flank of the White Mountains is one of California's most unusual mining operations. This excursion involves both four-wheeling, as well as a strenuous hike up a steep mule trail.
Time Required:	A visit to the Black Eagle Mine Camp is a full day excursion out of Bishop. To visit the actual mine workings, however, a two day outing is recommended, with a backpack into the lower mine camp to spend the first night, and the final ascent to the upper camp and return on the second day.
Miles Involved:	The one way distance from downtown Bishop to the road's end high above Jeffrey Canyon is 25 miles. From there, the one way hike to the Black Eagle Mine Camp is another two miles, plus more two miles to the mine workings and the upper camp.
Degree of Difficulty:	From Highway 6, the three miles of dirt road are Class II or better. The last 1.4 miles of the road steeply ascend the north side of the canyon and are mostly Class III.
Remarks:	The Champion Mine is shown as the "Jeffrey Mine" on the USGS topographic map, as well as the Inyo National Forest map. In common practice, however, the mine is more often called the "Champion Spark Plug Mine".

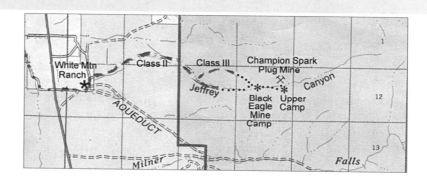

Many commodities have been mined from the White Mountains, not the least of which are gold, silver, lead and mercury. Even titanium is found in the sands of Jeffrey Mine Canyon, but in quantities far too small to economically extract. Perhaps the strangest commodity of value in the mountain range, however, is not a metal, but rather a rare aluminum silicate mineral known as andalusite. Like its close chemical cousin sillimanite, andalusite is a byproduct of intense metamorphism. Its value to man is that it can be made into a hard ceramic that resists destruction in very high temperature environments. Thus andalusite makes good thermocouple tubing, laboratory porcelain, and spark plug insulators.

Dr. Joseph A. Jeffery, the President of Champion Sillimanite, Inc. first found this unusual mineral in the White Mountains in 1919. The story of his find is recalled by Bill and Louise Kelsey in the October 1992 issue of *The Album*, a quarterly publication describing the times and tales of Inyo-Mono.

Jeffrey's find was located at an elevation of 9,000 feet, and was in a zone some two miles long, but only about thirty feet wide. Here an irregular quartz mass surrounded by schist contained the unusual mineral. The miners hired by Champion burrowed into the mountainside, creating large chambers where the andalusite concentration was high. The pieces extracted were hand-sorted, with bits of quartz and pyrite being broken off and discarded. The andalusite ore was then placed in sacks holding 95 pounds each. The sacks were carried by long strings of up to fifty mules (four sacks per animal) down the trail four and a half miles to the road's end, where they were emptied into ore bins. The material was then moved by flatbed truck another three and a half miles to Shealy Siding on the Southern Pacific's narrow gauge line. Here the ore was placed in long parallel rows of bins containing 2000 tons each. Every now and then, the stockpiled mineral was next put in narrow gauge rail cars for transport to the main line at Owenyo, where it was transferred to standard gauge rail cars. Ultimately, after being handled nine times, the andalusite ended up at the Champion Spark Plug Company Plant in Detroit, Michigan. The Champion Corporation actively mined the heavy blue-gray ore for a quarter of a century, from 1920 to 1945.

To find the place where this unusual mineral was mined, take Highway 6 north out of Bishop for about nineteen miles. Turn right onto White Mountain Ranch Road, noting your odometer reading as you turn. Proceed east 0.6 miles, passing the entrance to the White Mountain Ranch.

While it is called the White Mountain Ranch today, it was the Milner Ranch in 1919 when Dr. Jeffrey made his first excursions into the White Mountains. After finding his andalusite, Jeffrey bought the Milner Ranch. It would be his base of mining operations, and supply meat and produce for his miners as well as the feed for the pack mules. The creek from nearby Milner Canyon would be sent to the ranch through a stone-lined aqueduct (which is still there) to power a turbine to generate electricity for the ranch as well as the mine.

Turn left at the concrete block structure in the southeast corner of the ranch compound. Continue slightly more than 0.2 of a miles north, where you will want to turn right onto the Class I road heading eastward towards Jeffrey Canyon in the White Mountains. (This means you will take the second road to the right. If you turned right after slightly less than 0.2 miles, this Class II road will take you back onto the Milner Canyon Road described in Excursion #17.)

The road is generally quite good as it makes its way up the alluvial fan at the mouth of the canyon. About two miles from White Mountain Ranch, the road, by now Class II, drops down into Jeffrey Canyon and the scenery becomes more interesting. At a point 3.5 miles from Highway 6, look for a Class III road that cuts back sharply to the left. This is our route; however, before turning off here, you may wish to continue up the canyon bottom another half-mile to see where the mules were relieved of their heavy burdens. The last 0.4 miles are Class III.

Sacks of andalusite ore carried down the mountain by mules were emptied into this bunker to await being trucked to the rail siding three miles away.

From the road's end in the canyon bottom, a footpath starts up the canyon, to eventually climb high onto its north side. Your feet can eliminate a thousand feet of elevation gain if your go back down the canyon a half-mile, and take the side road previously mentioned. The road is steep and narrow requiring four-wheel drive and low range gears, but most SUVs should have no problem negotiating the grade. **Warning, this road is not recommended for vehicles with a high center of gravity.** After 0.7 miles the road comes to the top of the steep grade, and the country opens up. The road continues on another mile, but only proceed 0.6 miles more to where there is a small flat spot where people have parked in the past; stop here.

A foot trail now contours along the north side of Jeffrey Canyon. After a little more than a mile, it enters a grove of Jeffrey pine, and joins the old mule trail coming up from the canyon bottom. From here it is a steep, but relatively short climb up to the Black Eagle Mine Camp. The hike into this point should take most people an hour or so.

As you approach the camp, notice how the forest exists mostly in the deep crevice of the canyon, not out on the sunny slopes. Notice, too, how the pine trees are growing straight and tall. They have needles in clusters of three and produce relatively large cones. The three major pine trees of the White Mountains are absent here: the piñon pine, the bristlecone and the limber pine. Jeffrey Canyon is unique in the White Mountains as it has the only populations of Jeffrey pine *Pinus jeffreyi*, and nearly the only stands of ponderosa pine *Pinus ponderosa* in the entire mountain range. While the latter two trees are common in the Sierra Nevada, they are rare in the White Mountains.

Jeffrey pines at the Black Eagle Mine Camp.

The Black Eagle Mine Camp is a cluster of nine well-preserved structures (not counting a couple of outhouses), which were utilized by the Champion Corporation to house and feed mine workers. Four of the buildings are cozy weather-tight cabins, each equipped with a pair of beds, a table, and a wood stove. The central cookhouse, with its large stove that had to be dismantled and brought up in pieces, is equally well-preserved. It can easily feed a dozen people and has sleeping quarters for three. Other buildings in the camp are utilized as a shop and a museum. Only the bathhouse and one bunkhouse are in disrepair.

The reason that this camp is so well-preserved is that it has been adopted and maintained by Don and Margey Fraser and a group of dedicated volunteers from the Owens Valley. Visitors are welcome to stay in any of the cabins that happen to be unoccupied. If you do choose to visit the site, please contribute to its upkeep and maintenance. When you hike in, carry in your sleeping bag, of course, but also bring in a few supplies for the volunteers. Firewood is scarce, so a few manufactured fireplace logs and non-perishable food items would be welcome. Other thoughtful contributions might be a gallon of white gas or small propane cylinders for lanterns and camp stoves. Toilet paper, games, and even a few eight-foot long 2x4s would be useful, too. Once you get settled in, check out the shop building. It contains tools, materials, and a list of projects that need to be done. Upon leaving, pack out any accumulated trash. Be more than a passive visitor; be an active participant in the preservation of this unique facility! And above all, be super careful with fire. This unique and historic site cannot be replaced!

The Black Eagle Mine Camp

NOTE

THIS IS AN ALL-VOLUNTEER PROJECT. IF YOU ENJOY THE PLACE, PLEASE HELP BY DOING WHATEVER YOU CAN TO MAKE IT BETTER. (YOU DON'T HAVE TO BE A SKILLED CARPENTER OR MECHANIC, ANY SIMPLE LITTLE REPAIR, OR CLEANING JOB OR HAULING OUT SOME TRASH, ETC. HELPS A LOT.)

From the Black Eagle Mine Camp, the old mule trail climbs another 1500 feet higher to the upper camp and the mines at an elevation of about 9,000 feet. Unfortunately, all but one of the buildings of the upper camp burned in 1987.

The upper mine camp before the fire of 1987
(Laws Railroad Museum photo)

    This must have been one of the most unusual mining operations in California, if not the entire United States. There have certainly been higher mines. Just west of Bishop, the Pine Creek Mine extracted tungsten, molybdenum and vanadium from workings at 11,900 feet, and, as mentioned in *High Sierra SUV Trails Volume I – The East Side,* the Horton Creek Mine operated at 11,600 feet. But in both of those operations, there was a mechanical means to bring the extracted ore down the mountain for processing. Here at the Champion Mine, however, every pound of ore extracted was carried off the mountain on the back of a mule. This procedure continued up until the end of World War II, when a practical synthetic material was developed to replace the andalusite porcelain used in sparkplugs.

The Champion Mine, shortly after it ceased operation.
(Laws Railroad Museum photo)

(Historic photos courtesy of Laws Railroad Museum)

Postcard from the post World War I era
(from the author's collection)

Rich ore from the Champion Spark Plug Mine

17

The Awesome Milner Canyon Mudslide

Special Features:	Milner Canyon was the site of a sudden and massive mudslide that, while potentially deadly, was relatively harmless, because nobody was in its way.
Time Required:	This outing can be done in a couple of hours out of Bishop.
Miles Involved:	From downtown Bishop to the road's end in Milner Canyon is only 25 miles.
Degree of Difficulty:	Only the last five miles are dirt roads, and those are generally Class II or better.

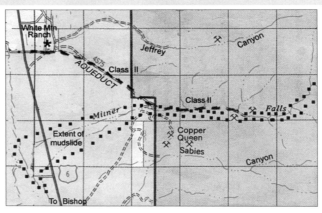

While Milner Canyon is as old as the White Mountains themselves, two or three million years old, the mudslide phenomenon here can be accurately traced back to one particularly severe thunderstorm that occurred on the afternoon of September 4, 1998. Curiously it was almost year to the day after the September 2, 1997, thunderstorm that washed away the historic site of Swansea on the shore of Owens Lake (see Excursion #36), and "the mother of all desert storms" that reeked havoc with Highway 14 going through Red Rock Canyon in eastern Kern County on September 3, 1997.

A low-pressure system over the Great Basin sucked up heavy tropical moisture-laden clouds off the Gulf of Mexico a thousand miles to the southeast.

When these clouds bumped up against the lofty White Mountains, they rose and cooled. With that cooling, their moisture precipitated out, falling in the basin between 14,246' White Mountain Peak and 13,040' Mt. Barcroft. Conditions were just right for a flash flood and one occurred, but a flood with a little different twist. The heavy rain runoff falling in this natural basin mixed with loose surface soil that had weathered out of metamorphosed volcanic rocks. The result was almost instantly a gooey mud. Because of the extremely steep slopes on the western side of the White Mountains, this muddy mess began to slide down the mountainside, picking up velocity and volume as it went.

Although nobody was present to witness the event, an examination of the debris suggests there were two phases of the mudslide. The first phase, in 1997, produced a thick viscous mud, filled with angular fragments of rock that had been plucked from the high slopes. This flow oozed down the canyon burying everything in its path, including portions of the Milner Canyon Road. The second phase, a year later, involved a thin, rock-free mud that attained considerable velocity as it flowed down the canyon.

The hardened second phase mudflow in Milner Canyon is on
the right, with the more viscous first phase debris on the left.

The natural topography of the upper basin channeled the now free-flowing mud into the lower confines of Milner Canyon. The first flow had a very thick consistency, and it sort of oozed down the canyon, moving perhaps only three to five miles per hour. While it carried the greatest amount of soil, it did not reach Highway 6. The second occurrence was different. The first mudslide had already solidified when it occurred. Most of the easily erodable soil had been stripped away in the first flood event. When the second severe rain occurred, there was much less available soil to mix with the water, hence the flow was much more liquid, and as such flowed at a faster speed. By the time the second flow had descended 3,000 feet to the 7,200-foot level where the road in the bottom of

Milner Canyon ends, the watery-mud was moving at the incredible speed of perhaps twenty to thirty miles per hour. The fast moving flow tore out trees from high on the mountain and carried them down into the Hammil Valley some 5,000 feet below. Where the canyon would bend, the centrifugal force of the fluid mud would cause the liquid mass to rise just like a racing car on a banked curve. In the canyon narrows just above the road's end, the flow was an estimated twenty feet thick. As it raced down the lower two miles of canyon, the walls spread out and the mud widened in its channel. At the mouth of Milner Canyon, the flow was forty yards wide and several feet deep.

At this point in the canyon the mudflow was only seven feet deep.

Once free of the restraints of the canyon walls, the flow widened even more to a width of eighty yards, and with this spread was a proportional drop in velocity. Still the mud kept coming. In less than an hour the mud had made its way three miles down into the bottom of Hammil Valley, a full 1,200 vertical feet below the mouth of the canyon. In the process, a debris channel crossed Highway 6 in two places, depositing mud, rocks and trees over a quarter of a mile. Traffic was blocked in both directions. It would be several hours before CalTrans would be able to reopen the highway.

Even after six years, vegetation has yet to reestablish itself on the hardened mudflow.

Although this phenomenon occurred several years ago, the now hardened muddy evidence of this flood remains in Milner Canyon as if it had happened just last week. To see if for yourself, take North Main Street (Highway 395) north from downtown Bishop, making a right turn onto Highway 6. Check your odometer here and proceed about seventeen miles north of Highway 395. Start looking for milepost 6 MNO 8.5. A quarter of a mile beyond, the debris from the mudflow can be seen on either side of Highway 6. Here the mudflow was up to a foot deep and nearly five hundred feet wide. Continue northward on Highway 6 another 1.9 miles to the White Mountain Ranch Road. Turn right here, passing the front driveway to this old ranch in a half-mile. The good graded dirt portion of the road soon ends, and a rough Class II road makes its way up the alluvial fan to the southeast. The road crosses a very old rock-lined ditch that once diverted Milner Creek down to the alfalfa fields of the White Mountain Ranch. The road parallels a two-strand power line that once took electric power to the Copper Queen Mine at the canyon's mouth.

Milner Canyon is entered at a point three miles from Highway 6. A quarter of a mile beyond is a good place to stop and examine the nature of the mudflow as it left the canyon. Notice the two distinctly different flows. The thick viscous flow is about one hundred yards wide and six feet deep. The subsequent thin and more fluid flow is only two feet deep and perhaps forty yards wide.

Continue to follow the road up Milner Canyon. At a point 3.7 miles from Highway 6, there is a spring surrounded by willows on the right. Just beyond, the road crosses the mudflow. The folks at the White Mountain Ranch had a tractor up here clearing the mud while it was still wet. A good decision, because when it dried, it became as hard as concrete.

At a point 4.1 miles from Highway 6, notice how, as the mud came around the bend in the wash, the centrifugal force of the second flow pushed the mud twenty feet higher on the north side of the canyon than on the south. A short distance up the canyon, the flow is only fifty feet wide, but twenty feet deep.

An adit and its tailing dump are passed on the left 4.7 miles in from the highway. At 4.9 miles we measured the mud at thirty feet above the channel on the north side, but only fifteen feet above the channel on the south side. A quarter of a mile more and the Class II road comes to another tailing dump, where the road now becomes Class III, and then soon comes to a dead-end.

If there is an underlying message to this backroad excursion it is: **Always be keenly aware of current local weather conditions. Flash floods happen every year in the Great Basin country, and the results can be deadly. Stay out of canyons, if there is current thunderstorm activity anywhere near!**

The same storm event also flooded Hwy. 14 below Red Rock Canyon.
(Photos courtesy of Bob Boyd)

Motorists have long had to contend with washouts in the Owens Valley.
This one occurred near Haiwee on August 23, 1925.

This washout occurred near Little Lake three days later.
(Laws Railroad Museum photos)

18

The Moulas Mine

Special Features:	This is an interesting scenic drive high onto the western slope of the White Mountains. Here are breathtaking views of nearly one hundred miles of the Sierra Nevada crest. Ideally, this is a trip to make in the morning, when the full sun is on the Sierra Nevada range.
Time Required:	This is an all day excursion out of Bishop.
Miles Involved:	The one way distance from downtown Bishop to the Moulas Mine is 21 miles.
Degree of Difficulty:	Large portions of the road are only Class II, but there is enough Class III to keep things interesting.
Remarks:	The 1994 Chalfant Valley topographic map at a scale of 1:24,000 is recommended, as it shows the road climbing up the north side of Piute Canyon. It does not, however, show the new graded road that follows the aqueduct up the alluvial fan.

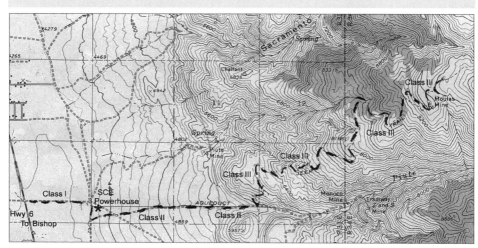

My research has never revealed just who it was that blazed this road up the western escarpment of the White Mountains to an elevation of nearly 10,000

feet. The feat was no doubt motivated by the lure of mineral wealth, although one wonders whether the road building costs were ever recovered.

To find the Moulas Mine and its magnificent view, take Highway 395 north out of Bishop to its junction with Highway 6; from there continue north on Highway 6. You will come to the Chalfant Loop Road 11.4 miles north of Highway 395. Turn right onto the wide graded road that heads east towards the mountains. Again note your odometer reading as you leave Highway 6. A "T" intersection is reached after 0.7 miles. Follow the graded road to the right, and immediately turn left again at the fenced building. This structure is a powerhouse, part of the Southern California Edison Company's hydroelectric project, which utilizes the water flowing down the aqueduct from Piute Creek. The road, still graded but more rough now, heads straight up the alluvial fan towards the canyon to the east.

Piute Creek Canyon is entered a little more than two miles from Highway 6. At the 2.8-mile point are the stone ruins of an old miner's cabin on the left. The lower reaches of Piute Canyon have been extensively prospected over the years. Before the aqueduct, the original road in the canyon bottom led to a number of old mining properties. They were the Monoco, the Golden Horse Shoe, and the Z and S Mines. This stone cabin no doubt once provided shelter to someone working in one of those mines.

The approach to Piute Creek Canyon

A tenth of a mile beyond the cabin ruins, a Class III road starts climbing the north side of the canyon. Turn left here, and engage your four-wheel drive. This is the way to the Moulas Mine. (If you continue on up the canyon another mile, the road will come to an abrupt end at a place where lively Piute Creek emerges from beneath a massive boulder field, only to be channeled into an SCE pipe.)

The narrow one lane road is steep, rocky, and offers poor traction for the next half-mile. Nevertheless, I rate the road as an easy Class III. In less than a mile, the country opens up a bit as a high bench is reached, and the road becomes only Class II again. That situation doesn't last long, however, for soon the road returns to Class III, as the grade steepens once more.

A curious situation occurs about five miles in from Highway 6. Here at about 7,500 feet, the silver or gold cholla cactus *Opuntia echinocarpa* is suddenly abundant along the side of the road. Then after another quarter of a mile, it is all gone. There must be something in the soil at that particular spot that the cacti like.

Silver or Gold Cholla *Opuntia echinocarpa*

Six miles in from Highway 6, there is a nice view down into the Piute Creek drainage to the east. The piñon pine forest is entered a half-mile beyond, and a quarter of a mile further is a dry, but otherwise nice campsite.

Finally, at an elevation of 9,600 feet and at a distance of about eight miles in from our starting point on Highway 6 (and 5,400 feet above the highway), we come to the ruins of an old stone cabin and the site of the Moulas Mine. The origins of this mine are obscure, and few mining records seem to have been kept. The 1:125,000 White Mountain topographic map, published in 1917, does not show any mine in this area, but it does show a pack trail following today's road alignment up the mountainside. That mule trail went all the way to the crest of the White Mountains at 11,400 feet, where it forked with branches going north, east, and south. The 1962 White Mountain Peak topographic map, at a scale of

1:62,500, does show the mine and the jeep trail leading to it. Presumably then, sometime in that forty-five-year span between 1917 and 1962, the old pack trail was turned into today's road, and the mine was developed.

There is a great diversity of valuable minerals found along the western flank of the White Mountains. A cursory inspection of the tailing dumps here will quickly reveal a wide spectrum of the copper minerals, malachite, azurite, chalcopyrite, and even the iridescent sheen of bornite. As common as those minerals are on the ore dumps, however, that was not what the miners were after. It was gold and silver that was of primary interest here. A 1987 publication of the South Coast Geological Society suggests that this mine has 22,000 tons of "marginal" gold and silver reserves. That may sound like a lot of ore, but under today's market conditions, the cost of extraction, transportation, and processing suggests that this mine will remain just as it is well into the foreseeable future.

The Moulas Mine

Mineral collecting notwithstanding, the real treasure to be gleaned by a walk out onto the tailings dumps is the magnificent view of the Sierra crest to the west. To the south, you can see all the way to Mount Williamson. To the west are Glass Mountain, Mammoth Mountain, and in the far distance, Mounts Banner and Ritter and the sawtooth ridge of the Minarets. Looking to the far north, one can see the various peaks on Yosemite's eastern boundary. Mornings at the Moulas Mine are magnificent and memorable.

19

Gunter's Grand View

Special Features:	This is yet another outing that takes one high up onto the western slopes of the White Mountains for spectacular views of the Sierra Nevada Range. Be sure to get an early start, so that you reach the Sierra viewpoints when the morning sun is still on the Sierra Crest.
Time Required:	This is an all day excursion out of Bishop.
Miles Involved:	The one way distance from downtown Bishop to the road's end is about eighteen miles. This includes about seven miles of asphalt, with the remaining distance over dirt roads.
Degree of Difficulty:	The road is mostly Class II, but with significant portions of Class III in the last three miles. Any high clearance four-wheel drive vehicle should make it with ease.
Remarks:	The 7.5 minute Laws topographic map is recommended for this outing, as it shows all of the various side roads in good detail. (There are several stores in Bishop that sell this map.)

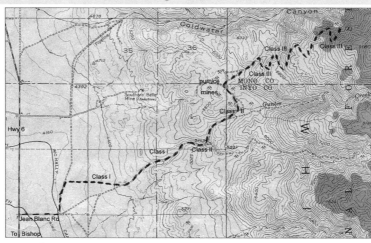

Our excursion up Gunter Canyon begins at the corner of Main and Line Streets in downtown Bishop. Proceed north on Highway 395 for 0.8 miles to the intersection with Highway 6. Turn right onto Highway 6, and proceed on up the Owens Valley for 5.5 miles to Jean Blanc Road. Turn right here, noting your odometer reading as you leave Highway 6. After a quarter of a mile the pavement ends where Joe Smith Road takes off to the right. Continue east on the now graded dirt Jean Blanc Road for another half-mile to where it crosses the North McNally Canal (likely to be dry). Once over the canal bridge, turn to the left at the crossroads beneath the huge cottonwood trees.

The road follows the east bank of the canal, and while it is technically only Class I, it has developed a washboard surface so that careful driving is required. At a point 1.9 miles from Highway 6, turn right onto the road that heads east towards the White Mountains. After only one hundred feet or so, stay to the left on the Class I road. In a little more than a mile, the road starts up a small draw that will eventually be Gunter Canyon. The road now deteriorates a little to Class II. Exposed on the right are banded layers of gray and brown limestone, a portion of the Campito Formation of early Cambrian Age.

The road forks at a point 4.5 miles from Highway 6. The right fork goes up the side canyon to dead-end at some prospect holes; stay to the left. The road twists and turns as it winds its way up through this narrow part of the canyon. The greenish colored slate exposed here is part of the Poleta Formation, also early Cambrian in age.

The canyon opens at the five-mile point, and a side road goes off to the right. Stay to the left on the main road. Within a quarter of a mile, a large tailing dump of what appears to be dazzling white sand appears on the left. This is not sand, but volcanic pumice, a very light ash that was being mined from several open pits in this area. This was part of the Hidecker property, a mine that operated here as early as the 1930s. Their crusher was situated at the base of the hillside at the highest point of the tailing dump. If you have any doubt that this material is pumice, select a fragment somewhat smaller than a baseball and give it the "float test". The sample should float! (Barite, another white colored mineral was also found and mined near here in the late 1920s, but it is quite heavy, heavier than quartz, and it certainly won't float on water.)

A waste dump of dazzling white pumice.

The float test. - pumice floats on water.

The road forks at the upper side of the tailing dump. You can take either fork, but for our purposes let's go to the left. The road climbs the low ridge above the millsite, and then turns north again heading for another gleaming white tailing dump less than a mile away. At a point 0.8 miles from the first pumice millsite, look for a side road to the right climbing up the hill. We will want to go to the right here, but a short diversion to the left will first take you to a large pumice quarry. If you do choose to go over there, return to this intersection and proceed up the mountainside. The amount of pumice removed from this area is incredible. Much seems to remain, but it is apparently not of the quality required by industry. A 1989 report published by the South Coast Geologic Society said that there are 9.6 million tons of sub-commercial pumice in this area.

Another commodity mined in Gunter Canyon is barite, a very dense mineral, often fine-grained and light gray to white in color. Barite has a wide variety of industrial uses, but its major use by far is for petroleum drilling mud (see *Glossary*). The mineral, from which the element barium comes, is also used as an important ingredient in the manufacture of glass, ceramics, enamel, and paint. In Gunter Canyon, barite veins two to eight feet thick were found in the Campito sandstone. Although our road does not go by them, the Gunter Canyon Barite Mine and the Hobo #1-8 claims shipped a considerable tonnage of barite in 1928 and 1929.

Seven miles in from Highway 6, our road now comes to a series of switchbacks that steeply climb the hillside, and in doing so the road now becomes Class III. Junipers begin to appear at the top of the steep grade. About eight and a half miles from Highway 6, the first sweeping views of Bishop, the Owens Valley, and beyond to the mighty Sierra Nevada are to be had. From this lofty vantage point one can get a hint of what might be seen as the road climbs ever higher. At nine miles, a side road right goes in to Gunter Canyon and ends; stay to the left. More switchbacks are encountered, and with each turn there are more grand vistas to the west. To the south you can see all the way to Mount Williamson and beyond. Looking west are Glass Mountain, Mammoth Mountain, and in the far distance, Mounts Banner and Ritter and the Minarets. Looking to the far north you can see Matterhorn Peak on Yosemite's eastern boundary. One is reluctant to leave these awesome belvederes, but the road continues to climb, and it beckons us onward.

Rabbitbrush *Chrysothamnus nauseous* lines the road to Grand View Point.

Before long, a piñon-covered shoulder of the mountain is crossed, and the Coldwater Canyon drainage is entered. Finally, ten and a half miles from Highway 6, the road comes to an abandoned mine and abruptly ends. The elevation here is 8,500 feet. I have not discovered who put this road in, what they were mining, or when they were working the property. The mine did have an ore bunker at the lower adit, so presumably some ore was trucked down the mountainside for processing. I would guess that mining took place here within the last fifty years, because the road and mine do not appear on the 15-minute Bishop quadrangle topographic map published in 1949, and no mention is made of it in the California State Report on the Mines and Mineral Resources of Inyo County that was published in 1951. **Warning: Stay out of the underground workings; they are not safe to enter!**

Mine at the end of the road.

20

Cottonwood Basin

Special Features:	This excursion will take you up to an elevation of 10,400 feet in the White Mountains east of Bishop. After passing through occasional groves of Bristlecone pine, the route drops one thousand feet into a beautiful basin where a lively stream nourishes lush green meadows filled with wildflowers and surrounded by groves of aspen. The fall colors are outstanding along Cottonwood Creek.
Time Required:	One can certainly drive from Bishop into the Cottonwood Basin and return in a single day, but this outing deserves at least a weekend visit.
Miles Involved:	From downtown Bishop to the first ford of Cottonwood Creek, the distance is a little more than 28 miles.
Degree of Difficulty:	Of those 28 miles mentioned above, all but five miles are over dirt roads generally graded to a high standard. Nevertheless, the last 3.5 miles to the road's end are Class III.
Remarks:	Deep snows are likely to close the higher portions of this road anytime from November well into early June. **People with cardiac and respiratory problems should realize that this is one of the highest roads in the entire United States, and breathing difficulties could be experienced.**

Our route to the Cottonwood Basin begins at the intersection of Line and Main Streets in downtown Bishop. Go north on Main Street 0.8 miles to where U.S. Highway 6 leaves Highway 395. Turn right here, following Highway 6 north and then east for 3.8 miles. Make a right turn off of Highway 6 onto the clearly marked Silver Canyon Road. Note your odometer reading as you leave the highway. In a quarter of a mile you will pass the Laws Railroad Museum on the right.

When investors formed the Carson & Colorado Railroad in May of 1880, their dream was to push a railroad into western Nevada to profit from the mining traffic, extending it on into the Owens Valley to pick up more mineral wealth, as well as agricultural commodities. Because the railroad would interconnect with the narrow gauge Virginia & Truckee Railroad at Mound House, Nevada, the new line would be narrow gauge as well. It took nearly three years to push those tracks as far as Laws. When the route for the narrow gauge tracks of the Carson & Colorado Railroad was selected, the decision was made to go south down the eastern side of the Owens Valley, thus bypassing such towns as Bishop, Big Pine, Independence and Lone Pine. Laws would become the station for Bishop, and rail service started here on April 1, 1883. The last day of service was April 30, 1960.

Today's Laws Railroad Museum, operated by the Bishop Museum & Historical Society, preserves those 77 years of rail service at Laws Station. The eleven-acre site shows off not only the depot, but also the agent's house, turn table, and a seven-car train behind steam engine #9 as well. A number of other historic buildings from Bishop have also been moved here to enhance the display. An hour spent here is a worthwhile investment of time. The museum hours are 10 a.m. to 4 p.m. daily.

The Laws Railroad Museum

Follow the paved Silver Canyon Road beyond Laws. Soon the pavement will end, but a high standard graded dirt road continues east toward the deep slash of Silver Canyon, a major defile in the White Mountains just ahead. Soon the canyon is entered, and two miles from Highway 6 the dirt road makes its first ford of Silver Creek, a year around watercourse. The water depth is usually not great. The bottom of the streambed is generally firm, and there should be no hidden boulders lurking beneath the water. Under normal circumstances, these fords in Silver Canyon should present no problems to the drivers of SUVs and other backcountry vehicles. **Warning: if you have any doubt at all about the water's velocity and depth, always stop to check it out before plunging in.**

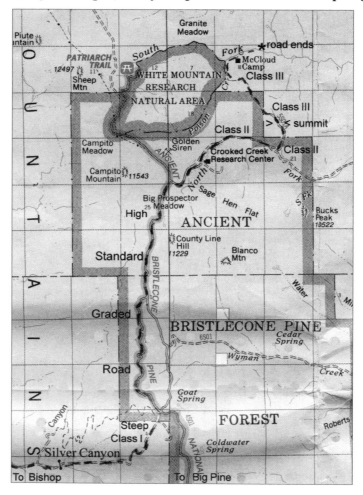

The roadway deteriorates slightly to Class I after the first ford. It steadily ascends the canyon floor for the next five miles, fording the creek a number of times. In those five miles the road gains 2,000 feet in elevation.

This stream of life-giving water not only supports a line of willows (some of which encroach on the roadway at times), water birch, and occasional cottonwood trees, but it also supports a wide variety of wildlife. Indeed, lower Silver Canyon is a good place to be on the lookout for Desert Bighorn sheep *Ovis canadensis nelsoni.*

Desert Bighorn *Ovis canadensis nelsoni*

More often than not, nature writers describe the Desert Bighorn sheep as living in the most rugged and inaccessible portions of the desert ranges. Supposedly, they move up and down the steep mountainsides with the seasons, ever searching out fresh plants on which to browse. They are described as being very shy of human contact, fleeing at the slightest sight or scent of man. Frankly, that is all bunk!

While those stereotypes may well apply to the Desert Bighorn's close cousins in the Sierra Nevada *Ovis canadensis*, our experience with the Desert Bighorn has been much different. We have seen herds of a dozen or more at low elevations in Silver Canyon and in Telephone Canyon in the Pilot Mountains of Nevada in the middle of summer. The conventional wisdom would dictate that they should be way up in the high country at that time of year. Further, when we have encountered Bighorn sheep along the sides of backroads, they pretty much ignore us if we immediately stop, turn the engine off, and remain reasonably quiet. A roadway would hardly be considered as the *most rugged and inaccessible portions of the desert habitat*, and we have had encounters with sheep in this manner several times. On one occasion, in August in Lower Silver Canyon, I came upon a group of fifteen Bighorns, mostly ewes, but with at least one ram and several lambs. They continued to graze quietly, no more than fifty yards from where I had stopped my car. Only when I got out did they seem a little wary, but even then they did not flee in fright. They simply sauntered away from me up the hillside, munching as they went and in no particular hurry. Ranger-Naturalist Charlie Callaghan of Death Valley National Park tells the story of a herd of Bighorn sheep in the Black Mountains standing on the rocks high above the highway, watching, and seemingly fascinated by, all the tourists stopping at Badwater. Such behavior might be considered as cautious, but certainly not frightening for the animals. In his book *Desert Wildlife,* veteran desert naturalist Edmund Jaeger tells of a Bighorn ram coming within fifteen feet of his camp breakfast table one morning, and later bedding down for the night within one hundred yards of his camp. He admits that is very unusual behavior for Bighorn Sheep, particularly a ram.

Silver Canyon is a giant gash in the western escarpment of the White Mountains. The rock sequence in the lower part of the canyon is part of the 550 million year old Campito Formation, highly metamorphosed sandstones and shales once deposited in the bottom of an early Cambrian age sea. As the road climbs higher, the rocks become slightly younger in age. Above the Campito Formation is the Poleta Formation, followed by the Harkless Formation. The latter two rock units are also marine sediments of early to middle Cambrian times. Although I have never specifically looked for fossils in Silver Canyon, all of these formations contain trilobites, hard shelled little critters which once scurried across the ocean bottoms. In addition, the Poleta contains fossil sponges, but their fossilized remains are sometimes difficult to recognize.

At a point 7.5 miles from Highway 6, the Class I road suddenly leaves the canyon bottom, and begins to steeply ascend the north wall of upper Silver Canyon. You will want to engage your four-wheel drive here, and possibly drop your transfer case into low range. Because of the steep grades and narrow roadway, there was once a time when the U.S. Forest Service designated Silver Canyon as a one-way road for downhill traffic only. The road has been greatly improved over the last fifty years, however, and while the grades are just as steep as they ever were, the road has been widened and the radius of the hairpin turns increased. The traction of your vehicle is greatly increased when you have power going to all four wheels.

The road gains 3,000 feet in the next 3.5 miles, as it steeply switchbacks up the mountainside. While the road surface is generally good, the grade is steep, and for that reason, at least four-wheel drive, if not low range gears are a good idea. (On the descent, low range gears are certainly recommended.) Once the top is reached, the road becomes Class I or better again. A crossroads in reached at 11.5 miles from Highway 6. The elevation here is a lofty 10,150 feet. In the last ten miles you have climbed five thousand vertical feet. Again note your odometer reading or reset your trip odometer to zero here at the top of Silver Canyon.

The graded road to the right goes 2.5 miles south to the Schulman Grove Visitor Center. Straight ahead, the road begins the descent of Wyman Canyon to eventually enter Deep Springs Valley (see Excursion #23). To visit the Cottonwood Basin, turn left onto Forest Road 4S01, the high standard dirt road that follows the crest of the range ten miles northward toward the Patriarch Grove. We are not going that far, however.

In the next mile or so, our road will climb even more to a 10,820' high point, and then switchback down a little through a grove of Bristlecone pines. The road through here essentially crosses the Campito Formation, but as our road leaves the intersection and begins to climb a little, the blue-gray limestone rocks on the left are part of the bottom layers of the Poleta Formation. If you seek trilobite fossils, you might look here.

There is a good view north of 13,040' Mount Barcroft (to far left) and 14,246' White Mountain (next to it in the far distance) from this 10,800-foot high point on the road.

The highpoint to the northeast is 11,278' Blanco Mountain, an easily climbed summit made of Reed Dolomite, the oldest of the Cambrian rocks found in the White Mountains. This rock formation is important, because the soil created from weathered Reed Dolomite is the favored habitat for the Bristlecone pine. Do not climb Blanco Mountain, however, if you are looking for Cambrian fossils. Except for some poorly preserved algae, it is remarkable devoid of fossils.

At a point 7.2 miles from the top of Silver Canyon, a Class I road branches off to the right. Continue straight ahead on Forest Road 4S01 another 2.5 miles to visit the Patriarch Grove, where the U.S. Forest Service has two easy self-guiding nature trails here at 11,200 feet. The quarter mile long Timberline Ancients Trail takes you past the Patriarch Tree. This tree is a relatively young fifteen hundred years old, but it is the largest of the Bristlecone pines ever found, with a circumference of nearly 37 feet. The half-mile long Cottonwood Basin Overlook Trail provides stunning views to the east. From the Patriarch Grove the road continues north, but deteriorates to Class II. Further progress is halted by a locked gate a couple of miles before reaching the Barcroft Laboratory at 12,400 feet.

We are going to visit the Cottonwood Basin, however, so we will be turning to the right here onto Forest Road 5S01. A sign announces it is one mile to the Crooked Creek Station and five miles to Cottonwood Creek.

For many years the University of California has maintained a series of high altitude research stations here in the White Mountains. Originally the facilities consisted of four parts: (1) the Owens Valley Laboratory, just east of Bishop at 4,080 feet, (2) the Crooked Creek Laboratory which you see to the right at 10,200 feet (3) the Barcroft Laboratory farther up 4S01, at 12,400 feet and (4) the Summit Laboratory on the very top of White Mountain Peak at 14,246 feet. (The last seven miles of road to the top of White Mountain Peak have deteriorated so that the Summit Laboratory is now little used and generally only accessible on foot or by helicopter.) At these facilities, graduate students and post doctorate researchers from a wide variety of scientific disciplines come and perform basic research involving high altitude adaptations.

The University of California's Crooked Creek Laboratory. The hillside behind the station is quartz monzonite, a granite-like rock of the Sage Hen Flat pluton.

At a point 1.6 miles off Forest Road 4S01, our road 5S01 comes to an unlocked gate in a drift fence. The gate should be closed when you reach it;

please close it again after passing through. You are now in country used for the summer grazing of cattle for well over one hundred years. Road 5S01 fords tiny Crooked Creek several times, as it makes its way down a draw. The dark rocks to the left are part of the highly metamorphosed 600+ million year old Wyman Canyon Formation of Precambrian age. The contrasting outcrops of white rocks are lenses of limestone and dolomite interbedded within the Wyman sequence. Like the slightly younger Reed Dolomite, the Wyman Formation is a poor place to look for fossils.

At a point two miles in from Forest Road 4S01 and 9.2 miles from the top of Silver Canyon, Forest Road 5S01 forks. The right fork is a Class II road that goes down Crooked Creek to eventually dead-end at about the 9,000-foot level just beyond Sage Hen Peak. At one time this jeep trail went on through Dead Horse Meadow to join the Wyman Canyon Road a couple of miles below Roberts Ranch. That through route is no longer passable. For the Cottonwood Basin, we will want to turn left at this fork.

Crooked Creek is cattle country.

Our Class II road now begins a gradual climb in the next mile and a half to the top of a 10,200' ridge, where there is a grand view north of White Mountain Peak. Here a USFS sign warns motorists that the road ahead requires four-wheel drive.

14,246' White Mountain Peak

As you start your descent into the Cottonwood Basin, engage your four-wheel drive, and put your transfer case in low range. While the road down is steep and a little rocky in places, it is no worse than Class III. The road descends some eight hundred vertical feet in the next 2.6 miles. Once in the valley below, the road improves to Class II again. Cottonwood Creek is forded for the first time three miles below the ridgetop. **The use of four-wheel drive is recommended for all these stream crossings.**

The trail turns east after the first ford, and begins to follow Cottonwood Creek downstream. The stream is forded again, and soon the two old log cabins of McCloud's Cow Camp are reached. History has forgotten when McCloud's Camp was first established, but it is clearly marked on the 1917 topographic map.

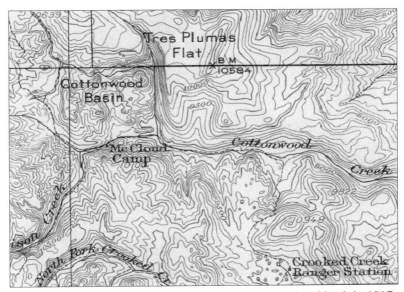

McCloud Camp is shown on this topographic map printed back in 1917.
Notice, at that time, there was a Ranger Station located down on Crooked Creek.

The larger of the two cabins at McCloud Camp contains a wood stove and a couple of beds, and might provide emergency shelter from a storm, if you do not mind sharing the premises with the abundant population of mice. There are three species of mice in the White Mountains, but the one that seems to have taken over this cabin is the common Deer Mouse *Peromyscus maniculatis.* Unfortunately these little critters can host the Hantavirus that can be passed on to humans through infected rodent droppings, urine and saliva. Trust me folks, the Hantavirus Pulmonary Syndrome is something you will want to avoid. The disease is often fatal! **My recommendation would be to stay out of these cabins. If you do go in, avoid all rodent droppings, and don't stir up any dust. Breathing the virus is the most common way of becoming infected!**

McCloud Camp

Below McCloud Camp the road fords Cottonwood Creek once again, but comes to a dead-end within a half-mile. In this last half-mile, the geology suddenly changes once again from the Precambrian metamorphic rocks to the much younger granite-like quartz monzonite rocks of the Beer Creek pluton. These igneous rocks are easily recognized not only by their coarse grained composition, but by the well-developed vertical joint system that runs through them.

Outcrops of quartz monzonite display a system of vertical joints.

Cottonwood Creek contains some small fish: Rainbow trout, Eastern Brook trout, and at lower elevations, brown trout. All of these species were probably introduced to these waters a hundred years ago by ranchers in Fish Lake Valley, and later by the Rainbow Club in Bishop. You may have heard about the rare and endangered Paiute Cutthroat trout also planted in Cottonwood Creek some years ago by the Department of Fish and Game. The rumors are true. This was done in 1946 with brood stock taken from the East Fork of the Carson River, where their habitat was seriously threatened. However, the transplants were put in the remote and nearly inaccessible North Fork of Cottonwood Creek, not here on the South Fork. **Fishing for the Paiute Cutthroat is still strictly prohibited. Violators face very stiff penalties. Don't do it!**

It should be noted that, at the urging of a wilderness advocacy group in Davis CA, U.S. Senator Barbara Boxer has introduced a bill in the Senate which would add nearly 2.5 million more acres of designated *Wilderness* areas to California's fourteen million acres of already existing wilderness. A similar bill has been introduced in the House. If passed, and signed into law by the President, this legislation would place 282,880 acres in the White Mountains under formal *Wilderness* classification. That amounts to more than 95% of the entire mountain range! As currently written, the bills would put the White Mountain Road into a non-wilderness corridor, but the road into the Cottonwood Basin would be forever closed. The Forest Service would not be able to drive in there for administrative purposes. The Department of Fish and Game would not be able to drive in here. Scientists with the White Mountain Research Station could not drive in here in pursuit of their research. Cattlemen could no longer drive in here. Campers and fishermen could no longer drive in here. Four-wheelers would be locked out. Everyone loses, except for a few politicians pandering to big city voters who have never been in here and never will be!

The road's end in the Cottonwood Basin makes a very pleasant place to car camp, but that soon may come to an end.

140

Before you plunge in ......

When your road encounters a water hazard such as a stream crossing, or even a large mud hole, there are three vital pieces of information you need to know **before you plunge in:**

Water Depth: How deep is the water? Is the water deeper than the height of your doorsills? If so, you may find water leaking into the interior of your vehicle. Worse yet, your vehicle may briefly float, with your wheels lifted off the bottom. Under those circumstances, the current could sweep your vehicle downstream. In even deeper water, the water could bend your radiator fan into the radiator core.

Water Velocity: Is there any current? If so, how strong is it? Is it strong enough to sweep your vehicle downstream?

Bottom Conditions: What is the roadway like under the water? Is it likely to be firm sand or bottomless mud and muck? Are there likely to be any large rocks hidden by the water?

Obviously, each driver should get out of the vehicle and carefully look at the water hazard before plunging in. Note the three factors listed above, and mentally plan where you want your wheels to be as you cross.

Other hints:

Look for fresh tracks on the other side of the water hazard, confirming that other vehicles have successfully driven through the water recently.

If one of the vehicles in your party has a winch, send the vehicles without a winch across first.

21

Bishop View

Special Features:	This is a short trip high into the White Mountains east of Bishop to a tungsten mine in the upper reaches of Redding Canyon, where there is a superb view of Bishop and its environs.
Time Required:	This outing can be done in two or three hours out of Bishop.
Miles Involved:	The distance from downtown Bishop to the road's end at the Gray Eagle Mine is a little over ten miles.
Degree of Difficulty:	The road into Redding Canyon is graded dirt Class I or better. The road climbs out of the canyon, however, and the last three miles are mostly Class II, but with a little Class III.
Remarks:	Except for the rare winter snowstorm, this trail is usually open throughout the year. This is an outing to be best taken in the morning, when the sun is on the Sierra Nevada skyline to the west.

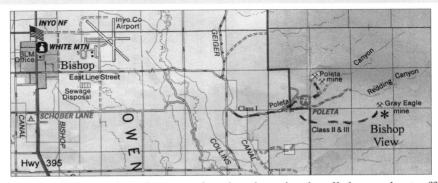

Looking for a quick and easy outing that doesn't take all day, and yet offers nice scenery and great views? "Bishop View" fills the bill!

From the intersection of Main and Line Streets in downtown Bishop, note your odometer reading, and take East Line Street east towards the White Mountains. After three miles the Owens River is crossed. A half-mile beyond on the right is the University of California's Owens Valley Laboratory, part of the White Mountain Research Station. Here scholars in a wide variety of scientific fields come to undertake research projects.

The road makes a wide turn to the south at the four-mile mark, and now becomes Eastside Road. The Eastside Road marks the western boundary of the "Poleta Open Area", a 2,500-acre area set aside for operators of off-road vehicles to roam the countryside at will. That explains the myriad of trails going all over the hills to the east. At 5.2 miles look for a Class I road on the left. A sign indicates it is the Redding Canyon Road. Note your odometer reading, and turn left here. After following the Redding Canyon Road for 1.1 miles, the road forks. Here a side trip can be made to the Poleta Mine by taking the left fork to Poleta Canyon. After nearly a mile, just past the picnic tables, there is a Class III road to the right that goes 0.7 miles up to the mine.

The Poleta Mine goes back to 1881, when a quartz-sulfide vein containing free gold was found between bedding planes in a limestone (which is part of the Silver Peak Group). The mine was most recently worked in the 1930s, but closed for good in 1941. Since 1900 the Poleta Mine has a recorded production of more than 2,000 ounces of gold and another 800 ounces of silver. Some say those production figures should be doubled. The main workings include a four hundred foot tunnel. Inside the adit is a 600-foot winze descending along the vein. **Warning: Don't even think about going in the underground workings. They are dangerous!**

The Poleta Mine

Our excursion is going to take us into the upper reaches of Redding Canyon, not Poleta Canyon, so we are going to keep to the right at the fork 1.1 miles off the Eastside Road. The Redding Canyon Road now deteriorates to something between Class I and Class II. At a point 1.9 miles from the Eastside Road, look for a steep, but otherwise Class II road climbing out of the south side of Redding Canyon. If you elect to continue straight ahead, the road passes the concrete foundation of a cabin and goes into the narrows. Here the road turns to Class III, as it goes through a wet area, where willow and other vegetation have all but overgrown the roadway.

The way to Bishop View and the Grey Eagle Mine is the side road to the right, before the old cabin site is reached. In a quarter of a mile the road has climbed up and out of the canyon bottom, and has turned to the east, where it forks again. Take the left branch this time. It ascends a smaller canyon through rocks of the 550-million year old Campito Formation. You had better engage your four-wheel drive, because the road is steep enough to be considered Class III.

Desert Needlegrass *Stipia speciosa* is very common along the road
to the Gray Eagle Mine. In the spring its tender young shoots
are a favorite brouse of Tule Elk and Desert Bighorn sheep.

The country levels out at a point three miles in from the Eastside Road, and the Class II road actually drops down a bit. A couple of small drainages are crossed, and at the 4.3-mile point a side road to the left is encountered. That road drops down to some old mine workings, but a cable across the road bars access by vehicles. Continue going straight ahead in a generally eastward direction.

The road to Bishop View.

Finally, five miles in from the Eastside Road, the geology suddenly changes, and the first workings of the Gray Eagle Mine are reached. (There are more tunnels around the hillside, but they are not accessible by road.) Here at 6800 feet, at the lower edge of the piñon-juniper forest, the bedrock suddenly changes from highly metamorphosed marine sediments to a granite-like igneous rock called quartz monzonite. Gold was the commodity originally sought here where quartz veins containing free gold penetrated the quartz monzonite. Yet a mile away at the Poleta Mine, the geology is quite different. There the gold-bearing quartz veins are in limestone, a sedimentary rock. In later years, around 1952, scheelite, the principle ore of tungsten, was also mined here. The large pit near the road's end shows where earlier tunnels at several levels were opened up into one large "Glory Hole". **Warning: The mine works are unsafe to enter.**

The real treasure to be had at the Gray Eagle Mine, however, is the terrific view of Bishop just to the west. While the broad expanse of the Sierra Nevada skyline is somewhat limited by the walls of Redding Canyon, a number of thirteen thousand footers can be seen on the skyline to the west. They include 13,118' Mt. Emerson on the south, going north to 13,983' Mt. Humphreys, 13,181' Basin Mountain, 13,652' Mt. Tom, 13,196' Mt. Julius Caesar, 13,704' Mt. Abbott and its close neighbor 13,451' Mt. Mills. A bit closer, in the valley below, lies the City of Bishop with its western suburbs. Upper Redding Canyon is only ten miles away, yet only a handful of Bishop's residents have ever seen their community from this perspective. Such a pity!

22

Black Canyon

Special Features:	This is another outing that is close to Bishop, and can be as short and easy, or as long and challenging as you choose to make it. The excursion ascends a major canyon in the southern end of the White Mountains, where prospectors have trod for years.
Time Required:	A full day should be allocated to fully explore the upper reaches of Black Canyon, but if you choose to go only as far as the second narrows, a couple of hours is adequate.
Miles Involved:	The one way distance from downtown Bishop to the second narrows is about twelve miles. Add another 26 miles to fully explore the upper reaches of the Black Canyon and return to Bishop.
Degree of Difficulty:	The lower portion of Black Canyon is usually Class II or better. The difficulty comes at the second narrows of the canyon just above the confluence of Black and Marble Canyons. Here are two hundred feet of rock strewn Class IV that often separates the men from the boys. Drivers of unmodified SUVs may choose to go no further. Drivers of short wheelbase vehicles with 33-inch tires should have no problem. Once this obstacle is overcome, the road beyond is generally Class II, and usually no worse than Class III.
Remarks:	**Keep in mind that summer thunderstorms above the White Mountains are potentially dangerous to anyone in the narrow canyons. At best, a sudden downpour can wash out the roads in a matter of minutes. In worst-case scenarios, flash floods occasionally occur, and can be fatal to anyone caught in their path. Stay out of Black Canyon when storm clouds gather over the high peaks!** Except for the rare winter snowstorm, the lower portions of this trail are usually open throughout the year.

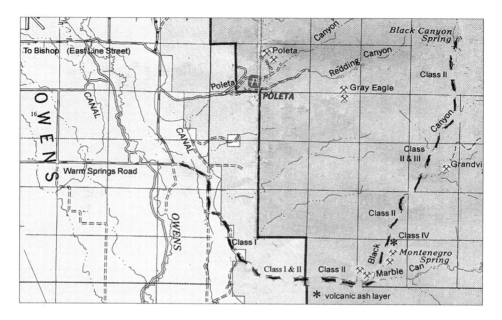

The Mexican Mine at the head of Black Canyon was discovered in 1862. Prospectors have been trudging through the canyon ever since. Surely those sourdoughs must have noticed the heavily mineralized quartz veins in the canyon's steep vertical walls. There are also lenses of cerrusite and galena between layers of schist and limestone. Claims were staked over the years, but it was not until decades later that any sort of serious mining was attempted. Interest in Black Canyon was renewed around the Turn of the 20th Century. Just before the Bank Panic of 1907, the Black Canyon Mine had a dozen cottages housing workers. Developers were running full-page ads in the Bishop newspaper promoting their stocks. A few residents in the Owens Valley still have these certificates, although there is not much left of the original mine. There has been some renewed interest in the canyon's mineral potential in recent years, and some core drilling and other prospecting has taken place.

From the intersection of Line and Main Streets in downtown Bishop, take Main Street (U.S. Highway 395) south in the direction of Big Pine. At a point 2.5 miles south of downtown, the Warm Springs Road starts east across the Owens Valley. Note your odometer reading, and turn left here. As you drive east along Warm Springs Road, keep your eyes open for Tule Elk. Some three hundred of these magnificent animals were first transplanted into the Owens Valley in the early 1930s in order to preserve their species due to loss of native habitat. They seem to be doing quite well. Their numbers are now up to about five hundred animals in several herds. The Tinemaha Herd sometimes roams this far north.

Tule Elk *Cervus elaphus nannodes* prefer to dine in
fields of alfalfa, but will also eat native vegetation.

Proceed eastward on Warm Springs Road 4.4 miles to the point where the pavement swings to the left and turns north. Leave the pavement here, crossing the cattle guard and going straight ahead on the graded dirt road. The road will turn to the south in a half-mile. At a point 2.6 miles from the end of the asphalt, you will find a Class I road going straight ahead, while the Eastside Road swings to the right. Continue straight ahead here. This Class I road climbs the alluvial fan, and soon enters Black Canyon. The elevation at the mouth of the canyon is 4,300 feet.

As you enter the canyon, notice the flat lying layers of fanglomerate sediment perched high on both sides of the canyon. This was deposited in early Pleistocene times just as alluvial fans are deposited today. However, the very noticeable white layer is volcanic ash, which varies in thickness from two to three feet. It was deposited when the Long Valley Caldera exploded some 760,000 years ago (see Excursion #11). Normally these fanglomerate beds would be buried in the ground beneath you. However, the White Mountains are being steadily uplifted, causing the streams to erode downward and thus exposing the beds.

The layer of white material embedded in these beds of fanglomerate is
volcanic ash blown out of the Long Valley Caldera 760,000 years ago.

The road gradually deteriorates from Class I to Class II as you cross the wash for the second time. Near here, cavities eroded out of the fanglomerate sometimes contain piles of twigs and other dry vegetation that have obviously been brought into these holes and cracks. These accumulations of vegetation are not the result of random floodwaters. Each stem and twig has been brought here and carefully put in place by our old friend the Pack Rat, sometimes called the Wood Rat. There are actually two species of Pack Rats in the White Mountains. There is the common *Neotoma lepida* found throughout the sage and piñon-juniper regions of Inyo County, and his bushier tailed cousin *Neotoma cinerea*, whose habitat has gone as high as the very top of 14,246' White Mountain Peak.

The nests, or middens, that these little critters build in the cracks and crevices are usually protected from the elements and often remain dry. Some can actually be tens of thousands of years old, and as such can be of enormous benefit to paleobotanists, who study prehistoric plant life. The Pack Rat selects one spot in his home in which to urinate and defecate, something it does often. During the animal's life, this perch is usually moist. Pollen blown in from nearby plants will adhere to the sticky surface. Thousands of years later some paleobotanist can come along, dissect the midden, and extract the pollen grains. A microscopic examination of the pollen can then identify the predominate vegetation around the midden at the time of the Pack Rat's life. Sometimes those results are surprising.

A Pack Rat and its home

The first narrows are reached at a point 2.5 miles in from the Eastside Road. The road is a little sandy at times, and can easily be washed out after a thunderstorm. Nevertheless, the first narrows are usually no more difficult than Class II. The elevation here is 5,300 feet. The light colored rocks on either side of the canyon at this point are the 560 million year old Deep Spring Formation.

The first narrows in Black Canyon.

The canyon swings to the north at a point five miles from the asphalt. Ahead is a black band of rocks from which the canyon gets its name. These highly metamorphosed rocks are part of the Campito Formation. They are slightly younger than the Deep Spring Formation, but both are from the early Cambrian Period, when life on earth consisted only of primitive marine organisms.

The remains of an old stone cabin and a quail guzzler are passed on the left. The latter is a device installed by the California Department of Fish & Game. It is designed to capture whatever sparse rainfall might fall here, and channel the water into a subterranean tank for long term storage. The life-giving water is then accessible to quail and other wildlife by way of a sloping ramp.

Just beyond the guzzler, a Class III side road climbs steeply up the hillside to the left to some mining claims. The canyon and road fork at a point 5.4 miles from the blacktop. The left fork is Black Canyon; the right fork with a solitary cottonwood tree is Marble Canyon. This fork dead-ends in about one hundred yards.

Here at the fork in the canyons, hidden amid the sage, can be found the stone walls and foundations of a half dozen structures, all part of a long forgotten mine camp of the World War I era. The Black Canyon road goes straight ahead deteriorating to Class III. A short drive up the canyon will reveal some of the diggings that supported the camp. As you make your way up the canyon bottom, keep your eyes open for bits and pieces of asphalt. As incredible as it may seem, at one time this road was paved! The principal mines in this area were the Mirage-Mariposa and the Hope. Both contain small amounts of gold, silver, lead, zinc, and tungsten, but not enough to economically extract at today's labor costs. **While at least one tunnel appears to be safe, do not attempt to enter any of these underground workings.**

A third of a mile above the fork in the roads comes the second narrows in Black Canyon. Here is the previously mentioned two hundred feet of rocky Class IV. Once it is surmounted, the road becomes significantly better.

Black Canyon above the second narrows.

There is a dependable year around spring about a mile above the second narrows. In the springtime, particularly in wet years, it may support a stream that can flow down the canyon a mile. Under these circumstances, Black Canyon is particularly delightful with a variety of spring wildflowers in bloom.

Beyond the first spring, the road continues on up the canyon for another five miles to an elevation of 8,800 feet, where there is a "T" intersection. You have now gained 4,500 feet since entering the canyon some nine miles back. The left fork of the road soon ends at an old mining claim. The right fork descends four hundred feet to Black Canyon Spring. While the topo map shows the road extending beyond Black Canyon Spring all the way to Reed Flat to connect with the paved White Mountain Road, the U.S. Forest Service has administratively closed the upper portion of this jeep trail. The USFS sign at the Reed Flat end says: "No vehicles to avoid damage to the road" (an interesting choice of words)!

23

White Mountain Traverse

Primary Attraction:	This backcountry excursion takes the reader 5,000 feet up the east side of the White Mountains via well-watered Wyman Canyon. Once on the 10,400' crest, our route steeply descends 6,000 feet down Silver Canyon on the west side of the range. Along the way are old mines, historic sites, and groves of ancient Bristlecone pines.
Time Required:	This is an all day excursion.
Distance Involved:	The total round trip mileage from Bishop, going up Wyman Canyon, and returning down Silver Canyon is 77 miles.
Degree of Difficulty:	The Wyman Canyon portion of this route is mostly Class II. However, there are several areas where poor traction makes passage easier if four-wheel drive is engaged. The Silver Canyon is Class II going downhill (but the steep upper 3.5 miles are safer taken in four-wheel drive, where all four wheels are holding you back). The upper Silver Canyon Road is definitely Class III when taken in the uphill direction. You might wish to stop at the White Mountain Ranger District office on north Main Street in Bishop to inquire about current road and weather conditions before attempting this outing.
Remarks:	Be sure that you have a full tank of gas before leaving Bishop. **Because of the high elevations involved, this route is generally impassable between November and June. People with cardiac and respiratory problems should realize that this is one of the highest roads in the entire United States, and breathing difficulties could be experienced.**

In recent years, the ancient Bristlecone pines of the White Mountains have become a nationally known tourist attraction. These rugged trees are the oldest living things known to man. The U.S. Forest Service has built attractive visitor displays at both the Schulman and Patriarch groves. The road to Schulman Grove has been paved, making it easily accessible to the family automobile. Your first trip to the White Mountains should be over this high standard road; however, there are more challenging routes. For the backcountry explorer, I suggest the ascent of Wyman Canyon on the east slope to the crest, and then the descent down Silver Canyon on the west side.

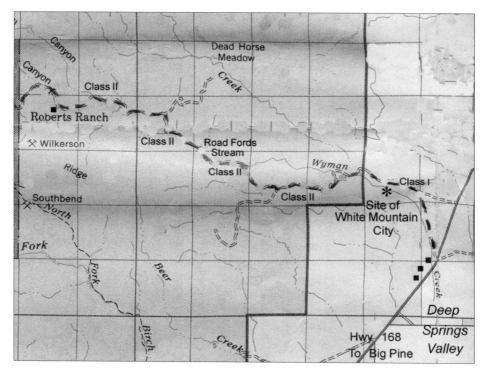

Take U.S. Highway 395 south from Bishop in the direction of Big Pine. About ten miles south of Bishop you will notice what appears to be a number of satellite dishes pointed to the sky. These were installed by the California Institute of Technology and the United States Office of Naval Research and are antennas used for deep space radio astronomy. For the last forty years they have provided researchers with valuable information about our solar system and beyond. The deep trough of the Owens Valley makes an ideal location for such a facility, because the high mountains on either side block out unwanted electronic interference created in urban environments.

Just before reaching the community of Big Pine, look for State Route 168 starting off to the left. The intersection is well marked, and there is a campground here as well as a U.S. Forest Service display on the Bristlecone pine trees. Leave

Highway 395 here going eastward on State Route 168, noting your odometer reading as you do so. The once mighty Owens River is crossed in 1.4 miles. This is the lowest point of today's journey, 3920 feet. If you think that the greasewood and atriplex that live on the sometimes hot, sometimes cold, sometimes salty and always arid floor of the Owens Valley survive in a harsh environment, you ain't seen anything yet!

Our road forks a little over two miles from Highway 395. The right fork crosses the Inyo Mountains and goes on into the Eureka and Death Valleys; stay left toward Westgard Pass.

Toll House Spring can be seen on the left side of the highway 7.7 miles from Highway 395. This was once a private road, and more than a century ago a toll taker's house stood here. The charge was one dollar per wagon with two animals and fifty cents for each additional pair. A horse and rider were charged a quarter. The tariff for cows was a dime each and smaller animals like sheep, goats, and pigs were a nickel.

A mile beyond you will reach the top of 7,271' Westgard Pass, named after A. L. Westgard, a tireless promoter of auto touring. In 1913 he led a caravan of twenty horseless carriages over the old toll road, while publicizing the route of his newly scouted Roosevelt National Highway. Geographers use this low point in the mountain range as a convenient place to separate the White Mountains to the north from the Inyo Mountains to the south. In reality, however, the White and Inyo Mountains are one single continuous range.

On the left at a point 27.5 miles from Highway 395 is a cluster of houses, which was once a Cal Trans highway maintenance station. Just beyond the perimeter fence, a dirt road heads northwest towards the White Mountains. Leave the pavement here, noting your odometer reading. The elevation at this point is 5,300 feet. In the next eighteen miles you will climb 5,100 feet.

Leaving the pavement the Class II road, sandy in places, heads west towards the White Mountains. After 1.3 miles, a Class I road on the right comes in from the highway. Proceed westward and within a half-mile you will begin to see the low stone walls that mark the site of what once was White Mountain City. A BLM sign indicates this is an "Area of Critical Environmental Concern."

It was around 1861 when Colonel Cralley, J.S. Broder, the Graves brothers, and Don Wyman came to this region looking for gold. In the election of that same year, the Deep Springs precinct (of which White Mountain City was the largest community) registered 521 Democratic votes without a single Republican vote. A suspicious Republican candidate came over to investigate and found only a handful of people in the entire precinct. Today stonewalls still mark the location of seven buildings, three corrals, and one reduction furnace. Petroglyphs on nearby rocks suggest that the site was used long before the Democrats came.

Ancient petroglyphs and stone ruins mark the site of White Mountain City.

Continue westward entering Wyman Canyon. You will be passing the site of White Mountain City on the left. At a point 3.3 miles from Highway 168, there is a side road to the right where Wyman Creek is crossed. Many years ago, the main road went to the right here, climbing a series of wet slippery rock stairs in the very bottom of the canyon. It was a Class IV and V route that washed out so frequently, and was usually in such bad condition, that more often than not it was impassable. A bypass route was eventually bladed out high on the south side of the canyon. This bypass is today's Class II road. After 3.2 miles it drops back down into the stream again to rejoin the former route.

The granite-like rocks all along this bypass, and continuing up Wyman Canyon another three miles, are part of the plutonic rocks that were intruded into the Cambrian marine sediments during the Jurassic Period some 150 million years ago. They no doubt came from the same deep-seated magma pools as those that fed the Sierra Nevada range just to the west.

Soon after rejoining the canyon bottom, the road enters the piñon forest. The elevation here is about 6,800 feet. After ascending Wyman Canyon another couple of miles, at a point eight miles from Highway 168, a side road to the right goes 1.4 miles over a ridge to drop into Dead Horse Meadows on Crooked Creek.

After proceeding up Wyman Canyon slightly less than a mile, the bedrock geology suddenly changes. The granitic rocks are left behind, and in their place is a rapid succession of much older rocks. First there is a thin band of the 550 million year old Campito Formation. Following it is an equally thin band of the 560 million year old Deep Spring Formation, followed by another thin band, this time the 570 million year old Reed dolomite. All are deposits accumulated in the sea bottom during Cambrian times. Finally the road crosses several miles of the Wyman Canyon Formation, another layer of old marine sediments that are Precambrian in age.

The road fords Wyman Creek in several places, but
the bottom is firm and the water usually not very deep.

At a point 10.4 miles from Highway 168 and at an elevation of 8,000 feet, the site of Robert's Ranch is reached. This was once a camp for the Wilkerson Mine just up the side canyon to the south. Two abandoned cabins survive from a more modern era, but what is of more interest is the old stone reduction furnace that has been subsequently modified with a door and a window. The furnace was no doubt built to reduce the complex sulfide ore, but judging from the relatively small amount of black shiny slag, not much ore was put through the device.

The road now improves to Class II and remains that way to the crest of the range. A meadow area is crossed, where there is sufficient flat land to camp. Wild roses have been very common along Wyman Creek for the last several miles, and they are abundant here. If you pass this way in the fall, you might collect some of the rose hips. They can be turned into a tasty jelly that is rich in Vitamin C.

Wild rose *Rosa woodsii*   Rose hip

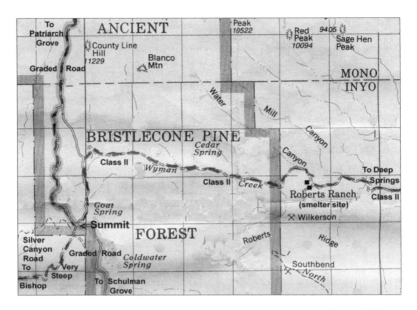

A half-mile above the Robert's Ranch site is a rather substantial gate. The U.S. Forest Service keeps this gate open during the summer and fall months, but closes it during the winter when the roads ahead are covered with snow. A Forest Service sign a half-mile farther indicates you are now entering the "Ancient Bristlecone Pine Forest".

The USFS has set aside a special botanical area of 26,529 acres for the study, protection, and visitor interpretation of this unique tree. **Vehicular travel is restricted to established roadways, and the gathering of wood is strictly prohibited.** In the several Bristlecone groves, there are about one hundred trees that are over four thousand years old. The Forest Service would like to protect them.

How To Tell The Difference Between the Bristlecone Pine and the Limber Pine

Both of these hardy pines grow at high elevations in the White and Inyo Mountains under the most harsh and inhospitable conditions imaginable. They are sometimes confused, because individual trees of both species are often twisted and contorted by the elements, and because both trees occupy the same ecological niche.

The Bristlecone pine *Pinus longaeva* (previously *Pinus aristata Engelmann*) has needles that are 1.0 to 1.5 inches long and in clusters of five. The needles are darker, spread out evenly on the branchlets, sometimes resembling a bottlebrush. The cones are two to three inches long, and have conspicuous quarter inch long prickles at the ends. The Bristlecone pine grows almost exclusively on calcium rich soils as is found in limestone or dolomite. Indeed, in the White Mountains, most of the Bristlecone pines are growing on the Reed Dolomite Formation.

The Limber pine *Pinus flexilis* also has needles in fives, but the needles are 1.5 to 3.0 inches long and lighter in color. Its cones are also longer, up to ten inches long, and larger in diameter than the Bristlecone. The Limber pinecone lacks the little incurved prickles so characteristic of the Bristlecone pine. Further, the branches can be very irregular, some being long, others quite short. The Limber pine is more widely spread throughout the White and Inyo Mountains, and it is not as picky about the soil it grows in. The tree derives its name from the fact that the small branchlets are so supple that they can be bent, twisted, and even tied in knots without breaking.

Bristlecone pine

Slightly over five miles above Robert's Ranch, 15.6 miles from Highway 168, an old log cabin is encountered, and here the road forks; stay right. The road to the left is a service road for the two Southern California Edison Company power lines that you have been following for the last fourteen miles. The Class II right fork switchbacks up the hillside for nearly a mile to encounter a high standard graded road on top.

At the top of Wyman Canyon

If you choose to turn right here, you can drive 7.5 miles further up the ridge to visit the Patriarch Grove at 11,200 feet. The Forest Service has two easy self-guiding nature trails here. The quarter mile long Timberline Ancients Trail takes you past the Patriarch Tree, which is a relatively young fifteen hundred years old, but it is the largest of the Bristlecone pines ever found. It has a circumference of nearly 37 feet. The half-mile long Cottonwood Basin Overlook Trail provides stunning views to the east. From the Patriarch Grove the road continues north, but deteriorates to Class II. Further progress is halted by a locked gate a couple of miles before reaching the University of California's Barcroft Laboratory at 12,400 feet. Beyond this High Altitude Research Station a jeep trail once continued seven more miles up the ridge to the very top of 14,246' White Mountain Peak; however, that route is now limited to hikers.

To complete our traverse of the White Mountain Range we will need to turn left upon reaching this graded road. The next important road junction is 1.6 miles ahead.

In looking around this high windswept plateau, one would guess that the prehistoric Indians would not have ventured up here much, other than an occasional hunting party. Seemingly the highest mountains of the Great Basin would be the last place that one might expect to find an ancient campsite, let alone the site of a small village. Yet here in the White Mountains, no less than eleven village sites have been found at elevations ranging from 10,400 to 12,640 feet. All the sites found are in meadow areas near permanent water sources. These villages had up to eight pit houses, surrounded by a low rock wall and covered by a roof of Bristlecone and limber pine boughs. They were probably inhabited only during the summer and fall months, but the astounding thing is that some of the sites may go back as far as 2,500 B.C. The 4,600-year-old Methuselah tree was only one hundred years old in 2500 BC! Clearly these sites were in use for well over a millennia when the Athabaska linguistic group Native Americans, from whom the modern day Paiutes have descended, first moved into the Great Basin. The Paiutes seemed to have adopted the ways of the ancient ones, however, and some of these sites were occupied as recently as 1836, when Joseph Walker first came into the Owens Valley.

At a point eighteen miles from Highway 168, a crossroads is reached. If you wish to make a side trip to see the Schulman Grove, turn left here, it is only three miles to the south. The Schulman Grove is the most developed site in the White Mountains. It has a USFS Visitor Center (staffed only from June through September) and three hiking trails that wind their way through these ancient trees. It is along the four-mile long Methuselah Trail that you pass the Methuselah tree, the oldest living thing known to man, dated at 4,600 years. The tree is no longer marked, because in the past people have cut bits and pieces off of it. Nearby are at least eight other trees over four thousand years old.

If, upon reaching the crossroads, if you want to continue your traverse of the range without any diversions, simply proceed straight ahead at the crossroads. A USFS sign indicates that Road 6S02 goes straight ahead to Silver Canyon. The elevation here on the ridge is 10,400 feet. Incidentally, don't be surprised if your rig doesn't seem to have the spunk it normally has. If you get out and walk around a bit, you won't have your usual spunk either! The atmosphere up here does not have as many oxygen molecules per cubic liter as you are accustomed to.

Road 6S02 forks after only 0.2 miles; stay to the right. The left fork soon dead-ends at a radio repeater site. For the next four miles, a good Class II road to the right steeply switchbacks down the mountainside into Silver Canyon. In this four-mile stretch, you will drop 4,000 feet. Because of the steep grades, only downhill traffic is recommended. This road is considered Class III coming up due to the loose traction afforded. I recommend the use of lower gears and four-wheel drive going down, too. It is easier on your brakes when you utilize your engine and have four wheels to hold your car back.

Once you reach the stream in the canyon bottom, the grade becomes much more gentle. A small stream dances its way through very old and highly metamorphosed rocks of the Harkless, Poleta, and Campito Formations. Along the stream are thickets of willows, wild roses, and an occasional cottonwood tree. From where the road first reaches the canyon bottom, it is less than six miles to the mouth of the canyon and two more miles to Highway 6. Laws is passed just before reaching the highway. This was once a station on the narrow gauge Carson & Colorado Railroad coming out of Mound House, Nevada. Even if you are not a railroad buff, a stop at the Laws Museum will top off a delightful day's outing (providing you get there before closing time at 4 p.m.). From here, Bishop is just four miles south on Highway 6.

Laws Railroad Museum

If You Should Break Down

What should you do if you are out in the backcountry alone and experience a serious automotive breakdown? Should you stay with your disabled vehicle or go for help? Should you split your group with the strongest member walking out for help, while leaving those less physically able behind? The conventional wisdom is to stay with your vehicle in the hope that someone will come along and find you. That may not be the best answer. Some of the trails described herein are in very lonely country, where it could be weeks before anyone would happen by.

Obviously, the best solution is to prevent such circumstances from occurring. It is always best to travel with companions in a second vehicle. It is also wise to keep your vehicle properly maintained. This will eliminate many potential mechanical problems. It is also important to always go prepared. If you carry the items listed in *Appendix D* a serious breakdown will certainly be inconvenient, but not life threatening. As an added bonus, by having some of the items listed, you might be able to improvise repairs sufficient to get you back. Did you give some thought to some sort of an emergency communication plan before you left home? A cellular telephone backed up with a CB or 2-meter radio could get you out of a potentially serious jam.

If your vehicle should become disabled, don't panic. Sit down with your passengers and together carefully analyze your circumstances. Do you have the means to communicate with someone in the outside world? If so, it would probably be best to call for help, and then all remain with the vehicle. If that is not an option, consider other alternatives. Did you tell anyone where you were going and when you expected to return? If so, are they likely to notify the Sheriff's Department if you don't return when expected? If that does not seem promising, you are going to have to think about self-rescue. How far is it to the nearest paved road or place of human occupancy where you might find help? Could your strongest member walk there? If so, how long might that reasonably take, and under what environmental conditions, such as darkness, extreme cold or extreme heat? What about water, food, and warm clothing for both those who might stay with the vehicle, as well as those who might go for help? Give the answers to these questions careful thought, and then rationally develop the *Rescue Plan* that has the best chance of success under your own particular circumstances.

Years Ago In Big Pine

The 1890s

The 1920s

The 1920s
(Photos courtesy of Richard McCutchan)

Chapter V

Trails Out Of Big Pine

For the outdoorsman, Big Pine, California is synonymous with hunting and fishing in the High Sierra or possibly mountaineering in the Palisades. However, there are also plenty of additional opportunities for backroad exploring in the White and Inyo Mountains east of Big Pine.

Big Pine's roots go back to 1869. Once the Owens Valley Indian Wars were over, small farming communities began to develop up and down the valley, and Big Pine was one of them. The community got a big boost in 1877-78, when an irrigation ditch system better distributed the waters of the Owens River, and farms flourished. That all came to an end in 1924, as the City of Los Angeles acquired the water rights, and the ditches dried up. Big Pine became relegated to being a bedroom community of its larger cousin, Bishop, just fourteen miles to the north.

Nevertheless, twelve hundred people still call Big Pine home. It has a market, two sporting goods stores, four places to eat and four motels. It also has a couple of service stations. Your fuel tanks should be topped off before heading east. Take advantage of these services, for there will be none where you are going.

Big Pine circa 1920
(Photo courtesy of Richard McCutchan)

24

The Warren Bench Circuit

Primary Attraction:	This is a low level excursion that can usually be done even when deep snow still blankets the high country. The route winds its way through picturesque weathered granite boulders. Along the way are fine views of the Palisades group of peaks in the upper Big Pine Creek Canyon. As an added bonus, the area is alive with wildflowers, should you make this outing in the springtime.
Time Required:	This is a two-hour excursion out of Big Pine.
Miles Involved:	The entire circuit is twelve miles long.
Degree of Difficulty:	The first 2.5 miles of dirt road are Class II, but the remaining 5.5 miles are Class III, some of it requiring low range gears.
Remarks:	Except for the rare winter snowstorm, this trail is usually open throughout the year.

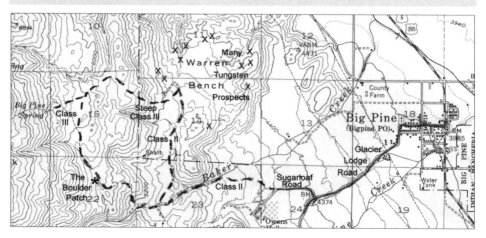

The Warren Bench circuit is one of those places that is usually accessible all year long, and offers a pleasant destination for a couple of hours of easy four-wheeling. Views of the Sierra Nevada skyline to the west are impressive, particularly in the winter when the peaks wear a mantle of snow.

To find the road to Warren Bench, take Crocker Street west from downtown Big Pine. Note your odometer reading as you leave Highway 395. Crocker Street turns into Glacier Lodge Road upon leaving town, and the highway swings to the left and passes beneath a double set of high power lines. As you head southwest along the roadway, there is a grand view of the Sierra skyline straight ahead. Left to right, we can see 12,790' Goodale Mountain, and behind it and slightly to the right is 13,397' Cardinal Mountain. Farther to the right is 13,665' Birch Mountain. Looking more westward we can see 14,040' Disappointment Peak and, below it, middle Palisade Glacier.

Turn right onto the paved Sugarloaf Road at a point 1.6 miles from Highway 395. After 0.6 miles turn right onto graded dirt Arc Road. A borrow pit is passed on the left, and a side road right goes over to Baker Creek on the right, but continue heading westward on the main road. Slightly more than three miles from Highway 395, the road crosses the Baker Creek culvert. Here the stream is lined with cottonwoods, water birch, willows, and wild roses.

The grading ends at the 3.2-mile point from Highway 395, but a narrow Class II road passes through the drift fence and continues on. The road forks at 3.5 miles. You may return via the left fork ahead, but for the moment take the right fork, which turns north and heads up a broad flat shelf known as Warren Bench. This is important winter range for deer forced down out of the mountains by snow. Another fork is encountered at 3.7 miles; again go right.

The well-weathered igneous rocks all around you are part of the great Sierra Nevada Batholith that was pushed up from the bowels of the earth during Jurassic and Cretaceous times. Related granite rocks of late Mesozoic age can be seen atop Mount Whitney, in the cliffs of Yosemite Valley, and in the glacier-scoured Desolation Basin west of Lake Tahoe. It was tungsten prospectors who put these roads in many years ago, but alas their efforts were for naught. No tungsten was ever mined here.

Weathered spires of granite stand tall and straight like prehistoric Easter Island statues.

Our Class II road forks at a point 4.4 miles from Highway 395. The right fork goes onto some prospect holes. Take the left fork that, within a quarter of a mile, will begin to climb the rocky hillside to the west. It is here that you should engage your four-wheel drive, and drop the transmission into low range. You will need them both for the next five miles.

The Class III roadway climbs steeply up the mountainside. The steep grade ends at the 5.1 mile point, and just beyond there is a nice view of Warren Lake down in the floor of the Owens Valley. A ridgetop is crested at 5.5 miles, and here tracks go off to the left to return to the 3.7-mile point mentioned previously. Stay to the right. Our road now drops down into a small valley, where at 6.1 miles yet another road goes to the left. The right fork goes four more miles to an 8,500' high point that I call "Glacier View" (described in *High Sierra SUV Trails Volume I - The East Side*). If snows do not block the route, the Class III side trip to the right is highly recommended. If you cannot go higher, turn to the left here. It is but two miles back to the fork in the road at 3.5 miles. Along the way the road winds its way through "The Boulder Patch", a picturesque maze of well-weathered granite rocks.

"The Boulder Patch"

25

The Grandview Mine

Primary Attraction:	This outing takes the reader to an old mine perched high on the eastern side of Black Canyon, where grand views of the Sierra Nevada skyline are afforded. It is also a good place to go "nutting" in the fall.
Time Required:	This is a half-day excursion out of Big Pine, but it is one that can be combined with Excursions #26, 27, 28, or 29 for a full day of four-wheeling.
Miles Involved:	The one way distance from downtown Big Pine to the Grandview Mine is twenty miles.
Degree of Difficulty:	The dirt roads into the Grandview Mine are generally no worse than Class II.

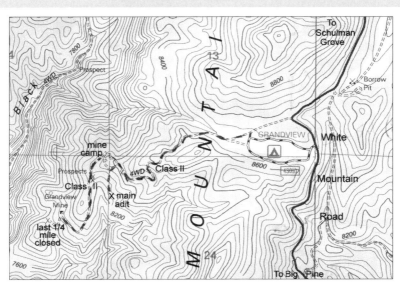

The Grandview Mine is one of those easy destinations for a pleasant drive and a picnic lunch amid the solitude of the piñon forest and the scenic grandeur of the Sierra skyline. It is not an excursion to drive all the way from Los Angeles to do, but anyone in the Owens Valley with a few hours to spare might wish to consider it.

From downtown Big Pine take Main Street (Highway 395) to the north edge of town, where you will want to turn right onto State Route 168. The intersection is well marked, and there is a roadside campground and Bristlecone pine display there. Note your odometer reading as you leave Highway 395 heading east across the Owens Valley. Just 0.4 miles beyond the Owens River Bridge, Highway 168 crosses the old right-of-way of the Carson & Colorado Railroad (later the Southern Pacific). Like most other towns in the Owens Valley, the railroad bypassed Big Pine. Zurich Station, located here, was Big Pine's nearest rail access. Alas, the tracks and station were removed in 1960.

A key road intersection is reached at a point 2.3 miles from Highway 395; keep to the left. Four and a half miles east of Highway 395 you may notice the horizontal layers of gravel and rounded cobbles. The White and Inyo Mountains were well in place when these lake sediments were laid down in Tertiary times. At 7.7 miles Toll House Spring can be seen on the left side of the highway. The precursor to today's Highway 168 was once a private road. More than one hundred years ago, tolls were extracted from folks traveling between the Owens Valley and Fish Lake Valley. At 12.4 miles from Highway 395, reset your trip odometer to zero and turn left onto the paved White Mountain Road, the same byway that goes up to the Schulman Grove of Bristlecone pines.

The White Mountain Road soon passes through the now disused entrance station and begins a winding ascent across Cambrian age rocks of the Campito Formation and slightly younger Poleta Formation. The Poleta can be easily seen at the "mini-narrows" 0.8 miles beyond the entrance station. After 3.2 miles, the road passes the Piñon Picnic Area, where there is a mile long nature trail that makes for a pleasant diversion. The entrance to the Grandview Campground is in two more miles, and here we will leave the pavement. Turn left, entering the sprawling 26-unit Forest Service campground, but then immediately turn to the right on the dirt road that heads through the camp in a westerly direction. Although rarely full, this out of the way campground has become quite popular in recent years, perhaps because there is no "Campground Host", and no fees are charged to camp here. (There is also no water and no refuse collection.)

After going 0.3 miles through the campground, you will come to a "T" intersection. Go to the right about one hundred feet, and then turn to the left onto a Class I road. Soon this road will deteriorate to Class II, as it climbs a short grade to a ridgetop. Still Class II, the road now switchbacks down the hillside.

A fork in the road is encountered at a point 1.3 miles from the White Mountain Road. This intersection is at the edge of an old miner's camp. If you take the right fork, the road will turn to the south and go down the hill another half-mile to the site of a second miner's camp. All that remains, however, is the foundation of the outhouse. The road once went on down the hillside another third of a mile to the diggings, but the U.S. Forest Service has scarified the last portion of the road.

Road to the Grandview Mine

To visit the Grandview Mine, however, go left at the intersection just before first miner's camp. After one hundred yards or so, go left again. The mine is but another quarter of a mile beyond.

There seems to be little doubt as to where the mine's name came from.

The Grandview Mine and prospect holes in a half-mile radius have had a number of different names over the years. The only real production from any of them seems to have been here where limestone, overlaying quartzite and slate, contains occasional lenses of galena (lead sulfide) and cerrusite, (lead carbonate), together with minor amounts of silver, zinc and copper minerals. Total production seems to have been about fifteen hundred tons, of which six hundred tons was produced in 1947. The ore was trucked down to the Southern Pacific narrow gauge line at Zurich siding, where five carloads were shipped off to the smelter. A diligent search of the mine's tailings dump today will still produce samples of the heavy lead ore, perhaps including a few specimens of the copper minerals malachite (bright green) and bornite (an iridescent metallic copper color). The main adit is wide open. While it may invite exploration, **my recommendation would be to stay out of the underground workings.**

The Grandview Mine today.

Whether one is into old mines or not, the area around the Grandview Mine is a good place to collect piñon nuts in September and October.

26

Mollie Gibson Canyon

Special Features: A little used four-wheel drive route to a little known mine. This is also a good place to collect pine nuts in the fall.

Time Required: This is a half-day excursion out of Big Pine, but one that can be combined with Excursions #25, 27, 28, or 29 for a full day of four-wheeling.

Miles Involved: The one way distance from Big Pine to the Mollie Gibson Mine is 18.6 miles.

Degree of Difficulty: The road into the mine is generally an easy Class III, but there is one Class IV pitch shortly before reaching the mine. The high point of this road exceeds 7,000 feet, making portions impassable during the winter months.

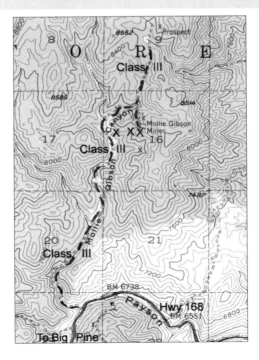

The Mollie Gibson Mine is one of hundreds of long forgotten mines in the White Mountains. Its charm is that it is so rarely visited that the Class III tracks in the wash leading to it are barely discernable. If you seek quiet solitude, this is the place.

From downtown Big Pine take Main Street (Highway 395) to the north edge of town. Here you will want to turn right onto State Route 168. The intersection is well marked, and there is a roadside campground and Bristlecone pine display there. Note your odometer reading as you leave Highway 395. Keep left where the road forks 2.3 miles east of Highway 395.

Army troops stationed at Camp Independence originally blazed a horse trail through this low point in the mountains. The route was called the "Old South Pass" at the time. With the mineral discoveries along the eastern side of the White Mountains, it became obvious that something more than a burro trail was needed. In the early 1870s three local men, W. A. Greenly, T.J. Hubbard and J.S. Broder, built a private road across the pass and charged people a fee to use it. Eight miles from Highway 395 is a spring, where the old toll taker's house once stood. The toll was twenty-five cents for a horse and rider. One dollar was charged for a wagon with two animals and fifty cents for each additional pair. The tariff for cows was ten cents each, and smaller animals like sheep, goats, and pigs were five cents each.

Toll House Spring and the toll taker's house circa 1918
(County of Inyo, Eastern California Museum photo)

For the next mile and a half, the rocks along the road are of the lower Campito Formation, of early Cambrian times. They were deposited in a shallow seabed some 550 million years ago.   Some of the oldest trilobite fossils in North America can be found here. At the second narrows in the canyon, the rock layers change from sandstone to limestone. This is the bottom stratum of the slightly younger Poleta Formation. In places it contains the fossilized remains of primitive vase-shaped sponges called *archaeocyanthus*, which lived on the bottom of the shallow Cambrian sea. They would eventually evolve into coral.

At a point 12.4 miles from Highway 395, a side road left goes to the Schulman Grove area of Bristlecone pines. Stay right on Highway 168, which now is headed straight north across Cedar Flat. A mile beyond here you will be on top of 7,271' Westgard Pass, and begin to cross Cedar Flat. The rocks exposed on the right are more strata of the lowest part of the Poleta Formation.

Once across Cedar Flat, the road begins to drop into Payson Canyon, and with it you descend back down through the Campito Formation. The road into Mollie Gibson Canyon is on the left, at a point 15.5 miles from Highway 395 (2.4 miles past the White Mountain Road). This side road is easy to miss, so be watching for it as you begin to descend Payson Canyon. (The GPS coordinates at the turnoff are 37°18'58" N – 118°09'15".)

The road enters Mollie Gibson Canyon, making its way up the rocky wash in a northerly direction. These dark rocks are of the Campito Formation. The route is an easy Class III. Some of the piñon trees here are unusually large. If you are looking for a good place to go "nutting" in the fall, this is it.

The canyon opens up after a mile, and soon you will pass a quail guzzler high on the bank to the right. After another mile a tunnel and some prospect holes in the Deep Spring Formation will appear on the right. The canyon forks at a point 2.6 miles in from State Route 168, and the road does, too. This fork is easy to miss, so watch for it 0.2 miles beyond the first tunnel.

The tracks to the left continue up the main canyon. This road deteriorates to Class IV in places, and eventually dead-ends at more prospect holes. To find the Mollie Gibson Mine, you must stay to the right where the canyon forks. A tricky pitch of Class IV bedrock is immediately encountered. Once over it, the road makes a sharp hairpin turn, and steeply climbs out of the wash and up a quarter of a mile to top the ridge just to the south. A large can dump on the ridge indicates the mine camp was here. Tracks lead one hundred yards to the right to a prospect hole. From the camp, the tracks to the left lead to the main adit.

History seems to have forgotten who Mollie Gibson was. She was probably the wife or daughter of the prospector who first staked his claims here. Did he find anything? The number of cubic yards contained in the tailing dump suggests a lot of digging went on. However, the absence of a millsite, or even an ore bunker, says that little wealth ever left the canyon.

Tailing dump of the Mollie Gibson Mine

A Word About Tires

The high road clearance, the added traction of four-wheel drive, and the carrying capacity of most SUVs make them a good general-purpose backcountry vehicle. SUVs are a reasonable compromise between the comfort and luxury of a conventional automobile and the spartan raw power of a farm tractor.

Unfortunately the stock tires your SUV came with do not share that compromise. They are probably "city tires" designed for ease of ride and comfort. They will probably be grossly inadequate to stand up to the rigors of rough roads. If you do much backcountry exploring, your first priority should be making sure that your vehicle has proper footwear.

It is not the size of the tire, or the tread design that should be your major concern, but rather the ability of the tire's tread surface, and sidewalls, to stand up to rocks and other road hazards. In 45 years of four-wheeling in this country and abroad, I quickly learned that a 4-ply passenger car tire is going to let you down, and at the worst possible moment. What is needed is a 6, 8, or even 10-ply truck tire. Shop carefully and talk to other four-wheelers before making your selection.

27

The Westgard Mine

Special Features:	The first half-mile of this trail provides spectacular views down Payson Canyon into Deep Springs Valley. Those same views may make passengers sitting on the right side a little nervous.
Time Required:	This is a half-day excursion out of Big Pine.
Miles Involved:	The one way distance from Big Pine to the Westgard Mine is twenty miles (but currently a rockslide blocks the last 1.5 miles).
Degree of Difficulty:	This dirt road portion is generally Class III.
Remarks:	This road is not shown on the 1993 Inyo National Forest map. In 1999 a rockslide covered about forty feet of the road at a point two miles in from Highway 168. The clearing of this debris would be a good service project for some four-wheel drive club, and with sufficient manpower might be accomplished in a single day. Until that day comes, however, the road will remain blocked.

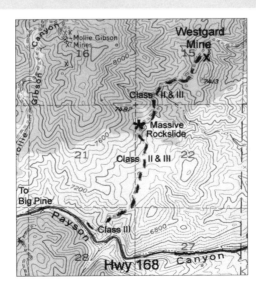

If you are one to recognize and appreciate the engineering and hard work that can go into a jeep trail, the road into the Westgard Mine should hold your attention. The route offers sufficient challenge so that the driver never becomes bored, and the scenery will delight the passengers who have the time to look at it.

From downtown Big Pine take Main Street (Highway 395) to the north edge of town. Turn right onto State Route 168, noting your odometer reading. Keep left at the fork 2.3 miles east of Highway 395. In another 1.3 miles Toll House Spring can be seen on the left side of the highway. This was once a private road, and more than a century ago tolls were extracted from folks traveling between the Owens Valley and Fish Lake Valley. For the next mile and a half, the rocks along the road are of the lower Campito Formation, of early Cambrian times. They were deposited in a shallow seabed some 550 million years ago. Some of the oldest trilobite fossils in North America can be found here.

At a point 12.4 miles from Highway 395 a side road left goes to the Schulman Grove of Bristlecone pines. Stay to the right on Highway 168, which now is headed straight north across Cedar Flat. A mile beyond here you will reach the 7,271' Westgard Pass, named after A. L. Westgard, a tireless promoter of auto touring. He led a caravan of twenty horseless carriages over the old toll road in 1913, while publicizing the route of his newly scouted Roosevelt National Highway.

The first SUV to cross Westgard Pass circa 1922.
(County of Inyo, Eastern California Museum photo)

Once across Cedar Flat, the road begins to drop into Payson Canyon, and you now descend back down through the Campito Formation. The road into the Westgard Mine is on the left, at a point 16.3 miles from Highway 395 (3.2 miles past the White Mountain Road). Look for a rusted iron pipe sticking up. Engage your four-wheel drive, and turn left onto the Class III road carved out of the rocky hillside. These rocks are also part of the 500 million year old Campito Formation.

As you climb steeply up this grade, your passengers will have a bird's-eye view of the highway below as it descends Payson Canyon. After only 0.7 miles, the top of the grade is reached. The road now starts northward across a secluded valley. Here, in the springtime, nature often puts on a superb wildflower display with fields of lupine accentuated with golden patches of Coleville poppies and crimson Indian paintbrush.

The Class III road climbing out of Payson Canyon.

Now mostly Class II, the road continues northward, as it contours around the hillside. The previously mentioned rockslide is encountered two miles in from the highway. If some kind sole has crafted a way across it, a ridge is crossed at the 2.4-mile point from the highway. Now the road starts down a small draw. An old miner's camp is just a half-mile below. The rusting remains of a vintage car, its 1929 license plates still in place, can easily identify this site.

Although the road continues on down the gully, I would suggest parking here, and going the rest of the way on foot. One can drive closer; however, the road is a steep and rocky Class IV, and the half-mile walk only takes fifteen minutes. Then too, there is the matter of a two-ton boulder that has rolled off the hillside to come to rest in the middle of the narrow road. One simply cannot drive around it, and there is no place to turn around, so the driver who makes his way in here will half to back up that last half-mile.

The road forks just before reaching the mine. The right fork leads to the lower camp, just around the bend. When we were first in here in the 1960s, the bunkhouse had already collapsed, but the mess hall, complete with a wood burning range, was still in place. One wonders if this spot was chosen as the mine camp, because of its grand view down into Deep Springs Valley each evening as purple shadows crept up the distant mountainsides.

The left fork leads to the mine. The head frame, hoist house, and ore bunker make an impressive sight as you come around a bend in the road. Although the main tunnel appears safe, **do not be fooled. Do not enter any of the underground workings. Likewise, the ladder going down the main shaft is not to be trusted. Use extreme caution around these mine workings.**

The two principal minerals worked here were galena (lead sulfite) and cerrusite (lead carbonate). The ore is found along a contact zone where the igneous quartz-diorite intruded into beds of limestone. The vein can easily be seen at the tunnel entrance. A foot trail crosses a nearby divide to other diggings in the next canyon north.

As of 2000, there were no *Keep Out* signs at the Westgard Mine. However, this is private property, and the visitor is urged to respect the rights of the owner. If vandalism becomes a problem, we are sure that *Keep Out* signs will be posted.

Lupine

Indian paintbrush

28

Furnace Creek

Special Features:	If you seek solitude, this is the place to come. Except for a few quail hunters in the fall, Furnace Creek Canyon is one of the least known and seldom visited canyons on the east side of the White Mountains.
Time Required:	From the vicinity of Dyer, Nevada, it only takes a couple of hours to go into Furnace Creek and return. From Big Pine, however, it is an all day excursion.
Miles Involved:	The distance is 48 miles from downtown Big Pine to the washed out end of the road in Furnace Creek.
Degree of Difficulty:	The passable portion of the route described is no worse that Class III.
Remarks:	Except for the rare winter snowstorm, this trail is usually open throughout the year.

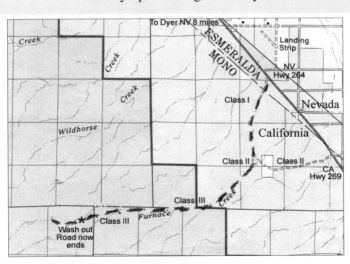

When I wrote *Inyo-Mono Jeep Trails* back in 1969, I described the roads going up Indian Garden Creek and Furnace Creek on the east side of the White Mountains. After an absence of 32 years, I rechecked those routes in the fall of

2001. To my disappointment, I found the jeep trails in both canyons washed out even more than they had been previously. Indian Garden Creek was accessible only to a point two miles off Highway 269. The jeep trail up Furnace Creek did take me four miles off the highway, but that is only half of the eight miles that it was in 1968. While I would hardly recommend that someone drive all the way up from Los Angeles to visit one of the most remote canyons in Mono County, Furnace Creek still makes an interesting destination, if one is already exploring the backroads of Nevada's Fish Lake Valley.

Take State Route 168 out of Big Pine over Westgard Pass and then Gilbert Summit. At a point 37 miles from Big Pine, you will come to a road junction at Oasis Ranch. Turn left onto California State Route 269 going in the direction of Dyer, Nevada. After eight miles you will cross the State line into Nevada. Continue north another two miles on Highway 264 to milepost 264 ES 2.00. Here, make a sharp turn to the left onto the Class I road heading south. Note your odometer reading as you leave the pavement. Although no sign marks the exact spot, California is re-entered again within a quarter of a mile. The good road continues south for two miles, passing an occasional Joshua tree *Yucca brevifolia*. This is about the northern limit of this species, a member of the Yucca family, and indicator plant of the Mojave Desert. To my knowledge, this is the only place in Mono County where Joshua trees can be found. The fact that they are even this far north seems to be a botanical oddity.

This is as far north as Joshua trees grow.

Upon going 1.9 miles south of Nevada Route 264, a Class II side road to the left will take you back to State Route 269. To visit Furnace Creek, however, continue straight ahead. Our road will soon cross the wash coming out of Furnace Creek Canyon and deteriorate to Class II. At a point 2.2 miles in from the highway, the road now starts up the wash and deteriorates even more to an easy Class III. The mountain straight ahead is 10,316' Station Peak, with its core of lava. Soon piñon and juniper trees begin to appear, as do some very large specimens of Great Basin sage. During the spring and summer months, melting snows in the high country permit surface water to flow this far down the canyon, giving life to the line of willows that line its course.

Basalt capped 10,316' Station Peak towers over the trail into Indian Creek.

At the 2.8-mile point, the stream is forded, and there is a short but steep ascent that will require low range gears. The first of the cottonwood trees will appear in another quarter of a mile. At the four-mile point, just as things look promising for further progress, the tracks go around the corner and a large washout is encountered. In 1968 the road continued on up the canyon several more miles to end at a series of springs at an elevation of 9,200 feet. Until some public service minded four-wheel drive club adopts this trail as a restoration project, the road will forever end here at an elevation of 6,600 feet.

29

The Piper Corridor

Special Features:	If you like desert solitude, this little used road should be appealing. It is the only vehicle route that directly connects the Deep Springs Valley and the Eureka Valley.
Time Required:	Make this an all day outing, because of the distances involved.
Miles Involved:	It is 33 miles by Highway 168 to Gilbert Summit. From there expect fourteen miles of dirt roads before reaching the asphalt again at the Eureka Valley Road. It is 34 miles from this point back to Big Pine.
Degree of Difficulty:	Of the nearly fifteen miles of dirt road running through the Piper corridor, all but about a mile are Class I or II. The few Class III sections you are likely to encounter are short and should not pose any great difficulties. The last five miles are Class I.
Remarks:	Piper Mountain and Piper Peak are two different summits identified on the 15-minute Soldier Pass and Piper Peak quadrangles respectively. Except for the rare winter snowstorm, this trail is usually open throughout the year.

Back in October of 1994 in the waning days of the 103rd Congress, at the urging of various national environmental groups, the Democrat controlled Congress passed the so-called *California Desert Protection Act of 1994,* which created 69 new Wilderness Areas covering a whopping 3.6 million acres in the California Desert. Generally four-wheelers and those who like to explore the desert's backroads took a big hit by the passage of that legislation. Enthusiastically signed by President Clinton, the bill closed more backroads and jeep trails in California than all the previous wilderness closures combined! More than one third of the 9.5 million acres in the California desert administered for multiple use by the Bureau of Land Management was suddenly off limits to motor vehicles. This was just another example of how ineffectual the off-road recreation lobby in Washington D.C. really is. Indeed, since the *Wilderness Act of 1964* was initially passed, four-wheelers, rockhounds, hunters, fishermen, and RVers have all been fighting a losing battle to keep public lands open and accessible, thus preserving their particular form of recreation. Green advocacy groups (GAG) are not satisfied with what they have, and are currently mounting yet another congressional campaign to lock up in wilderness even more acreage in Inyo and Mono Counties.

Having said all of that, the losses could have been worse, and I suppose we should be grateful for the few bones thrown to us by Congress. In a few areas, non-wilderness corridors have been left out of a few wilderness areas to accommodate backroad recreation. One of those corridors was the Steel Pass route connecting the Saline and Eureka Valleys. It is described in *Death Valley SUV Trails*. (That same publication also describes the road corridor in the Surprise Canyon Wilderness, although in recent years environmental groups have succeeded in getting a Federal judge to close the route.) The narrow corridor left open in the Mokelumne Wilderness is described in *High Sierra SUV Trails Volume I - The East Side,* and the Dusy-Ershim corridor is described in *High Sierra SUV Trails Volume II - The Western Slope*. For reasons that remain unclear, two narrow road corridors were left running through the 72,575-acre Piper Mountain Wilderness. In this outing, we will explore the longest segment of that road.

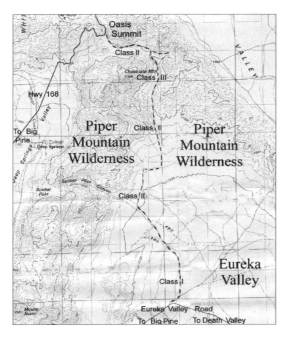

We begin our wilderness odyssey at 6,300' Gilbert Summit, some 33 miles east of Big Pine on State Route 168. Here a Class II dirt road leaves the highway heading south and a little east towards 7,703' Piper Mountain, the high point in the Chocolate Mountains (not to be confused with 9,450' Piper Peak in the nearby Silver Peak Range). Note your odometer reading as you leave Highway 168.

Soon the road swings into a more easterly direction, as signs mark the wilderness boundary to either side of the roadway. In some cases, these block pre-1994 roads. The road gradually descends into a small valley, where a fork is encountered at a point 1.6 miles in from Highway 168. The left branch continues straight ahead 0.4 miles to some mining claims and a ridgetop from where there is a stunning view east down into the southern end of Fish Lake Valley. While this side trip is a worthy diversion, we will want to turn right at this fork. It might be a good idea to reset your trip odometer at this junction, as all other distances shall be measured from this wye.

Still Class II, the road turns to the south and begins its gradual descent of some 2,500 feet into the Eureka Valley. After a quarter of a mile, the road passes a cattle trough and water tank on the right. While the *Wilderness Act* does not prohibit cattle grazing in wilderness areas per se, the long-term goal of the environmental lobby is to get cows, and their support facilities such as this, out of wilderness areas.

Two miles beyond the water tank a light gray banded limestone can be seen on the left. This is an outcrop of the Mule Spring Limestone, a thick layer of shell fragments deposited in the bottom of a seabed during early Cambrian times some 530 million years ago. In places, this formation has yielded the fossil remains of trilobites and other marine animals.

Soon the road enters a defile where the geology changes. Here layers of reddish brown quartzite are standing on end in a dramatic fashion. The quartzite started out as a layer of sand on the sea bottom. It consolidated into sandstone, a common sedimentary rock. At some time in the great geologic past, this sandstone was subjected to great heat and pressure, causing it to be changed into quartzite, a metamorphic rock. These may have been the same dynamic forces that thrust the once flat-lying sandstone up onto its side. Geologists call this the Harkless Formation. It is slightly older than its upper neighbor, the Mule Spring Limestone, being some 550 million years old.

Layers of dark reddish brown quartzite are standing on end.

The narrows are reached 2.6 miles from the wye. At 2.7 miles the canyon is left, and soon we get our first views south of the Eureka Valley Sand Dunes. Most sand dunes in North America are, in one way or another, products of the Pleistocene Ice Age. That is true here in the Eureka, too, although the links are not quite as strong as in other areas. Over the last 10,000 years, the prevailing winds have picked up loose sand particles throughout the valley and have deposited them here. These dunes cover an area only three miles long and one mile wide, yet they are the tallest sand dunes in California, possibly the tallest in all of North America. They rise suddenly more than 680 feet above the dry lakebed at their western base. If you have not visited the dunes, made a Natural National Landmark by the Bureau of Land Management in 1984, by all means visit them at the end of this excursion.

The Eureka Valley Sand Dunes

As we drop into the Eureka Valley below the 4,500-foot contour level, creosote becomes very abundant. This hardy desert shrub, affectionately known to the botanist as *Larrea divaricata*, is very adaptive to the desert's harsh environment. Naturalist Edmund Jaeger noted that creosote bushes in the Mojave Desert near Bagdad lost all their leaves during the extreme drought years of 1909-1912, when not a single drop of rain fell for 32 consecutive months. Yet when those rare desert rains did return, the hardy creosote leafed out and flowered, resuming its normal life cycle just like nothing had happened.

The hardy creosote *Larrea divaricata*

As one descends farther into the Eureka Valley, the road makes a horseshoe-type swing to the right, and for a short distance turns back north again. At a point 6.2 miles beyond the wye, a point of rocks is reached, and here the road turns north again. This point of rocks has served as a landmark and a campsite for desert travelers for nearly 150 years. Old stone walls enclose the open portions of a natural rock shelter. Whoever drafted the wilderness boundary made certain that this old campsite was several hundred yards within the wilderness to discourage continued use for car camping.

This sheltered rock defile has been used as a campsite
for hundreds, perhaps thousands of years.

The road now improves somewhat, but still remains Class II as it continues to make its way ever southward. After another 1.5 miles (7.7 miles from the wye), a wilderness boundary sign now blocks a road heading off to the northwest. This road once led into the east side of Soldier Pass, a low gap in the mountains used to reach Deep Springs Valley. The main road south now turns in a southeasterly direction and improves further. Soon it will become mostly Class I.

A major intersection is reached 11.5 miles from the wye. Here another Class I road comes in from the left. This is the Horse Thief Canyon Road, which after passing through Horse Thief Canyon goes northeast into the southern end of Fish Lake Valley.

For all other destinations, stay to the right. The high standard Eureka Valley Road is but 1.2 miles to the south. Here, 14.3 miles from Gilbert Summit, the pavement is reached again. By turning left, one can visit the Eureka Valley Sand Dunes (21.5 miles) or go on into the northern end of Death Valley (46 miles to Grapevine Ranger Station). By turning right, you will return to Highway 395 and Big Pine in 34 miles.

30

Around Andrews Mountain

Primary Attraction:	This lonely corner of the Inyo Mountains offers miles of backroads to explore. There are old mines and unusual rock formations. The entire area is part of Inyo National Forest. Camping and collecting wood for campfires are permitted anywhere. (Be sure to pick up a free *Campfire Permit* at any Ranger Station.) This is also a good place to collect piñon nuts in the fall.
Time Required:	This is an all day excursion out of Big Pine.
Miles Involved:	The round trip distance from Big Pine is 53 miles. The off-highway portion is 26 miles, not counting the miles of side roads that invite more exploration.
Degree of Difficulty:	The backroad portion is mostly Class II, with about five miles of generally easy Class III. During the winter months much of this route is closed by snow.

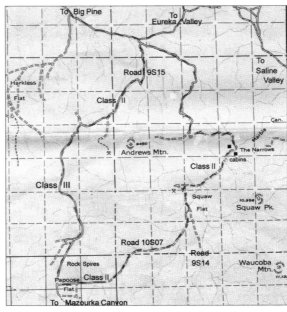

The White and Inyo Mountains are full of secluded little spots which, in and of themselves, have no particular significance, except to offer scenic destinations for a day's outing. One such trip is the loop around Andrews Mountain in the northern end of the Inyos. The roads are mostly Class II, with a little bit of Class III. Over-crowding is not a problem here. The area has no inhabitants, and you are not likely to meet many others back here. Dove, quail, grouse, and chukars can be found in the sage-covered valleys, and larger game abounds in the piñon-covered hills. I first described this route in *Inyo-Mono Jeep Trails*, published by La Siesta Press in 1969. Thankfully, a recheck of this same route thirty years later has revealed that absolutely nothing has changed.

Take California State Route 168 east out of Big Pine. At a point 2.3 miles east of U.S. Highway 395, keep to the right on the Eureka-Saline Valley Road. Eleven miles beyond this fork (three miles above the Devil's Gate narrows) a U.S. Forest Service sign points south towards the Papoose Flat Road; turn right. This road forks after 0.2 miles. Keep right on Forest Road 9S15 (formerly called Hines Road). Upon completion of this loop trip, you will come out at this same spot via the left fork.

The right road crosses a large treeless valley heading straight for 9,460-foot Andrews Mountain. The road swings to the west, crosses a wash, and soon enters the piñon forest. The first good campsite is but 2.6 miles in from the highway. The elevation here is 7,600 feet.

The road enters a small canyon, where there is a tenth of a mile of easy Class III. Exposed here are some of the oldest rocks in the Inyo Mountains. In the next mile you will pass through sections of the pre-Cambrian Deep Springs Formation, the Campito and Poleta Formations, both of very early Cambrian Age. These rocks are 550 to 600 million years old.

The road forks at the top of the canyon. Explore the left fork, which goes to some mining claims, if you wish, but return to 9S15 going to the right. A second intersection is encountered a mile beyond. At this second intersection you will want to keep left on 9S15, starting up the switchbacks just ahead. Before doing so, however, you might wish to check out the right fork which passes through an old miner's campsite to dead-end, in a quarter mile, on a ridge overlooking the Owens Valley. There are good views north to Big Pine and Bishop, and of 13,652' Mt. Tom dominating the Sierra skyline. Below in the foreground is Harkless Flat.

At a point 4.2 miles in from the pavement, you will come to a series of switchbacks. While the road is technically no worse than Class II, you may wish to engage your four-wheel drive and drop to your lowest gears in order to ease up the grade slowly.

After climbing the grade for a mile, a side road to the right is encountered. This is a relatively new route that goes down to Harkless Flat (see Excursion #31). Stay left on 9S15, and within a tenth of a mile you will be on the ridgetop, the high point of this backcountry excursion. The elevation is 9,100 feet. From here there are magnificent views of the Sierra crest to the southwest. Looking from north to south, one can see 13,125' Mt. Baxter, 13,005' Mt. Gould, 13,632' University Peak, 13,289' Mt. Bradley, 13,977' Mt. Keith, 14,375' Mt. Williamson, 14,086' Mt. Russell, and behind it, the Whitney group, including 14,025' Mt. Langley.

The descent off the south side of this ridge is an easy Class II. At a point seven miles in from the highway, yet another intersection is reached. Road 9S15 to Papoose Flat goes to the left. The two side roads to the right pass a remote weather station installed by the California Institute of Technology, and soon dead-end. There are some nice campsites in this area.

Continuing left along 9S15, notice the numbers of young junipers becoming established in flat areas where there are no mature trees. This suggests that the forest is not only healthy, but also expanding.

At a point 9.8 miles in from the highway a gentle ridgetop is reached, overlooking the surreal landscape of Papoose Flat. Stay left and soon you will be entering Papoose Flat, with its unique granite pinnacles. Notice how the geology suddenly changes. For the last ten miles, the road has been going through country where the rocks were old metamorphosed sediments of Cambrian age. Here at Papoose Flat, the bedrock geology suddenly turns to quartz monzonite, a granite-like rock of Cretaceous age, very similar to the rocks found throughout much of the Sierra Nevada. It seems likely to assume that the granite rocks of the Inyo and White Mountains came from the same deep-rooted source in the earth as that of the Sierra Nevada. The spires are the products of differential erosion. Differences within the quartz monzonite caused some to weather and decay sooner, leaving the harder more resistant rock.

The road into Papoose Flat in 1968 and it
hasn't changed a bit in the last 35 years!

Although there is no water, Papoose Flat is a good place to find a secluded campsite for the weekend. A side road to the right goes out to a deer hunter's camp and a scenic overlook. Below you is the Owens Valley, and beyond the Sierra skyline. It is in this area where our annual piñon nut gathering takes place each fall. The elevation here is 8,400 feet. At a point 11.3 miles in from the highway, in the heart of Papoose Flat, there is an important road intersection. The road straight ahead is a Class IV route to Badger Flat. From here one can descend via Mazourka Canyon to come out in the Owens Valley near Independence.

Forest Service Road 10S07 goes to the left. To complete our tour around Andrews Mountain, this is the way we must go. The roadway is well defined at first, as the road heads eastward. But as the trail turns northward again, it drops down into a twisting, narrow sandy wash where the sage brush tower over each side of the roadway. You will generally follow this wash for the next eight miles, all the way to the head of the Marble Canyon Narrows. This portion of the trail is generally an easy Class II.

If you should pass this way in the fall, you cannot miss the clusters of bright yellow blossoms of rabbit brush that is very common and present everywhere. Other plant species in this area, which are far from common, are the rare Jaeger's Caulostramina *Caulostraminia jageri,* the Wildrose Canyon Buckwhat *Eriogonum eremicola,* the Inyo Rock Daisy *Perityle inyoensis,* and the Bristlecone cryptantha *Cryptantha roosiorum.* The Inyo Mountains have some very unique flora. The scenery, too, is grand in a quiet way. Far to the north is 9,460' Andrews Mountain. On the ridge to the northeast is 10,358' Squaw Peak. Due east on this same ridge is 11,123' Waucoba Mountain.

Five miles beyond the road intersection in Papoose Flat, another intersection is reached. To the right is Forest Road 9S14, which climbs south into the hills to dead-end near Squaw Spring. Stay to the left on 10S07, and soon you will be crossing Squaw Flat.

My field notes indicate that on May 25, 1968, I first climbed Waucoba Mountain starting from Squaw Flat. The 3,300 feet of gain was tiring, and the round trip hike took all day. Had I started the ascent from Squaw Spring, I could have saved 1,000 feet of climb and started a couple of miles closer.

The next intersection is a mile away. Follow Forest Road 10S07 to the right. Upon leaving Squaw Flat, the bedrock geology once again changes back to very old metamorphic rocks. These rocks are of Precambrian age, laid down in the sea bottom more than half a billion years ago. At that time, life on earth consisted of only the most primitive marine plants and animals.

From the crossroads in Squaw Valley, it is another 2.2 miles down to the old miner's camp at the head of the Marble Canyon Narrows. When I first visited this site in 1968, the two cabins were dilapidated, but one was useable, if you didn't mind sharing it with the mice. In the last thirty years the structures have deteriorated further, and today one is not far from collapse. These structures seemingly go back to the depression years of the 1930s, when miners eked out a living working the sands of Marble Canyon for placer gold. Although many have searched for it, the source of this placer gold has never been found.

The old miner's cabin in upper
Marble Canyon has seen better days.

Passing the two cabins, the road climbs the rocky canyon bottom for two miles of easy Class III driving. The road turns to Class II at the top, and remains that way. A large treeless flat is traversed, followed by a ridge crossing. For about a mile, prospect holes appear to the left and right. At a point 6.4 miles from the cabins, you will find yourself back at the very first intersection, which is only 0.2 miles south of the paved highway. Your loop around Andrews Mountain is now complete. The total distance you have traveled is 26 miles.

This mine headframe in lower Marble
Canyon dates back to the 1930s.

31

To The Top Of The Inyos

Primary Attraction:	Wildflowers, fossil collecting, old mines, peculiar rock formations, high altitude scenery and the ever-present High Sierra skyline make this a very enjoyable excursion. The entire area is part of the Inyo National Forest. Camping and the collecting of wood for campfires are permitted anywhere. (Be sure to pick up a free *Campfire Permit* at any USFS Ranger Station.) In addition, piñon nuts can be collected here in the fall.
Time Required:	To go from Big Pine to Independence via Harkless, Papoose, and Badger Flats and on down Mazourka Canyon will make a full day of off-roading adventure.
Miles Involved:	This excursion is 58 miles long, of which dirt roads make up 42 miles.
Degree of Difficulty:	The dirt road portions range from Class I to Class III. However, large portions of this route are made impassable by snow during the winter months.

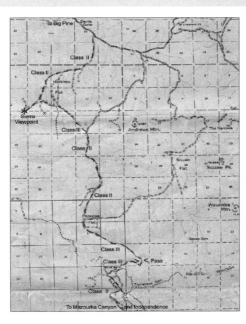

The intersection of U.S. Highway 395 and State Route 168 is on the northern edge of Big Pine. Check your odometer reading, and go east on Highway 168. At a point 2.3 miles east of Highway 395, keep to the right on Waucoba Road (sometimes called the Eureka-Saline Valley Road) as Highway 168 swings to the left. Proceed nine miles beyond this fork (just one mile above the Devil's Gate narrows) to where a U.S. Forest Service sign points right towards the Inyo Mountains. A second USFS sign identifies this road as 9S13. The elevation here is 6,700 feet. Eventually you will climb another 2,800 feet to reach a high point of 9,500 feet.

Turn right on this Class II road, gently climbing into the hills to the south. While the predominate plant is sagebrush, spring and early summer often produce a profusion of Indian paintbrush, scarlet pentstemon, desert mallow and prince's plume. If you are lucky, you may also find the prickly pear cactus *Opuntia erinacea* in bloom. Even the most bedraggled prickly pear turns into Cinderella when it blossoms in the springtime. They are common along this route.

In the next mile, keep to the right at each of the three forks you encounter. At a point 2.9 miles in from the pavement, a side road to the right goes up the hillside to some prospect holes dug into the Wyman Formation, a siltstone and limestone of pre-Cambrian age.

Continuing straight ahead across Harkless Flat, notice the vegetation pattern. Slopes facing the southern sun are devoid of trees, while those on the north facing slopes produce piñon pines. Moisture is the key difference here. The south facing slopes have the sun beating down on them at a right angle much of the year. These soils dry out very quickly. The sun hits the north facing slopes at a much more oblique angle, and the soil retains its moisture much longer. Here the seeds of the piñon are able to germinate, grow and survive in this arid land.

In the late 1990s, a consortium of universities sought a Special Use Permit from Inyo National Forest that would allow them to construct a series of radio telescopes on 462 acres in Harkless Flat. A botanical survey was performed in the late summer and early fall of 1998 as a part of the review process. Botanists Mark Bagley and Dan Pritchett made a startling discovery; they found no less than 31 rare or endangered plant species in the general area, with fourteen of those species within the immediate project area. One example is the Inyo milk vetch *Astragalus inyoensis,* a rare perennial herb found only in the Inyo Mountains. The study also revealed six plant species not previously known to grow in the Inyo Mountains. Because of these findings, the local chapter of the California Native Plant Society brought sufficient political pressure to get the project shelved, if not scrapped altogether. In this case, off-roaders can offer thanks to the environmental community for keeping things just the way they are.

No road graders will upgrade the existing primitive road through Harkless Flat.
No field of parabolic antennas will fill the basin.

Harkless Flat lies at 7,300 feet.

At a point 3.6 miles in from the pavement, the tracks drop down into a
gully and fork. Keep left, going up the draw through the piñons. In little more
than a quarter of a mile you will climb back out of the draw, and here the first
junipers appear. There are two different kinds of junipers in the White and Inyo
Mountains: the Western or Sierra juniper *Juniperous occidentalis,* and the Utah
juniper *Juniperous osteosperma.* The former is rare in these mountains, the latter
common. These are Utah juniper.

Native Americans, the Paiutes and their prehistoric forbearers, depended
on the very nutritious piñon nut for sustenance to get them through the winter
months. However, they also utilized the juniper for a variety of purposes.
Juniper berries were sometimes roasted and ground into a mush, or dried for
later use. They were also used to make a tea. Medicinal purposes of the berries
included their use for fevers and colds. The bark was utilized as a treatment for
constipation.

Stay to the right at the fork encountered one half-mile after coming out of the
draw, and pass through a shallow basin of very silty soil. Just as you come out of
it, continue straight ahead, but notice the road coming in behind you on the left.
We will return to take that road, but let's first climb the ridge a half-mile ahead
for a magnificent view of the Sierra crest. The Class II road passes an old cabin
of unknown origin just before getting there.

From this 7,200' ridge, one can look down into the Owens Valley onto Tinemaha Reservoir and beyond it to the lava flows on the western side of the Owens Valley. At least five very distinct volcanic cinder cones can easily be picked out. But the real attraction is the serrated skyline of the Sierra Nevada. Going from left to right, far to the south is 14, 375' Mount Williamson. As you cast your eye northward along the skyline, you will see a long series of thirteen thousand footers: 13,977' Mt. Keith, 13,289' Mt. Bradley, 13,005' Mt. Gould, 13,289' Black Mountain, 13,125' Mt. Baxter, and 12,790' Goodale Mountain. Looking straight across Tinemaha Reservoir is another lofty trio: 13,397' Cardinal Mountain slightly to the south, 14,058' Split Mountain in the center, and 13,490' Mt. Prater slightly to the north. It is little wonder that there are several unimproved campsites at this vantage point. The first rays of the sun striking these Sierra peaks are a sight to be long remembered.

The Sierra Nevada from the edge of Harkless Flat.
Tinemaha Reservoir is shown on the valley floor.

Enjoy the grand view as long as you wish, but when you are ready to move on, backtrack down the road 0.7 miles. Just before reaching that area of silty soil, go to the right. A crossroads is reached after 0.3 miles; continue straight ahead. The Class II road soon swings to the east, and zigzags through the piñons for half a mile to where a "T" intersection is reached. Turn to the left and within a quarter of a mile you will come to another "T" intersection. This time turn right on the well defined Class II road as it makes its way up a draw in the piñon and juniper forest.

The roadway leaves the draw after a mile and begins to climb the steep hillside. The road technically remains Class II, but the poor traction warrants engaging your four-wheel drive here. In another quarter of a mile, the road will truly become Class III. The 1.5 miles from the bottom of this grade to the top are generally steep. These rocks are part of the Harkless Formation, shale and quartzite of early Cambrian age.

At a point 4.3 miles from the Sierra viewpoint, a "T" intersection is reached. This is Forest Road 9S15 coming in from the western side of Andrews Mountain (see Excursion #30). You may wish to recheck your odometer reading. Stay right on 9S15, and within a tenth of a mile you will be on a 9,100' ridgetop. From here there are more great views of the Sierra crest to the southwest. You can see all the way south to the Whitney group, including 14,025' Mt. Langley.

The road improves for the next five miles. The descent off the south side of this ridge is an easy Class II. After traveling southward on 9S15 for nearly two miles, yet another intersection is reached. Follow Road 9S15 to the left. The two side roads to the right pass a Forest Service remote weather station and soon dead-end. There are some nice campsites in this area, too.

Continuing left along 9S15, notice the numbers of young junipers becoming established in flat areas where there are no mature trees. This suggests that the forest is not only healthy, but also expanding.

During the late Pleistocene and early Holocene Epochs, the Utah juniper was the dominant tree in the Great Basin. Not only were junipers present in great numbers, but their habitat was much broader. In those more moist times, the junipers grew at much lower elevations than they are found today. We know this from the amount of juniper pollen found preserved in packrat middens. Then relatively suddenly, in the middle Holocene about 6,500 years ago, the piñon pine began to appear and it quickly spread. Today the piñon is more common in the higher mountains of Inyo County area than is the juniper.

After following 9S15 four miles, you reach a gentle ridgetop overlooking the surreal landscape of Papoose Flat. Stay left, and soon you will be entering this valley with its unique granite pinnacles. Notice how the geology suddenly changes. Since leaving the pavement, the road has been going through country where the rocks were very old metamorphosed sediments of Cambrian and pre-Cambrian age. Here at Papoose Flat, the bedrock geology suddenly turns to quartz monzonite, a granite-like rock of Cretaceous age, very similar to the rocks found throughout much of the Sierra Nevada. Indeed, it seems likely to assume that the granite rocks of the Inyo and White Mountains came from the same deep-rooted source in the earth as those in the Sierra Nevada. The spires are the products of differential erosion. Differences within the quartz monzonite caused some portions to weather and decay sooner than others, leaving the harder more resistant rock.

Although there is no water, Papoose Flat is a good place to find a secluded campsite for the weekend. A side road to the right goes out to a deer hunter's camp and a scenic overlook. Below you is the Owens Valley, and beyond the Sierra skyline. It is in this area where I have often gathered piñon nuts each fall. The elevation here is 8,400 feet.

After you have followed 9S15 for five miles, the road forks again. The left fork goes easterly across the flat and then turns north again to go to Squaw Flat and the upper reaches of Marble Canyon (see Excursion #29). Keep right here, actually going straight ahead. Road 9S15 is now left behind. A Forest Service sign announces that the road ahead is for four-wheel drive vehicles only. You may wish to again note your odometer reading here. After 0.2 miles keep left. The right fork leads to some campsites with a view of the Sierra (there are other nice campsites overlooking Papoose Flat less than a mile ahead). Engage your four-wheel drive here. You will be using it for the next five plus miles.

The geology here is very complex. To the immediate left of the roadway are the upper few feet of the Poleta Formation and lower few feet of the Harkless Formation. But a short distance to the north, you have the igneous quartz monzonite pluton seen in Papoose Flat. Just to the right, going up the ridge, is a narrow wedge of the Monola Formation, followed by the Bonanza King dolomite. To complicate the geologic picture even further, the entire region is broken up by small faults that generally lie at a right angle to the roadway. These faults cut through the early Paleozoic formations, as well as the much younger quartz monzonite.

Papoose Flat lies at 8,400 feet.

A little over a mile beyond Papoose Flat you will encounter a short grade up a rocky ridge. While it appears to approach Class IV in severity, I nevertheless rate it as Class III. A half-mile beyond this section, you cross a low divide. The ridge to the left is quartz monzonite, while the ridge to the right is the Bonanza King dolomite.

The Bonanza King dolomite is named for a mine of the same name in the Providence Mountains west of Needles, California. This particular rock formation can be found throughout the Death Valley region. Its outcrops can be seen in the Panamint and Argus ranges, and east of Death Valley in the Grapevine, Nopah, and Resting Spring Ranges well into Central Nevada. Here in the high Inyos, the formation is 2,800 feet thick. Often this dolomite displays a "zebra striping" of different colored bands. It is thought to be middle Cambrian in age, about 530 million years old. Trilobites were a major marine fauna in those times; however, here for the most part only algae are preserved as fossils.

As you follow this road to the southeast, notice the trees coming down off the ridge to the right. They are Limber pines *Pinus flexilis,* a high altitude species with widespread distribution throughout the Great Basin. They grow as high as 12,000 feet, and often can be found growing with the Bristlecone pine *Pinus longaeva.* When young, these five needle pines have a smooth white-silver bark, which turns to a dark broken bark as the tree matures. Often they grow on the sunny dry south side of these high desert peaks. Here a healthy stand seems to be doing quite well on the shaded northern slope.

At a point 3.7 miles after leaving Road 9S15 back on Papoose Flat, a side road left once went out to Sidehill Spring and beyond, to approach within two miles of the summit of 11,123' Waucoba Mountain from the south. This road was closed by the U.S. Congress in 1994 with the creation of the 205,000 acre *Inyo Mountain Wilderness,* a part of the California Desert Protection Act. The road we can use turns south now and begins the Class III ascent of the nearby ridge. In a half-mile you will top out at 9,500 feet. This is Mazourka Pass. If you expected great views of the Sierra skyline, you will not be disappointed. The open flat area below to the south is Badger Flat. From here there is another mile of Class III road down to Badger Flat and from there, twenty miles of Class I road down Mazourka Canyon to Independence (see Excursion #33).

Badger Flat lies at 8,700 feet.

Historic Independence

Photographer J. W. Bledsoe took this photo of downtown
Independence sometime after the disastrous fire of 1886.

Bandhauer's store in Independence circa 1925.

The fourth Inyo County courthouse at its opening ceremony in 1921.
(County of Inyo, Eastern California Museum photos)

Chapter VI

Trails Out of Independence

Independence is the seat of Inyo County, but it remains a sleepy little hamlet hardly affected by the steady stream of tourists and recreation seekers heading up and down Highway 395. Most people pass right through without stopping, and that is a shame because the Eastern California Museum at 155 Grant Street does a very nice job of explaining the history of Inyo County, and should not be missed. Other nearby historical attractions are the Army Commander's House (at Edwards and Main Streets) and the home of writer Mary Austin (at Market and Grant Streets) who lived here for many years.

History tells us that one Charles Putnam settled on Little Pine Creek in 1861. Putnam built a sturdy stone house and operated a modest trading post out of it. Soon others were settling along the creek, and the site became known as Little Pine. There were Indian troubles in the Owens Valley, however, and Putnam's store was fortified against a possible attack. In 1862 the U.S. Army built a camp about a mile away. The fort was established on July 4th, 1862, and appropriately took the name Camp Independence. Its immediate purpose was to pacify the Indian deprivations in the valley, but the solders' presence also dampened the enthusiasm of local Confederate sympathizers, of which there were many. By 1866 the settlement had two stores, a hotel, blacksmith shop and four saloons. A plot map of lots and streets was drawn up, and the town's name was changed from Little Pine to Independence. About this same time there was a mass exodus from the nearby communities of Bend City and San Carlos. A few months later, when Inyo County was established, Independence became the county seat.

The first courthouse, a two story brick building, had been in use only two years when it was destroyed in the great earthquake of March 26, 1872. The second courthouse, a wooden two-story structure burned on June 30, 1886, along with 37 other buildings in town. The third courthouse, a two-story wooden structure was completed in 1887, but it was much too small. It was torn down after the present courthouse was built in the early 1920s. The most notorious outlaw to be brought into court here for legal proceedings was Charles Manson. He was arrested in Goler Wash on October 12, 1969, and brought to Independence, pending the filing of a long laundry list of criminal charges (which later included the Tate-LaBianca murders for which he and his followers were convicted).

While Independence remains a bedroom community, it is possible to fill your gas tank, get a room, buy some groceries, or get something hot to eat. There are several U.S. Forest Service campgrounds to the west of town on the road to Onion Valley.

32

The Eastside Road

Special Features:	This outing is along the western base of the Inyo Mountains, with, a bit of history, a few old mines, and opportunities for rockhounding.
Time Required:	This backroad adventure can be done in half a day, perhaps longer if you are rockhounding.
Miles Involved:	This is a loop trip of 28 miles.
Remarks:	Except for the rare winter snowstorm, this trail is usually open throughout the year.
Degree of Difficulty:	The dirt roads along this route are generally Class II or better. Although four-wheel drive is generally not needed, vehicles with high clearance are recommended. **While these areas should be accessible most of the year, do not attempt this route if the roadway is wet; there could be some bottomless mud holes.**

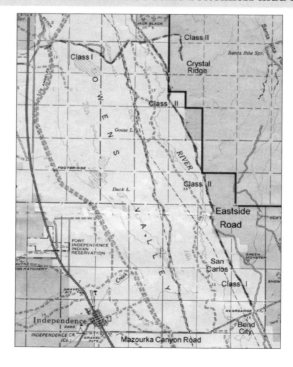

From downtown Independence take Highway 395 to the south edge of town, where you will want to turn left onto Mazourka Canyon Road. Note your odometer reading as you leave Highway 395. At a point 3.2 miles from Highway 395, the road suddenly encounters a big dip. This is the fifteen-foot fault escarpment created during the 1872 earthquake that devastated Lone Pine. This north-south fracture in the earth's surface can be traced for many miles.

The current channel of the once mighty Owens River is crossed after another half-mile, and a half-mile beyond that is the site of Bend City, a short-lived boomtown. Miners established this community in 1863, just like they did its neighbor San Carlos just three miles up the river. By December of that year the community had twenty-five to thirty houses and a ferry across the Owens River. If you lived in Bend City, the ferry ride was free; if you lived in rival San Carlos upstream, there was a charge! The following year Bend City boasted of having up to sixty or seventy houses, two hotels, and even a "circulating library". But there were major Indian troubles in the Owens Valley at the time, and many people felt safer living nearer to Camp Independence just four miles to the east. By 1866 when Independence became the Inyo County seat, Bend City's remaining population had moved westward. Not a single ballot was cast from Bend City in the election of 1867.

In 1932 this was all that remained in Bend City.
There is even less today. (Eastern California Museum photo)

If anyone had any plans to reoccupy and revive Bend City, they came to an abrupt end at 2:30 a.m. on the morning of March 26, 1872, when a major earthquake struck. The devastation experienced in Lone Pine was just as bad here. That earthquake would register 6.5 on today's Richter Scale. In retrospect, the decision the townsfolk made in 1865-66 to move was a wise one. Many of Bend City's un-reinforced adobe houses collapsed when the 1872 quake struck. Had those houses been occupied with sleeping citizens, the death toll would have undoubtedly been even higher than the 26 who did die (24 of whom were in Lone Pine). To make matters worse, the earthquake created a fifteen-foot escarpment that caused the Owens River channel to move a quarter mile west. When State Geologist W.A. Goodyear came through here in 1886, he found the ruins of 33 houses, a mill, a water wheel, and two arrastras. Today there is precious little to see.

In a few hundred yards, at 4.3 miles, the asphalt ends on Mazourka Canyon Road. If you look to the right and left here, and if you have a keen eye, you can see the old roadbed of the Carson & Colorado Railroad, (later the Southern Pacific) whose narrow gauge tracks served the Owens Valley from 1883 to 1959. Kearsarge Station once stood here, where passengers bound for Independence would disembark for their final 4½ miles by horse drawn buggy. The rails were pulled up in the 1960s, and nothing remains of the old station. If you want to see an old C&C station you are going to have to drive 34 miles south to Keeler (see Excursion #37) or fifty miles north to Laws (see Excursion #20).

Just before the cattle guard, turn left off the Mazourka Canyon Road onto the wide graded road (with a washboard surface) that heads north along the old railroad right-of-way. A mile and a half beyond the pavement one cannot help but notice the rocks to the right that are standing on end. These are 280 million year old sediments originally laid down in the bottom of a late Pennsylvanian to early Permian sea. They are part of what geologist's call the Keeler Canyon Formation. The oldest layers of this formation are noted for their black chert nodules, described by some as "natural golf balls".

At a point two and a half miles from the Mazourka Canyon Road (seven miles from Highway 395) the four tailings dumps of the Green Eyed Monster Mine can be seen on the right. The mine is mentioned as early as 1863 by the newspaper in Visalia. Exposed copper minerals easily attracted the prospector's attention, and the mineral float here must have been noticed early in the settlement of the Owens Valley. It is here that the copper mineral chrysocolla is found in a garnetized zone within a limestone member of the Keeler Canyon Formation adjoining an aplite dike. The orebody has been explored by several tunnels, but the only actual known production took place around 1900, and then the amounts produced were quite small. The miners did not know it at the time, but the only significant copper that would ever come from Inyo County would be as a by-product of the Pine Creek tungsten mine. By looking around the tailings dumps you might find a few pieces of blue azurite or bright green malachite. **Warning: Stay out of the underground workings.**

Beyond the Green Eyed Monster Mine, the graded road continues north skirting the base of the mountains. At the next promontory, where the Inyo Mountains jut out into the Owens Valley, three miles from the pavement (7.5 miles from Highway 395), is the site of old San Carlos. A Class II side road to the right takes you back to the Green Eyed Monster Mine. A Class I road to the left puts you in what once was downtown San Carlos, where you might find a few badly weathered bricks, but little else.

In the 1860s the community of San Carlos was the rival of Bend City, just three miles down the river. The San Carlos Mining Company erected a boiler to provide steam to operate a five stamp mill at the corner of Romelia and Silver Streets. On July 4, 1864, this nation's birth was celebrated in San Carlos by incessant hooting of the whistle on the mill's steam engine, horse racing, and, of course, a grand ball. A few weeks later, on August 27th, the first shooting in San Carlos occurred when a merchant by the name of Lentell was shot while throwing a man named Johnson out of his store.

The good folks of Bend City established a ferry to get across the Owens River. Not to be out done, the city fathers of San Carlos put in a bridge. Like their neighbors three miles down the river, the folks of San Carlos decided to move into Independence by 1865 after marauding Paiutes burned down the Union Mill south of town. Goodyear's 1886 observations of San Carlos noted the ruins of 26 houses and the decrepit state of the stone structure housing the San Carlos Mill. The nearby Ida Mill was also in a state of dilapidation. A life long Independence resident and very accomplished botanist, Mary DeDecker recalled visiting San Carlos in the 1930s and seeing still well-defined adobe building outlines and the mill still recognizable as a stone structure.

From old San Carlos follow the Eastside Road northward. The road is Class I as it leaves the site of San Carlos, but soon deteriorates to Class II, as alkali dust swirls high in the air behind you. A sandy stretch is reached about 2½ miles north of San Carlos, where you might be more comfortable in four-wheel drive. You will encounter several drift fences along the way. If you find the gates closed, please leave them that way after you pass through. Ranchers who graze their cattle in the river bottom don't want their livestock wandering off.

A crossroads is reached at a point 9.9 miles north of Mazourka Canyon Road (14.4 miles from Highway 395). If you are a rockhound, you may wish to turn right here and proceed two miles east and a little south on the Class II road to "Crystal Ridge". In the July 1972 issue of *Desert Magazine*, rockhound writer Mary Frances Strong described how she and her husband Jerry found one to three inch long quartz crystals here that were stained with chlorite and hematite. The crystals are imbedded in veins that were intruded into the surrounding granodiorite during the late stage cooling of the Santa Rita Flat pluton. In order to obtain the best specimens, the Strongs had to dig into the veins with a pry bar and a chisel to uncover fresh pieces. The last time that I visited this site was in the fall of 2000. It was my observation that a lot of rock hounds had dug at the site since that 1972 article first appeared. While the most easily obtained material has been taken, there are still a lot of crystals yet to be found here. **Warning: Be sure you wear gloves and have adequate eye protection before you start chipping out mineral specimens.**

Crystal Ridge

Back at the crossroads on the Eastside Road, one has two other alternatives for which way to go. If you continue straight ahead, the remains of the Jack Black Mine are less than a half-mile ahead. Beyond the mine, the Eastside Road continues north, where after 4.4 miles it joins the Aberdeen Station Road taking you back to Highway 395, just 1.2 miles to the west.

If you turn left at the crossroads, the Class I road passes some sloughs and winds around some cattle pens to rejoin Hwy 395 after 2.8 miles. Just before reaching the highway you will notice some buildings to the right. The California Department of Fish and Game has utilized some natural springs here to build a series of trout rearing ponds. Rainbow, Eastern Brook, and German Brown trout are hatched at the Mount Whitney Fish Hatchery outside of Lone Pine, and then brought here until they reach sufficient size to release in the streams and lakes of the Eastern Sierra. Visitors are welcome at the Black Rock facility, but please do not disturb the residents in the houses.

Once back on Highway 395, it is a little over eight miles back to Independence. If you are heading north, it is about eighteen miles to Big Pine, and 32 miles to Bishop.

33

Mazourka Canyon, Peak, and Pass

Special Features:	This road will take you to the top of Mazourka Peak, or if you choose, you can follow a jeep trail over a pass in the ridge and eventually come out at Big Pine. Along the way are old mines, fossil collecting and plenty of high desert and high mountain scenery.
Time Required:	Although the distances are not great, you will want to make this an all day outing, particularly if you cross Mazourka Pass and go on to Big Pine. The ascent of Mazourka Peak can also be combined with Excursion #34 for a full day's outing, returning to Independence.
Miles Involved:	It is 22 miles from downtown Independence up Mazourka Canyon to the top of either Mazourka Peak or Mazourka Pass.
Degree of Difficulty:	The road to Mazourka Peak is Class I, negotiable even for a modern passenger vehicle. If Mazourka Pass is your destination, the last two miles on the south side of the pass are Class III, with even more on the other side.
Remarks:	While the lower areas are generally accessible all year around, the higher portions are likely to be buried in snow during the winter months.

Mazourka Canyon is in the Inyo Mountains just east of Independence. It is somewhat unusual in that it does not start at the edge of the mountain range and then run directly into the crest at a right angle like most canyons do. Mazourka Canyon starts as all canyons do, but then it soon makes a 90-degree turn and runs parallel to the crest of the range for about seven miles before ending.

From downtown Independence take Main Street (Highway 395) to the south edge of town, where you will want to turn left onto Mazourka Canyon Road. Note your odometer reading as you leave Highway 395. This paved road will take you east across the Owens Valley 3.8 miles to where it crosses the Owens River. The elevation here is 3,740 feet. The elevation of Mazourka Peak is 9,412 feet, and Mazourka Pass is 9,460 feet, so expect to climb more than a mile in the next 22 miles. Continue following the paved road to the northeast another 0.6 miles to where the asphalt ends but the graded Mazourka Canyon road continues. By looking north and south here you can still see the old roadbed of the Carson & Colorado Railroad, (later the Southern Pacific) whose narrow gauge tracks served the Owens Valley between 1883 and 1959. Kearsarge Station once stood here, where passengers bound for Independence would disembark for their final 4½ miles by horse drawn buggy. The rails were pulled up in the 1960s, and nothing remains of the old station. If you want to see an old C&C station, you are going to have to drive 34 miles south to Keeler (see Excursion # 37) or fifty miles north to Laws (see Excursion #20).

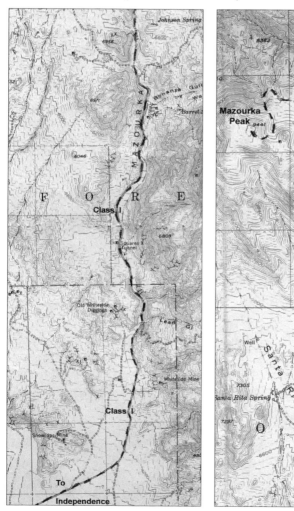
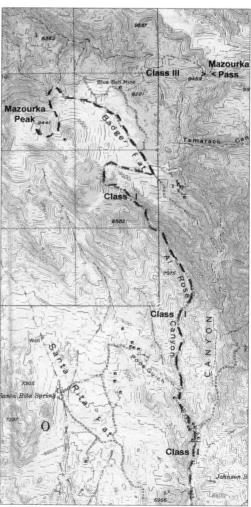

The graded road now crosses the equally old McGiver Canal (its water long ago sent south to flush the toilets of Los Angeles) and heads northeast towards the Inyo Mountains. In a little more than a mile the road turns to the north, and within a couple more miles you will enter Mazourka Canyon.

Lower Mazourka Canyon

At a point 7.1 miles from Highway 395, a side road to the right goes to the Whiteside Mine. The late Mary DeDecker researched this mine, suggesting this entire operation might have been a fraudulent promotional scheme designed only to attract investors' money. Whether that is true or not, these tunnels dug into the Tamarack Canyon Dolomite were once deemed to be safe enough that they were designated by Civil Defense authorities as an emergency fallout shelter during the peak of the cold war in the 1950s and 1960s. **The author, who has worked underground as a geologist, has looked at these tunnels recently and has concluded that they are no longer safe. The portal has partially collapsed, and some of the supporting timbers have burned midway through the main adit. My recommendation would be to stay out of the underground workings!**

About 1.3 miles north of the Whiteside Mine turnoff, there is another side road right. This Class II road climbs steeply some 2400 feet up the east wall of the canyon on its way to the Alhambra Mine, the Black Eagle Mine and the Betty Jumbo Mine at the head of Bee Springs Canyon. (See Excursion #34 for a description of that interesting road.)

Inyo National Forest is entered at a point nine miles from Highway 395, and the Squires Tunnel is passed on the right a half-mile beyond. For the next 2½ miles the layered rocks on the left side of the road are part of the Rest Spring shale of late Mississippian age. Although these siltstones and mudstones do contain fragments of ammonite fossils, fossil hunting is actually not very good, because the strata was metamorphosed with the intrusion of the Santa Rita pluton in the late Jurassic.

Barrel Spring, at the mouth of Water Canyon on the left, is 11.8 miles from Highway 395. This has proven to be a reliable source of water. For more than 125 years, miners have set up camp here while trying to eke out a living from this harsh land. Bonanza Gulch, just to the north, has had its gravels washed for placer gold. In spite of its optimistic name, the gulch was reluctant to give up any great riches.

A half-mile above Barrel Springs, yet another Class III side road to the right goes up Mexican Gulch to Johnson Spring. These rocks, too, are part of the Rest Spring shale. Your search for Mississippian fossils might be more productive here. At one time a pack trail climbed steeply above Johnson Spring to an unnamed pass at 9,500 feet, where it descended to Seep Hole Spring on the other side before dropping down Lead Canyon all the way to the Saline Valley. The author has briefly tried, without success, to find this old trail. Its relocation would be a good project for the *Friends of the Inyo Mountains Wilderness,* whose trail-finding efforts have been so successful a little farther south in the range.

A tenth of a mile beyond Mexican Gulch, a Class I road goes left through a breach in the Keeler Canyon Formation. This is Forest Road 13S05A, which goes across Santa Rita Flat to a spring of the same name. The basin is surrounded by granodiorite of Jurassic age. The area has been used for cattle grazing for well over a century. Beyond Santa Rita Spring this side road deteriorates to Class II, as it descends into Pop's Gulch, where it eventually rejoins the main Mazourka Canyon road.

Beyond the side road left to Santa Rita Flat, the Class I Mazourka Canyon road passes mounds of washed gravels and shafts dug down into the alluvium along the canyon bottom. In this area, and in Pop's Gulch still ahead on the left, destitute men eked out a living dry washing this sand for placer gold during the "Great Depression" years of the 1930s. Interestingly, the lode source from which that gold came has never been found. Most of their shafts and squirrel holes have long ago collapsed, but a few still remain open and unguarded. **Under no circumstances should any of these shafts or tunnels be entered!**

The turnoff to the left into Pop's Gulch is 14.3 miles in from Highway 395. Keeping to the right on the main road, Forest Road 13S05, the next three miles are called Al Rose Canyon. At first the road passes through a couple of miles of generally uninteresting Rest Spring shale, followed by a narrow band of the Perdido Formation. The piñon and juniper forest begins here, and the canyon no longer seems as dry and desolate.

Starting about seventeen miles from Highway 395, along the last mile of upper Al Rose Canyon, the road climbs up into the Sunday Canyon Formation, a shale rich in lime. Look here if you are collecting fossils. Graptolites have been found in this formation's lowest beds. These now extinct marine creatures lived in Paleozoic oceans from Cambrian to Mississippian times, but reached their zenith 420 million years ago in the Silurian Period, when these layers accumulated on the sea bottom. Graptolites, of which there were many different genera, floated upon the surface of the sea in colonies. For the most part, they were composed of soft tissues that were not well preserved in the fossil record. However, they did leave an elongated portion that resembles a thin single or double-sided hacksaw blade. It is this hard *rhabdosome* that is preserved as a fossil.

At a point eighteen miles in from Highway 395, the road climbs out of Al Rose Canyon and starts to cross Badger Flat. The narrow ridge of exposed bluish rock on the left is a thin outcropping of Ely Springs dolomite. It is of late Ordovician age. In eastern Nevada near Pioche, exposures of this rock contain coral and other fossils. Here those ancient life forms are few and far between.

A prominent outcrop of Ely Springs dolomite at the south end of Badger Flat.

Badger Flat is a high mountain valley, situated between 8,700 and 9,000 feet. It seems to be named not after the cantankerous animal, but after a man named Badger who was one of the founders of the Russ Mining District in 1863. Upon entering the flat, a side road to the right once went up Tamarack Canyon to a miner's cabin. The creation of the *Inyo Mountains Wilderness Area* in 1994 has now forever closed that road.

A short distance beyond, Forest Road 13S05 turns off to the right. This is one way to reach Mazourka Pass. If you plan to do that, I suggest you continue straight ahead on the main road another 0.8 miles, and take the road that turns right there.

At a point 19.3 miles from Highway 395, an important crossroads is reached. If your objective is to ascend Mazourka Peak, stay to the left on the Class I main road. It will climb up through the dark rocks of the Rest Spring Formation to reach the road's end in another two miles. The summit of 9,412' Mazourka Peak is festooned with three different antenna sites. The view is grand in spite of these man made intrusions. You can clearly see the entire Sierra Crest for thirty miles in each direction. You can see as far south as 14,375' Mt. Williamson (which blocks the view of Mt. Whitney) and as far north as 13,652' Mt. Tom. To the northwest Mt. Sill and the various high peaks of the Palisade group really stand out from this vantage point.

Rocks of the Rest Spring Formation near the top of Mazourka Peak.

The 9,441' summit of Mazourka Peak is festooned with antennas.
The view of the Sierra Nevada crest is breathtaking.

If your day's objective is not to merely drive up to Mazourka Peak, but to traverse the length of the mountain range and come out at Big Pine, then you will want to turn right at the 19.3 mile point. This latter route will take you up to Mazourka Pass via the Blue Bell Mine, less than a half a mile up the hill. The low stone walls of the several mine structures give no clue as to when this claim was first worked, but it is thought to date back to the 1860s. **Warning: The shaft is unguarded and dangerous; stand well back!**

The open shaft of the Blue Bell Mine.
Stay well back from the edge!

From the Blue Bell Mine the road makes one final steep ascent of Mazourka Pass. The last 1.8 miles from the mine to the pass are all Class III. This portion of the trail takes you across the 540 million year old Bonanza King dolomite of Middle Cambrian age. That formation is 2,800 feet thick in this area. This dolomite does not contain much in the way of fossils, except for some algae and some fucoidal markings that resemble wormholes.

The view from the top of 9,460' Mazourka Pass is also grand. From the pass the route north is just about all downhill, all the way to Big Pine. It is thirty miles to Big Pine via Papoose and Harkless Flats (see Excursion #31) with the next thirteen miles being Class III. If you choose to go to Big Pine via Papoose and Squaw Flats, (see Excursion #30) the distance is also thirty miles, but with only the first four miles being Class III. The choice is yours, depending on how much time you have.

34

Betty Jumbo Mine

Special Features:	This excursion takes you along a spectacular road climbing high onto the western flank of the Inyo Range, from which you can explore several old mines.
Time Required:	This is an all day excursion out of Independence, particularly if you drive on up to the summit of Mazourka Peak (see Excursion #33).
Miles Involved:	The total distance from downtown Independence to the Betty Jumbo Mine is slightly over sixteen miles.
Degree of Difficulty:	The first 8½ miles of dirt road have a good graded surface, followed by a little over six miles of sometimes-steep Class II. Only the last 1.4 miles to the Betty Jumbo Mine are Class III.
Remarks:	Except for the rare winter snowstorm, this trail is usually open throughout the year.

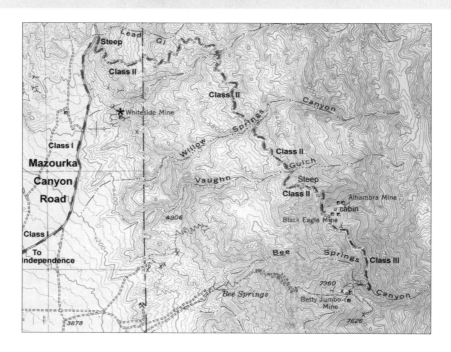

From downtown Independence, take Main Street (Highway 395) to the south edge of town, where you will want to turn left onto the paved Mazourka Canyon Road. Note your odometer reading as you leave Highway 395. The road soon crosses the Los Angeles Aqueduct, descends the 1872 earthquake fault escarpment and crosses the once mighty Owens River. In 1913 the City of Los Angeles Department of Water & Power began diverting water from the Owens River, sending it to Los Angeles via the massive aqueduct. As a result, lush fields and farmland from Bishop down to Lone Pine dried up. In an effort to restore the riparian habitat and at least partially restore some of the former wetlands, the DWP voluntarily drafted a plan in 2002-2003 to send more water down the Owens River. Those new releases should begin in 2004.

The Owens River near Independence. The City of Los Angeles
has promised to send more water down the river.

As you are driving east, notice the line etched onto the upper slopes of the Inyo Mountains just ahead. That road high in the Inyos is our destination. Notice, too, ahead and a little to the left, a spire of rock barely discernable on the distant skyline. It is Winnedumah Monument, but more about that curious feature later.

The pavement ends 4.4 miles from Highway 395, but the Mazourka Canyon Road continues on, with its good surface of graded dirt. Soon the road turns to the north, and within a couple of miles you will enter Mazourka Canyon.

At a point 7.1 miles from Highway 395, a side road goes right to the Whiteside Mine. The half a mile of tunnels in the mine were deemed to be adequately sound enough to be designated an emergency fallout shelter during the 1950s and 1960s at the peak of the cold war. Today, however, the portal has partially collapsed and a fire midway through the main tunnel has burned many of the timbers. **Stay out of the Whiteside Mine!**

The entrance to the Whiteside tunnel has partially collapsed.

Continuing up the graded Mazourka Canyon Road, the turnoff to the Betty Jumbo Mine is but 1.3 miles beyond the Whiteside Mine (8.4 miles from Highway 395). Here a road on the right makes a sharp turn back to steeply climb out of the wash. You may wish to recheck your odometer reading as you leave the Mazourka Canyon Road. Anticipating steep grades and loose traction, many drivers will engage their four-wheel drive. That is not a bad idea; however, the road is actually better than it first appears and turns out to be no worse than Class II. The road quickly climbs out of the canyon bottom and soon swings to the east, where the country begins to open up. Within a half-mile from the Mazourka Canyon Road, the banded layers of the Bonanza King dolomite begin to appear on the right. This "zebra striping" is a characteristic element of that particular formation. Ever since these beds were deposited in the bottom of a Cambrian Age sea some 525 million years ago, they have undergone a lot of metamorphism.

At a point 1.6 miles from the bottom of Mazourka Canyon, the road leaves the Paleozoic sedimentary rocks and climbs into igneous rocks of the Paiute

Monument pluton. Even those with no particular geological knowledge will notice the abrupt change. Think of these new rocks as a silica rich form of granite. They came from deep within the earth and were intruded into the overlying Paleozoic marine sediments during the early Cretaceous Period about 130 million years ago. They probably came from the same general magma chamber as the granitic rocks in the Sierra Nevada.

As the road climbs ever higher, the country becomes more interesting. At a point nearly five miles from the canyon bottom, the road forks; stay to the left. A half-mile more will bring you to the bottom of a series of steep switchbacks. Again, the road is not as bad as it looks and remains Class II. By the time you reach the top of those switchbacks, three quarters of a mile later, you will briefly be back into Paleozoic sediments again, this time seeing a small portion of the Johnson Spring Formation with its beds tilted up and standing on end. Following it, you get an even quicker glimpse of the Badger Flat limestone. Both formations are of Ordovician age, about 450 million years old.

By this time, you have climbed some 2,000 feet since leaving the canyon bottom. Here at 6,800 feet there are unobstructed views west of the Sierra Nevada skyline. Stop a moment and take in the scenery. The small dip in the Sierra crest to the west, (and very slightly to the south), is Kearsarge Pass. With an elevation of only 11,823 feet, the Kearsarge Pass Trail is very popular with backpackers into the backcountry, because it is the shortest, lowest and easiest pass out of the Owens Valley. The hike to its top is only four miles by trail with an elevation gain of 3,000 feet. Towering over the pass, the peak just to the north is 13,005' Mt. Gould. The highest peak immediately to the south of the pass is 13,289' Mt. Bradley.

The road ahead now contours around the mountainside and within a quarter of a mile reaches the tailings dump of the Alhambra Mine. Time and the elements have treated the Alhambra Mine well. The head frame remains in place, and up the draw the miner's cabin would still keep out the wind and rain on a stormy night. **Warning: The portal of the lower adit has collapsed and the ladder descending the shaft has broken rungs. Stay out of the underground workings!**

Here, and at the Black Eagle Mine on the point just a few hundred yards down the road to the south, gold was found where the quartz monzonite, the Tamarack Canyon dolomite and the Barrel Spring Formation all come in contact with each other. The complex geology is made even more complicated by faulting. The workings suggest that some ore was produced at both mines, although neither mine had an on-site mill, probably due to the lack of water. In the past, ore had been treated at Barrel Spring in Mazourka Canyon, and perhaps that was the destination of this ore.

The miner's cabin at the Alhambra Mine could still offer shelter in a storm.

The Alhambra Mine is often used as the jumping off point for hikers wishing to climb up to the Winnedumah Monument (also called Paiute Monument on some maps). That massive finger of quartz monzonite (a silica rich form of granite) is about a four-mile hike north of the Alhambra Mine, but the total elevation gain is only about 1,200 feet. That is much less of a climb than from anyplace else. The Paiute peoples of the Owens Valley have several stories about this rock spire. One of those oral traditions is that they were attacked by a tribe, who came over the Sierras to raid their villages. Overwhelmed and defeated, the Paiutes fled to the crest of the Inyo Mountains, where medicine man Winnedumah prayed to the Great Spirit for help. Suddenly a great storm appeared out of nowhere, and the ground shook. The invaders became frightened and fled westward back over the Sierra Nevada. Winnedumah was turned into a tower of stone, where he continues to watch over his people to this day.

The monolith named "Winnedumah Monument"
(County of Inyo, Eastern California Museum photo)

The Black Eagle Mine is 6.3 miles from the Mazourka Road (14.7 miles from Highway 395). The road ahead can be seen clinging to the mountainside, but here a U.S. Forest Service sign indicates that travel ahead is not recommended even for 4x4s. The problem is not generally with the roadbed itself, but the loose talus and boulders that have rolled down from above. The timid may wish to go no further, but when I last scouted the route in the fall of 2001, it was a perfectly useable Class III road for the entire 1.4 miles from the Black Eagle Mine to the Betty Jumbo Mine. True, it was necessary to maneuver through tight spots created by boulders too big to move. In order to do this, drivers may wish to have a passenger get out and guide them through.

It is a very interesting road, which took considerable engineering skill to build. Not only is the road interesting to drive, but the views straight down into Bee Springs Canyon are breathtaking. Above the Betty Jumbo Mine, the road climbs a short distance to cross a low ridge, where several branches dead-end at more prospect holes.

Road to the Betty Jumbo Mine.

Like the first two mines, the ore deposits of the Betty Jumbo Mine are found in contact-metamorphic rocks called tactite, adjoining the Pat Keyes pluton of the Hunter Mountain quartz monzonite. A two-foot wide quartz vein not only contains small amounts of gold and silver, but also scheelite, the principal ore mineral of tungsten. A 120-foot tunnel and a 240-foot deep inclined shaft have accessed the orebody, but in spite of the enormous road building costs, and all this digging, there seems to have been little production. Like so many mining ventures, a lot more seems to have been put into this ground than was ever taken out. **Warning: Stay out of the underground workings.**

Because the road comes to a dead-end at the Betty Jumbo Mine, one must return by the same route.

Ore bunker at the Betty Jumbo Mine

The Very Versatile Hi-Lift Jack

All automobile manufacturers provide a jack with their vehicles. This device is barely adequate for the job and is marginally useful only under optimum conditions. Experienced four-wheelers long ago came to appreciate the versatility and usefulness of the Hi-Lift jack. Not only will it elevate your vehicle so that a tire can be changed, but it will do so under extraordinarily difficult circumstances. It will also do much much more.

While alone and miles from any help, I have self-extricated myself from a bottomless mud hole in Baja California by using a Hi-Lift Jack and an abundant supply of fence posts. On another occasion, while in the while wilds of Western Chihuahua, I broke a rear spring shackle on my Scout. I used a Hi-Lift jack as a come-along to reposition the rear axle so that it could be temporarily affixed to the frame rail. As a rescue and extrication specialist with the fire department, I was trained to use the Hi-Lift jack to force open car doors and pull steering wheels off the laps of pinned-in drivers. Needless to say, whenever I am out four-wheeling, I always have my faithful Hi-Lift jack with me.

Hi-Lift jacks are not a new product. They have been around since 1895! Current models are tested to 7,000 pounds, but that is a very conservative rating. For economy of weight and ease of storage, I use the shortest model, one with a bar of only 36"; however longer models are available with bar lengths of 42", 48" and 60".

Whatever model the four-wheeler selects, it should be securely fastened to the vehicle so that it will not bounce around. This is more easily done on some vehicles than others, particularly if you have an SUV. I have placed mine on top of the vehicle using the factory installed roof rack. There it is secure and handy, yet it does not take up valuable interior space.

The Bloomfield Manufacturing Company which produces the product, also makes a number of accessories that could be useful to the off-roader. One is a larger base plate for added foundation. SUV owners should look at the curved bumper attachment. Bloomfield also makes an off-road kit.

Hi-Lift jacks are sold at larger hardware stores, particularly those catering to agricultural customers, and through four-wheel drive stores nationwide. For specific questions, call Bloomfield at (800) 233-2051.

The Lone Pine of Yesteryear

Lone Pine in the 1880s.

Lone Pine in the 1920s.

Lone Pine in the 1940s
(County of Inyo, Eastern California Museum photos)

Chapter VII

Trails Out of Lone Pine

Lone Pine's beginning goes back to the Civil War years of 1862-63, when it became a ranching and farming community, supplier to the scattered mines. At that time water from the Owens River had not yet been diverted (some say stolen) by Los Angeles and the floor of the Owens Valley was a green and fertile place.

The peaceful tranquility of the community was broken at 2:30 a.m. on March 26, 1872, when a major earthquake suddenly struck without warning. The town was nearly destroyed. In a matter of seconds Metsan's General Store and Juan Ybaceta's Union Market were flattened. Worse yet, the Munzinger & Lubken Brewery was reduced to rubble. Twenty-four of Lone Pine's citizens were killed in the collapsing adobe buildings. The twenty-foot fault scarp left by that earthquake can still be seen at the north edge of town. For a better understanding of Lone Pine's past, you may wish to visit the small Southern Inyo Museum sponsored by the New Coso Heritage Society, located just a half block off Highway 395 at 127 Bush Street.

Although still a small community of only 2100 people, Lone Pine today caters to tourists moving up and down US Highway 395. There are eight motels, several restaurants, four service stations, a market, two auto parts stores and even a small hospital. There are also several campgrounds nearby just off the road to Whitney Portal.

All of the outings described in this chapter are on BLM administered federal lands where camping and campfires are permitted anywhere. Rock hounding is also permitted. Be sure to stop at the Inter-Agency Visitor Center just south of town at the junction of Highways 395 and State Route 136. They have some interesting displays, and can provide the latest road information.

For the very latest in road information, stop at the
Inter-Agency Visitor Center just south of Lone Pine.

35

Union Wash

Primary Attraction:	A place where you can collect 235 million year old ammonite fossils, with a little more recent railroad history thrown in as well.
Time Required:	This is a half-day excursion out of Lone Pine (or all day if you are seriously collecting fossils).
Miles Involved:	From Lone Pine to the end of the road in Union Wash is ten miles.
Degree of Difficulty:	The road is generally no worse than Class II.
Remarks:	Except for the rare winter snowstorm, this trail is usually open throughout the year.

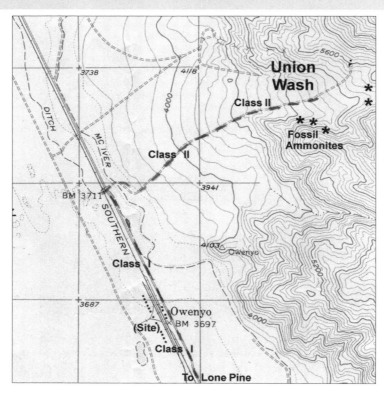

The Triassic Period, sometimes known as the beginning of the Age of Dinosaurs, has left relatively few sedimentary rocks in California. There is, however, a narrow band of Triassic sandy limestone and mudstone along the western flank of the Inyo Mountains. Known as the Union Wash Formation, these sediments were deposited in the bottom of a shallow sea some 235 million years ago. That sea teemed with marine life, particularly a type of shellfish called ammonites. These creatures were not limited to the sea bottom, but could float and propel themselves about by expelling a jet of water. When they died, they sank to the mud and ooze at the bottom of this primeval sea, where their shells sometimes accumulated in great numbers. Those shells became buried in the sea bottom sediment and today are preserved in the fossil record. If you would like to find some for yourself, Union Wash is the place to look.

Ammonites were hard shelled marine animals and are often well preserved fossils.

To find Union Wash from downtown Lone Pine, head north on Highway 395. Just before leaving town, turn right onto Narrow Gauge Road. Note your odometer reading as you leave Highway 395. This paved road will take you east for a mile and a half, where it makes a sharp left turn. Ahead is Lone Pine Station, a reminder of the 1910 to 1990s era when the Southern Pacific's tracks extended up into the southern end of the Owens Valley. The former station is now a private residence. We will avoid it by following the road to the northeast. After a half-mile, what is left of the Owens River is crossed, and within another 1.3 miles we will come to the old railroad grade of the Carson & Colorado Railroad, a narrow gauge line which extended 294 miles south from Mound House, Nevada (just east of Carson City). Construction was started on this railroad on May 31, 1880, and the tracks reached their terminus in Keeler in July of 1883.

Our paved road follows along one side of the railroad right-of-way for the next 1.3 miles, then crosses the old road grade to follow the other side for another two miles. The site of Owenyo is 6.7 miles from Highway 395. Here from 1910 to 1959 (the old C&C narrow gauge rails were torn out in 1960) was the interchange between the Southern Pacific's narrow gauge operation going north, and their standard gauge tracks going south. At Owenyo freight and bulk commodities from one line could be transferred to the waiting cars of the other line. Unfortunately, the buildings were razed when the tracks were pulled out, and you have to look close to even see the site. Only a few concrete foundations and the cement piers upon which the water tank rested remain.

Owenyo Station in 1947. Note that the old semaphore signaling system was still in use. (County of Inyo, Eastern California Museum photo)

Continue north from the site of Owenyo along the east side of the old railroad grade for another 1.2 miles. Here, nearly eight miles from Highway 395, a Class I road turns off to the right, immediately crosses the old McGiver Canal, and begins to climb the alluvial fan coming out of Union Wash. The road deteriorates to Class II, but remains passable to most vehicles. As you climb up the alluvial fan, you may notice the large clusters of Cottontop cactus growing here. They obvious like the hot and dry west-facing slope.

At a point 9.8 miles from Highway 395, the rock outcrop on the right is your first introduction to the marine sediments of Triassic age. This is where this sequence of marine sediments was first studied by geologist James Perrin Smith, who published his findings in 1914. He gave them the name "Union Wash Formation". Although the sequence is not completely exposed here, it has been measured with a total thickness of at least 2,800 feet. The formation can be further subdivided into three parts or "members": upper (the youngest), middle, and lower (the oldest). Here you are looking at rocks of the middle member. If you climb up the scree slope on the south side of the canyon, you may well find the fossilized remains of *Parapopanoceras haugi,* the most common of the eight ammonite species found here. BLM regulations allow amateur paleontologists to take reasonable quantities for their own personal collections. The *Parapopanoceras* layer is only three feet thick, so if you do not have the motivation or energy to climb two-thirds of the way up the steep scree slope, look at the loose material that has weathered out of the bedrock and is sliding downhill. The *Parapopanoceras* layer is of a dark gray to nearly black limestone, so pay particular attention to rocks of that description. **Be careful: the steep scree can be hazardous in that it offers poor footing, slides easily, and can endanger people below you.**

By continuing up the road to its end, and then walking up the canyon less than a mile to the east, one gets into layers dominated by yet another ammonite species *Meekoceras gracilitatus.* This area lies within the Southern Inyo Wilderness, and here the BLM rules are slightly different. Private collectors can still gather marine fossils found on the surface, but digging for specimens is prohibited. These *Meekoceras* beds were discovered in 1896 by paleontologist Charles Doolittle, who passed his collection on to James Smith for further scientific study.

The ammonites found here are relatively small, generally less a half inch to two inches in diameter. They can best be seen with the use of a 10X geologist's hand lens. I have found some real whoppers along the west coast of Baja California in Mexico, where no magnification was necessary. Some were nearly three feet in diameter!

Ammonites

Once you have had your fill of ammonite collecting, return to the old Carson & Colorado Railroad grade to turn to the northwest heading up the Owens Valley. After 3.4 miles turn left onto the Manzanar Reward Road. Highway 395 is but four miles to the west, and from there, another 7.5 miles back south to Lone Pine.

Cottontop cactus Echinocactus polycepalus in Union Wash

36

The Swansea Grade

Primary Attraction:	A narrow road corridor cut through the Inyo Mountain Wilderness that offers a very challenging alternative access route to the nearly two mile high crest of the Inyo Mountains. In the fall, this is also an excellent place to gather delicious and nutritious piñon nuts. This outing can easily be combined with Excursion #37 to make a complete loop.
Time Required:	This is an all day excursion out of Lone Pine.
Miles Involved:	From Lone Pine to the crest of the Inyo Range via the Swansea Grade is 33 miles. Add another nineteen miles if you chose to return to Lone Pine via Cerro Gordo, descending the Yellow Grade.
Degree of Difficulty:	Most of the thirteen-mile off-highway portion of the route is Class III, but there are several Class IV, and two short Class V sections to contend with. **This is a very difficult ascent in places, made a little easier if you elect to take it downhill. This route is not recommended for four-wheel drive vehicles that are overly wide, or ones with a long wheelbase. Likewise, this is not an outing for the casual or inexperienced off-road driver.** Snow often closes the upper portion of the route anytime between November and May.

This old wagon road was built in 1911 as part of the salt tram construction project. How mules could haul heavy timbers and miles of cable up these steep grades defies belief. Equally incredible is the fact that this old wagon road wasn't completely washed out in the last ninety years. The flash flood that occurred late in the afternoon of September 3, 1996, sent large boulders floating down the lower three miles of the route, covering the canyon bottom with several feet of new alluvium. That event did wash out the road; however, by December new tracks had been blazed up the wash, and the route re-established. Today the lower portions of the road are as good as they ever were.

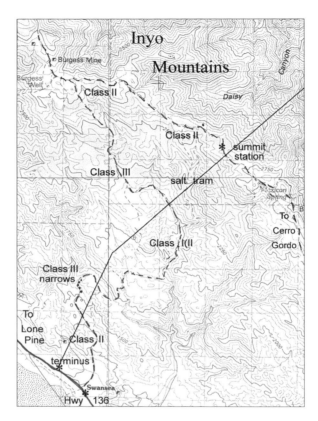

The road up the Swansea Grade starts here.

To find the start of the Swansea Grade from downtown Lone Pine, go south on Highway 395 two miles. Turn left onto State Route 136, going southeast another 9.6 miles to Swansea, a small cluster of buildings astride the highway.

Named after an historic metal-smelting town on the south coast of Wales, Swansea got its start in 1869, when the Owens Lake Silver-Lead Company built two blast furnaces here to smelt ore from the San Felipe Mine at Cerro Gordo. Under the leadership of its Superintendent, James Brady, the company began aggressively buying into other mines on the hill. This in turn lead to an intense rivalry between the Owens Lake Silver-Lead Company and the mines and smelters run by Victor Beaudry and his partner Mortimer Belshaw.

It was Belshaw who constructed the first road to Cerro Gordo in the summer of 1868, a route that was to be known as the infamous *Yellow Grade* after the rock formations through which it passed. Belshaw collected a toll on everything that moved up or down this road, including ore going to Swansea. After the Owens Lake Silver-Lead Company bought controlling interest in the Santa Maria Mine in July of 1870, Brady set out to build two more smelters at Swansea, which would double his capacity. In response, Belshaw attempted to shut his competitor down by stopping maintenance on his toll road, while increasing the tolls for ore wagons. Because the Owens Lake Company was the only one hauling ore down, Belshaw's motives seemed clear.

Besides overseeing the smelting furnaces at Swansea, Brady had other irons in the fire. When Remi Nadeau's contract to haul freight from Cerro Gordo and Los Angeles expired, Brady stepped in to fill the void at a lower rate. This put Beaudry and Belshaw in the strange position of using their archrival, Brady, to ship their ingots to market. As a spin-off, Brady also built a steam-powered boat to carry freight across Owens Lake to Cartago Landing, thus cutting several days off the shipping time to Southern California.

The next mischief experienced by Brady was not caused by Belshaw, but by Mother Nature. The great earthquake of March 26, 1872, which all but leveled Lone Pine, caused the eastern shore of Owens Lake to rise about two feet, while the western shore sank the same amount. Brady found the dock at Swansea was now 150 feet from water deep enough to accommodate his boat. The pier had to be extended. Meanwhile, the opposite dock at Cartago was nearly submerged.

In 1873 Belshaw changed the lower four miles of his toll road. It now reached the shore of Owens Lake some three miles north of Swansea. The road between Cerro Gordo and Lone Pine still ran through Swansea, but the heavily laden wagons of bullion never did. Brady simply shifted his boat, the *Bessie Brady*, to the end of Belshaw's new road. This site would soon become known as Keeler.

By early 1874 the Owens Lake Silver-Lead Company was in serious financial trouble. Operations at Swansea were suspended. The final blow to Swansea occurred a few months later, when a summer thunderstorm over the Inyo Mountains sent a wall of water, mud and debris down upon Swansea. The smelters were buried in several feet of fresh sand and rock. The damage was sufficient so that the smelters never reopened. Those few residents, who had not yet left Swansea, did so now.

For many years, the ruins of the old furnaces on the west side of the highway were items of historical interest, marked by a bronze plaque set back off the highway. The flash flood of September 2, 1997, sent more tons of silt, sand and stones across the highway into the smelter site. Similar occurrences have happened at least two other times in the past 125 years. What little is left is slowly, but surely being buried under the wind blown sand.

Swansea today

Our road to the crest of the Inyo Mountains begins opposite the Historical Marker, where a rough Class II dirt road starts up towards the hills. Note your odometer reading as you leave the highway. Soon the well-defined road reaches the alluvial wash left from the 1997 flash flood. When I drove up the wash in early 1998, there were just a few tire tracks in the sand and four-wheel drive was needed all along the route. A recheck in the summer of 2002 revealed the road had been re-established by use, and the road was mostly Class II.

As you carefully make your way up the wash, keep an eye out for the many members of the Buckwheat boys, who are known to inhabit these parts. There is the granddaddy, of course, California Buckwheat *Eriogonum fasciculatum* var. *polifolium,* and its more uppity neighbors Skeleton Weed *Eriogonum deflexum* and Mat Buckwheat *Eriogonum caestitosum*. If you are lucky and have your Munz or Jepsom reference with you, you might even be so lucky as to come upon a Nodding Buckwheat *Eriogonum cernuum* or perhaps even a Heermann

Buckwheat *Eriogonum heermannii* var. *argense*. But the two buckwheats I guarantee you will see are the spreading "Glandular Buckwheat" *Eriogonum brachypodum* and its cousin the Desert Trumpet *Eriogonum inflatum*. Their dried out skeleton remains long after the plant has gone through its normal life cycle.

Desert Trumpet
Eriogonum inflatum

Glandular Buckwheat
Eriogonum brachypodum

At a point two miles above the highway, the road passes under the route of the old salt tram for the first of three times. Unfortunately, the time and the elements have taken their toll in the last twenty years, and the cables and towers on the western slope of the Inyos are largely down. The Saline Valley Salt Company took two years building the 13.4-mile long electric powered tramline. At the time, this wonder of engineering was the longest and highest tramline in the world. The tramline had 39 high towers and 123 shorter towers that kept the 27 miles of cable off the ground. The tram had nearly three hundred buckets, each having a capacity of about 750 pounds. The tramline could move twenty tons of product per hour. It took two hours to move a bucket through the entire 27-mile circuit. Between 1913 and 1933, the tram carried salt products from the Saline Valley 7,500 feet up Daisy Canyon, over the Inyo Mountains, and 5,000 feet down the other side to a point on Highway 136 about a mile northwest of Swansea. At its Owens Valley terminus, the salt was put into Southern Pacific narrow gauge gondola cars for further transport to market.

A lonely tower on the salt tram tower overlooking Owens Lake.

At a point three miles up the canyon above the highway, the first serious challenge is reached: a dry bedrock waterfall a few feet in height. **Scout the route ahead on foot before proceeding. Plan carefully where you will place your wheels.** In 1968 and again in 1998 I rated this obstacle Class V going up, or Class IV coming down. By 2002 enough people had been over it, and had filled in the holes, that the rating had dropped to an easy Class IV in both directions. The next three similar obstacles should be no problem, if you can easily make it up and over this piece of bedrock all right. The canyon narrows further, and soon a second dry cascade is reached. Its rating, too, has been downgraded to Class IV. How will you find the trail? That all depends on Mother Nature. All it takes is one severe thunderstorm over the Inyos, such as that which occurred on September 2, 1997, and the lower five miles of this trail are gone.

An easy Class IV pitch along the Swansea Grade.

At a point 3.3 miles from the highway, the route leaves the lowest wash system and passes beneath the salt tram for the second time. The trail now improves to well-defined road, and it pretty much remains so from here on. It is Class II for the next half-mile, but soon turns to Class III, as the road steeply climbs the hillside for the next half-mile. A divide is crossed and 4.7 miles in, a second wash system is entered. This part of the wash escaped the 1997 flashflood, and the road here remains Class II for the most part.

The tram is passed beneath for the third and final time 7.7 miles above the highway. By this time you have gone from 3,600 feet at Swansea to 6,800 feet here. Just around the corner the first piñon trees will begin to appear. For the next four miles the piñon forest will offer a number of dry, but otherwise nice campsites, where firewood is available, and there are beautiful views of the Sierra crest to the west. One of these campsites covers an acre or so, large enough to accommodate a jeep club.

The road is well defined, but the grades are steep and sometimes deeply rutted. Traction is often poor. There are at least three Class IV pitches before the top is reached, but the worst is behind you. Finally, at a point twelve miles from the highway, the road again improves to Class II. The 9,200-foot crest of the Inyo Range is but a half-mile beyond. In the last 12.6 miles, you have made a vertical ascent of more than a mile.

No matter how hot it is in the Owens Valley or in the Saline Valley, the crest of the Inyos is always cool and breathtaking. If you have not done so already, this is a good place to stop and look around. The Sierra skyline to the west is magnificent. Although it sits well back from the crest, the 14,495' summit of Mount Whitney can be clearly seen at the northern end of a sawtooth-like ridge. To the north is the 10,668' summit of New York Butte (easily climbed from the end of the road). To the east and far below are the parched white salt flats in the bottom of the Saline Valley. On the skyline beyond are Dry Mountain and Panamint Butte. By turning to the south, 9,690' Pleasant Mountain is down the ridge, and beyond it a little to the right, is 9,184' Cerro Gordo Peak.

The salt tram descending to Owens Lake, circa 1950.
(Central Nevada Museum photo)

Once on the rounded crest, a "T" intersection is reached. To the left the Class II road goes to the Burgess Mine, just 0.7 miles to the north. Once called the Ironsides, the Burgess Mine is the southern-most mine in the Beveridge Mining District. Located at the very top of the Inyo Range, it commands superb views of the Sierra skyline to the west. Although the gold bearing quartz veins ran only $20-$40 per ton, several thousand feet of tunnels were dug here. The headframe over the main shaft has collapsed, but the remains of several buildings can still be seen in various stages of ruin.

Beyond the Burgess Mine, the Class II road continues north yet another 0.7 miles to end at 9,800 feet. Here is a sheltered campsite at the southern base of 10,688' New York Butte. From here a little used and difficult mule trail continues north along the ridge on its way to Beveridge, an isolated mining camp of yesteryear. While a backpack trip into Beveridge Canyon should be undertaken only by the physically fit, the one-mile climb up to New York Butte could be done by nearly anyone. There is a breath-taking view from its summit down into Hunter Canyon to the east.

By turning to the right upon reaching the crest, a Class II and III road goes south to the salt tram Summit Station, and on to the graded county road at Cerro Gordo, some eleven miles to the south east (see Excursion #37). From here you can descend the old "Yellow Grade" back down to Highway 136.

The salt tram summit crossover station in 1965.

37

The Crest of the Inyos

Primary Attraction:	A historic mining camp, coupled with great views of the High Sierra peaks to the west, and the Saline Valley to the east. This outing can be easily combined with the Swansea Grade route (Excursion #36) to make a complete loop.
Time Required:	Cerro Gordo and the Inyo Crest are an all day trip out of Lone Pine.
Miles Involved:	From downtown Lone Pine it is 23 miles to Cerro Gordo, and then another thirteen miles to the end of the road beyond the Burgess Mine.
Degree of Difficulty:	The county road up to Cerro Gordo is very steep, but nevertheless of graded dirt and Class I or better. From Cerro Gordo northward along the ridge, the route is mostly Class II, but with enough Class III to keep the casual tourists out. Snow can fall on the Inyo crest anytime from November through April, with deep drifts sometimes remaining well into May.

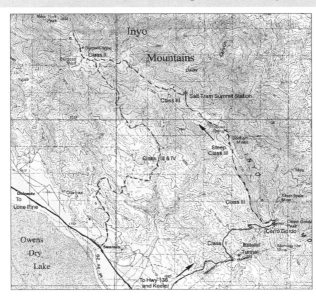

It is surprising that the Inyo Mountains do not get more backcountry visitors than they do. They have much to offer in the way of history and scenery. For the four-wheeler, they also offer an interesting and spectacular jeep trail high on the mountain's crest.

From downtown Lone Pine, go south on Highway 395 two miles to State Route 136, then turn left going southeast another 12.5 miles to Keeler. This small community was originally known as Hawley, but later changed to Keeler after Captain J.M. Keeler, who refurbished the Stevens flume across the lake in Cottonwood Canyon. Keeler once thrived as the transshipment point for everything from silver to salt. Before starting up the mountain, however, turn right on Malone Street and go down a couple of blocks to look at the old wooden station which served as the southern terminus of the Carson & Colorado Railroad, (and later the Southern Pacific) between 1883 and 1959.

The old Keeler station survives to this day.

From the old station at Malone and Railroad Streets, return to Highway 136, and continue south another 0.3 miles, where the graded Cerro Gordo road goes off to the left. The 8.5-mile piece of Class I road between Keeler and Cerro Gordo was known as the infamous "Yellow Grade". Originally it was a toll road over which sweating mule teams would toil and struggle with heavy loads. Wagons of wood and supplies went up the canyon, and these same wagons loaded with silver bullion would come skidding down, with their wheels chained. Although the old toll road is now graded, the route has not changed much since it was constructed well over a century ago. The 4400 feet difference in elevation has not changed either.

The county road heads to the northeast, as it leaves Highway 136 and begins its climb up the bajada. In a half-mile you will notice stone foundations off to the right. This was the site of the enormous Four Metals Mining Company's smelter. It was this firm that built the first aerial tramline down from Cerro Gordo. The smelter was completed late in 1908, with the tram in operation by early 1909.

While the smelter had a capacity of 120 tons per day, the tram could deliver only fifty tons of ore per day. Mule drawn ore wagons continued to ply the Yellow Grade until Four Metals ceased operation in 1914.

As the road enters the canyon a couple of miles in from the highway, the old road to Swansea can be seen to the left, climbing out of the wash. In a little more than three miles from the highway, the road starts through the narrows where the beds of limestone are standing up on end. These beds are part of the Owens Valley Formation of Permian age. The road climbs steeply up the canyon for the next 1.5 miles. Suddenly the canyon opens, and before you are the ore bunker and lower terminus of a second aerial tram. This one brought ore down from the Morning Star Mine, some 2000 feet above.

As the road makes a sweeping turn to the left and passes the bunker, a second side road appears on the right. This road goes to the amazing Estelle Tunnel. This tunnel was started rather late in the mountain's history. The tunnel had three objectives: (1) to cut into the rich silver-bearing Castle Rock vein, (2) to tap into the inferred deep extensions of the Morning Star Mine some 3,000 feet above, and (3) to seek downward continuations of the Jefferson chimney, another potential source of wealth. The Estelle Mining Company was formed for this purpose and the tunnel was begun in 1908. By 1923 the tunnel had penetrated straight into the mountain well over a mile, 8,100 feet to be exact. A vein containing silver was hit near the tunnel's end, followed by raises and tunnels another half mile. But after fifteen years of burrowing into the mountain, only 2,700 tons of ore was produced and that yielded a meager twenty ounces of silver per ton. The $80,000 recovered was far less than the cost of the venture.

The portal of the Estelle Tunnel penetrates the Keeler Canyon Formation, limestone of late Pennsylvania and early Permian age. This rock formation is quite firm and the tunnel required practically no shoring for the first 3,470 feet. The tunnel is wide enough at its entrance so that in the 1960s I was able to drive my International Scout quite some distance into the mountain. I stopped only when it dawned on me that there was no place to turn around and I was going to have to back out. In 1998 a large *KEEP OUT* sign was posted on the access road to the tunnel. **Please respect such signs.**

Beyond the turnoff to the Estelle Tunnel, the county road faces a gentler gradient as it climbs the next 2.2 miles to the Sunset Mine at an elevation of 7,250 feet. This is the lowest of Cerro Gordo's mines. The main tunnel was 385 feet long and tapped into a couple of fissures containing galena (lead) associated with some silver. In spite of its surface appearance, this mine was not a major producer. **Warning: Stay out of these old tunnels and shafts.**

Above the Sunset Mine, the county road climbs more steeply again, and there are great views of the Sierra crest to the west. Finally, at a point eight miles from the highway, downtown Cerro Gordo is reached.

The great silver and lead ores of Cerro Gordo were discovered by Mexican prospectors sometime before 1865, but it was not until 1866 that the Owens Valley Indian Wars were resolved and it was safe to wander about. History says that one Pablo Flores made a rich find high on 9,000' Buena Vista Peak in the Inyo Mountains. He named the site Cerro Gordo, which means "Fat Pig" in Spanish. As word of the strike got out, miners started flocking in to stake their own claims. Soon Pablo was not alone on his lofty mountaintop.

The first real mines to open were the San Lucas, the San Ygnacio, the San Francisco, and the San Felipe, the names of which reflected the Mexican heritage of their operators. At first, very little capital was required to mine the rich silver. Ore was dug out from surface pits and trenches using only hand tools, and placed into crude ovens made of rocks and adobe. The ore was "roasted" in the heat, with the silver and lead melting into puddles.

Before very long, the operation at Cerro Gordo caught the attention of a French-Canadian, Victor Beaudry, a merchant in Independence. Beaudry recognized the potential of Cerro Gordo and in 1866, opened a store on the mountain. He sold his merchandise to the cash-poor miners on credit, and if they were unable to pay their bills, he gained ownership of their claims.

Cerro Gordo became a true town. In time, many of the hundreds of claims were purchased and consolidated into two rival mines. Each had its own smelter. By 1870 the reduction furnaces were turning out ingots at the remarkable rate of nine tons a day. The silver-lead pigs could not be shipped out as fast as the mills poured them. For four or five years, life on this high and windswept hill was very exciting.

It was not until 1875 that production began to slow down, and Cerro Gordo's population began to drift away. By 1879 most of the mines had closed. Cerro Gordo seemed destined on a course to oblivion. News of Cerro Gordo's death was premature, however. In 1907 new veins were opened up, and the following year a six-mile long tramway was started to connect Cerro Gordo with a new smelter in Keeler. The tram was completed in 1909. When it wasn't broken down, it could deliver fifty tons of ore each day. In 1911, a zinc orebody previously thought to be worthless was mined, breathing more life to the mountaintop town. Between 1915 and 1919 some 33,000 tons of old smelter slag were re-worked, producing nearly a half million dollars in metal which had been lost in the crude methods of earlier ore dressing.

In 1916 electric power lines came up the mountain to Cerro Gordo, and electricity replaced steam as the means to power the hoists and mills. The camp experienced enough of a revival that the American Hotel, by now fifty years old, was renovated. Next door an ice plant was erected. In 1920, the Morning Star

Mine, passed on the way into town, finally hit pay dirt and shipped ore worth more than $100,000. About this same time, the Estelle Mining Company was shipping a little ore down the mountain to Keeler where a fifty-ton mill had been built. By 1924, however, the last mill was closed, and there was little mining on the hill. In 1929 a lessee opened a new vein, and shipped 10,000 tons of ore by rail between 1929 and 1933. With the great depression, a silence fell over Cerro Gordo. The rowdy old camp retains its slumber to this day.

The old mining camp of Cerro Gordo is now private property, but reservations can be made for overnight accomodations in the Belshaw House built in 1868, in the American Hotel built in 1871, or in the "new" bunkhouse built in 1904. In addition, two-hour walking tours can be arranged on weekends by calling ahead. Photography and mineral collecting excursions can also be arranged. You can write to Mike Patterson or Jody Stewart at P.O. Box 221, Keeler CA 93530. The number to call is (760) 876-5030.

Those interested in learning more about Cerro Gordo, and seeing photos of its colorful past, should look for an excellent book entitled *City Makers*, published by TransAnglo Books. It was written by Remi Nadeau, the great grandson of a desert freighter of the same name who made a substantial contribution to Inyo County's silver camps of the 1870s. Another publication worth having is *From This Mountain – Cerro Gordo*, by Likes and Day. It is available at the Inter-Agency Visitor Center on the south end of Lone Pine.

To the left as you enter town are the stone ruins of Victor Beaudry's slag furnace built in 1868. To the right a little further on is the two-story American Hotel. Downstairs was largely kitchen and dining facilities, with dormitory style accommodations upstairs. On a large tailings dump overlooking the town are the metal clad buildings of Belshaw's smelter, with its efficient reverberatory furnace.

Cerro Gordo

The county road passes through the heart of town and immediately comes to the crest of the Inyos. The road crosses the summit and starts down Lucas Canyon, to eventually join the Saline Valley Road in Lee Flat. However, the Inyo Crest trail is one of two roads taking off to the left here; turn left, but take the lower of the two roads.

The Class II road doubles back above the townsite as it contours westward around Chinese Hill, where there are great views of the Sierra Crest and of the Yellow Grade far below. A BLM sign warns that there are steep grades ahead, and this road is for four-wheel drive vehicles only.

A saddle is reached at a point 1.3 miles from Cerro Gordo. To the left is a scenic viewpoint. To the right a trail heads north along the pipeline coming from Cerro Gordo Spring and Mexican Spring. Until Mortimer Belshaw built this pipeline in 1870, the lack of water had been a real problem in Cerro Gordo. A pump lifted the water 1,800 feet and brought it four miles to Cerro Gordo. This pipeline could deliver 1,300 gallons a day. If you walk along the pipeline for about a mile, you will come to one of the intermediate pumping stations (which can be seen from the road below).

Road along the crest of the High Inyos.

The jeep trail crosses the saddle and begins a mile-long descent into the valley below. Along the way, there are more grand views of the Mount Whitney area of the high Sierra. Going from south to north behind Lone Pine, the major peaks that stick out in front are 14,025' Mt. Langley and 12,944' Lone Pine

Peak. Sitting back a ways at the north end of the saw tooth ridge is 14,495' Mount Whitney. Also to the rear and just to the north of Mt. Whitney is 14,086' Mt. Russell. Farther yet to the north is 14,375' Mt. Williamson. You won't get a better view of these giants than from right here.

By backroad standards, the jeep trail going down into this valley is not bad. The same cannot be said for the climb out on the far side. Traction is poor and the grade is steep, but most four-wheelers should be able to make it. It is certainly Class III, with perhaps only a few short Class IV pitches. But once on top, there is a rolling open meadow area, and the road improves to Class II once again. For those who want to stretch their legs a bit, just a half-mile to the east 9,690' Pleasant Mountain is an easy climb. Views from its summit are quite nice, and the peak even has Bristlecone pines on the east side of its knife-edge ridge. These are certainly the oldest living species of tree. Some of these trees may have been growing here 2,000 years ago.

A short distance beyond the meadow on the jeep trail there is a prominent rock outcrop on the right. If you stop here for a moment, you can look down upon Mexican Spring and the Bonham Talc Mine beyond. The road, still Class II, continues northward along the gently rolling crest of the range.

Seven miles from Cerro Gordo, you will reach the salt tram summit station. The elevation here is 8,800 feet. The Saline Valley Salt Company took two years building the 13.4-mile long tramline. At the time, this wonder of engineering was the longest and highest tramline in the world. The tramline had nearly three hundred buckets with a capacity of about 750 pounds each. The tramline could move twenty tons of product per hour. It took two hours to move a bucket through the entire 27-mile circuit. Between 1913 and 1933 the tram carried salt products from the Saline Valley 7,500 feet up Daisy Canyon, over the Inyo Mountains, and 5,000 feet down the other side to a point on Highway 136 about a mile north west of Swansea. At its Owens Valley terminus, the salt was put into Southern Pacific narrow gauge gondola cars for further transport to market. The tram cable was moved by five large electric motors that powered each of its five sections. Here at the summit station, section three coming up from the Saline Valley ended, and section four began.

In October of 1967, I was up here with some backcountry companions, scouting the trail for *Inyo-Mono Jeep Trails*. It was a pleasant autumn day, and we climbed not only Pleasant Mountain, but New York Butte as well. We had not planned to camp this high, but the shortened day caught us here at the salt tram summit station just before dark. A cold west wind began after the sun went down. We feared that sparks from an open campfire might be blown quite some distance, so we loaded the bottom of a 55 gallon steel drum with dry, downed piñon branches and soon the drum was glowing cherry red. The side of our bodies facing the drum was toasty warm. The next morning we awoke to a light dusting of snow over our camp.

When I rechecked this trail in 1998, I was a little apprehensive about what I would find at the summit station some thirty years later. To my very pleasant surprise, I found the summit crossover structure had changed very little. In looking at those 1967 photos (see page 236), I noticed a few sheets of corrugated metal missing now, but otherwise the sturdy timbers holding the structure up have survived the time and elements well. Unfortunately, the same cannot be said of the house occupied by the tram tender. In 1967 the roof was still intact and somewhat functioning. Today the heavy snows of the last thirty years have caved in the roof and collapsed the deck.

Looking down Daisy Canyon from the salt tram Summit Station.

From the summit station the road, still Class II, continues northward along the ridge. A mile and a half beyond the salt tram, there is a short quarter mile section of Class III, but soon the road improves to Class II again. Ahead of you to the north along this same ridge is 10,668' New York Butte, and beyond that is 11,107' Keynot Peak.

At a point eleven miles from Cerro Gordo, a side road goes to the left, climbs a slight hill and then begins a 5,600-foot descent back down to Highway 136 on the eastern shore of Owens Lake. This is the so-called Swansea Grade (see Excursion #36) built in 1911 to aid in construction of the salt tram. By turning right here, you have an alternative route off this mountain, thus making a complete circle. If you choose to go down the Swansea Grade, however, expect several Class IV sections of road (two of which are Class V coming up from the other end).

Beyond this fork, the main road up the ridge continues northward, and soon forks again. The left fork soon dead-ends at the Burgess well and millsite. By staying to the right another 0.7 miles, the remains of the Burgess Mine are reached. The rocks all along this portion of the Inyo crest have been late Pennsylvanian and early Permian limestones of the Keeler Canyon Formation. Here at the Burgess Mine, however, the geology suddenly changes to younger marine sediments of Triassic age, coming in contact with metamorphosed Jurassic volcanic rocks. Quartz veins, possibly related to the Cretaceous granite just to the north, intruded along the contact zone of the two rock units. A smattering of gold was found here, along with other metals. Several thousand feet of tunnels were dug, but the deposit was relatively low grade, with the ore yielding only $20 to $40 per ton. The headframe over the main shaft has collapsed, but the remains of several buildings can still be seen in various stages of ruin. One must wonder if the investment was worth the effort.

The road continues 0.7 miles beyond the mine to a dead-end. There is a nice campsite here, at an elevation here is 9,800 feet. From the end of this jeep trail, 10,688' New York Butte is an easy cross-country walk of a mile. This is also the start of a century old, but little used pack trail into the isolated site of Beveridge, another old mining camp hidden deep in a canyon far to the north accessible only on foot. In the 1960s I took BLM State Director Russ Penny into Beveridge in an effort to obtain some sort of historic site protection. Not much happened at the time. Thirty years later, in 1989, a group of dedicated hikers started locating and mapping the old miners' trails around Beveridge. Although many had been overgrown and washed out, the group, nevertheless, identified more than fifty miles of these old trails. With the BLM's blessings they are hard at work restoring them. One result is the 40-mile long Lonesome Miner's Trail along the crest of the range.

Whether on foot or four-wheeling, I have always found my days in the Inyos very enjoyable.

The Saline Valley terminus of the salt tram

Old Olancha

This is where Olancha got its start, the site of the old Farley ore mill.

The old Walker house in Olancha was built in 1870. It survived the great earthquake of 1872 and went on to be used as a stage stop, a general store and a post office.
(County of Inyo, Eastern California Museum photo)

Dick's Café was a roadside landmark for travelers on Highway 395 for many years.
(Photo courtesy of Richard McCutchan)

Chapter VIII

Trails Out of Olancha

Today Olancha is a minor inconvenience where motorists on Highway 395 must slow down a little as the roadway temporarily goes from two lanes in each direction down to one. Truckers may stop here for a bite of lunch, and motorists heading east toward Death Valley top off their gas tank, but life is pretty quiet in little Olancha.

History did a poor job in recording the historic roots of Olancha. We do know that paleo-Indians have lived around the shores of Owens Lake for nearly ten thousand years, and a small band of Native Americans were living along the southwest shores on Owens Lake in the early 1860s. It was then that prospector Minnard H. Farley ventured into the Owens Valley while searching for the "Lost Gunsight Mine", discovered and lost a decade before. One source credits Farley with finding and naming Olancha Pass, a route between the Owens Valley and Monache Meadows on the South Fork of the Kern River. Presumably it was Farley who corrupted a Paiute word giving us the name Olancha. Yet another source indicates Olancha was named by Mexican miners from Cerro Gordo who named it for a small village in Central America.

The community of Olancha probably had its beginnings in 1861 when Farley found gold and silver in the volcanic rocks near Coso Hot Springs. He named a nearby high point "Silver Mountain" and called his mine the Olancha. Farley hand sorted his best ore, and packed it by mule six miles across rugged lava where it could be put into wagons and transported another twelve miles to Olancha Creek just west of Owens Lake. Here, in 1862, he built a stamp mill to crush the ore and a furnace to reduce it and smelt out the precious metal. It was the first ore mill to be built in the Owens Valley. He cut cottonwood and pine trees from the nearby canyons to the west and with the wood, fired a steam boiler that powered the mill. One source says the Farley Mill was burned in 1867 during an Indian uprising, but that seems doubtful because the Owens Valley Indian Wars were over by 1866.

By 1868 a seemingly endless string of Remi Nadeau's freight wagons were transporting the silver ingots from Cerro Gordo's mines south to Los Angeles. Their route was called "The Bullion Trail". All that freight went through Olancha, and here an overnight rest stop was established for the teamsters. Large corrals and a hay lot were built for their mules. A small country store also developed, followed soon after by a stage stop to accommodate Owens Valley and Cerro Gordo bound travelers. In 1870 there was but one stage a week, but within a year there were two stages a day going up the "Yellow Grade" to Cerro

Gordo. A post office was established in Olancha in September of 1870 (and it remains open to this day serving the area's couple of hundred residents). In 1875 Nadeau's teams began transporting two daily wagonloads of silver bullion from the Darwin Mines. That freight, too, went to Olancha before starting south.

In the fall of 1910 Olancha became a siding on the Southern Pacific Railroad's standard gauge line that extended from Mojave, north up the Owens Valley as far at Owenyo. Here it interfaced with their narrow gauge line that came down from Nevada. The S.P. abandoned their Owens Valley narrow gauge line in 1959, but standard gauge service to Lone Pine Station continued until 1982. It was not until 1998 that the rails through Olancha were removed and salvaged.

Olancha siding after the Southern Pacific pulled out its tracks.

It is claimed that these cottonwood trees along Highway 395 sprouted from fence posts driven into the ground 100 years ago.

38

Fossil Canyon

Primary Attraction:	A vertebrate fossil locality where one can camp in seclusion amid badlands containing the bones of prehistoric creatures.
Time Required:	This is an easy excursion of an hour or two out of Olancha.
Miles Involved:	From the intersection of Highway 395 and State Route 190 at the south end of Olancha, it is 4.7 miles to the turnoff at Dirty Socks Spring, and from there it is but another three miles into Fossil Canyon.
Degree of Difficulty:	The route is normally only Class II if the sand in the wash is moist or firm. It the sand is dry and chewed up by the passing of other vehicles, then four-wheel drive might be required. Even under those conditions, it is an easy Class III, providing you maintain your forward momentum, and do not become bogged down.
Remarks:	This trail is usually open throughout the year.

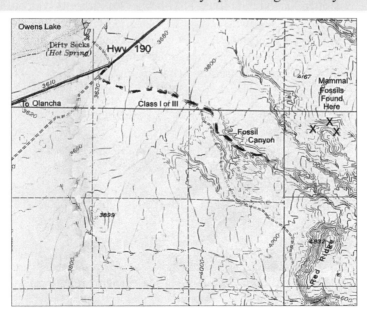

The name *Fossil Canyon* does not appear on any map. This is because it has no official name. It was I, not the U.S.G.S. Board of Geographic Names, who named it. If you want to call it something else, be my guest. Nevertheless, it is a good name that aptly describes local geologic features. The locality is south of Lone Pine, at the north end of the Coso Range.

Fossils are not particularly rare in Inyo County; the limestones of the White and Inyo Mountains are full of them. They are mostly corals, trilobites, and other small creatures that once lived in the sea. Vertebrate fossils, the remains of larger animals having a backbone, are much more rare, particularly those which lived on land. These animals are less likely to become preserved as fossils. Nevertheless, there is one place in Inyo County where vertebrate animals have been found in some numbers. The site is not accessible by conventional vehicles.

From the service station in downtown Olancha, go south on Highway 395 for a quarter of a mile. Turn east onto State Highway 190 and note your odometer reading. Soon, on the right, you will pass the Olancha Dunes, a small area of sand dunes, which have formed since the Owens Lake dried up after the last Ice Age. The BLM has designated these dunes as an *open area* where off highway vehicles can roam freely.

At a point 4.7 miles from Highway 395, you will come to a gravel road on your left, leading to Dirty Socks Spring just a quarter of a mile off the highway to the north. It is not a spring at all, but an artesian well that was drilled in 1917 to serve a nearby soda plant. When warm water was struck at 1,200 feet, a health spa was envisioned. A concrete lined circular pool with steps was built, as were changing rooms and picnic facilities. The structures are now gone, the water has cooled, and only the circular bath remains. The dark murky algae-filled water appears to be so foul that nobody swims there any more, although the site does serve as a makeshift campground for people passing through.

Dirty Socks Springs circa 1968. The changing rooms and
other structures have subsequently all been torn down.

The road to Fossil Canyon turns south off Highway 190 opposite the access road to Dirty Socks Spring. If you are heading east as you would be coming from Olancha, turn right, opposite the road to Dirty Socks Spring. The dirt roadway immediately circles to the west. A hundred yards or so from the pavement, turn left crossing over a berm built to protect the highway from flash floods. A well-defined Class I desert road heads south 0.4 miles where it forks. Keep right and you will soon enter a wide desert wash. Here the tracks may disappear altogether, or there may be tracks everywhere. It doesn't matter. Simply engage your four-wheel drive, and head up the wash. **This sand can be treacherous at times, so keep your speed up.**

Watch the soft sand!

Within a mile you will enter the hills and the sides of the wash will begin to get higher and close in on you. These soft sediments are part of the Coso Formation laid down in the waning years of the Pliocene and early stage of the Pleistocene.

At a point 1.6 miles from the highway, the wash forks; keep left in the main branch. The softly eroded sediments on either side of the wash take on a badlands appearance. Soon the wash narrows and the cliffs on either side get higher. I can recall on one occasion in the spring when Loris and I passed this way, stirring up an enormous barn owl with its pure white underside and thirty-inch wingspan. These magnificent creatures of the night like to nest in the cliff-side cavities found here.

Fossil Canyon

As you proceed up the canyon, the sediments change from a dull brown to colorful bands of pink, red and tan sandstone. Then three miles in from the highway the canyon suddenly comes to a dead-end. The rocks here are the very old metamorphic core of the Coso Range. Resting on top of them are the three million-year-old sandstones and siltstones of late Pliocene age. When you place your hand on the contact between these two rock formations, there is a missing span of a hundred million years or more.

In order to find fossils of the vertebrate animals that walked on this land in the late Pliocene, you are going to have to leave your car and wander through these badlands on foot. That is what Cal-Tech students did in the 1930s, when many interesting finds were first made.

The vertebrate fossils found here are mostly mammals. They include prehistoric meadow mice, rabbits, hyena-like dogs, peccaries, long-tined pronghorns, primitive horses, and yes, even mastodons. These animals roamed the region during the beginning of the Plio-Pleistocene Ice Age, a million years ago. At that time the Sierra Nevada Mountains had been formed and were in place, but much of what is desert now was savanna or grasslands then. Paleontologists know this from the high-crowned teeth in the fossilized remains. These teeth are most often found in grazing type animals. The colorful rock formations at Red Rock Canyon, some sixty miles to the south, were formed at the same time and under the same geologic circumstances as this stratum. The best fossils were found in the soft material lying just below a hard arkostic sandstone. Do not expect to encounter a twenty-foot museum piece. If you are lucky you may see a few clusters of tiny bones. You never know, however; at least one large jawbone was found here, complete with million year old molars.

Although the Maturango Museum publishes a small book that seems to encourage vertebrate fossil collecting, it is clearly unlawful to do so without a permit. Because vertebrate fossils are of great scientific importance, normally these permits are only issued to scientists and institutions. For further information contact the Ridgecrest BLM office.

A mammoth molar

39

Centennial Canyon

Primary Attraction:	Centennial Canyon makes a pleasant outing on a warm weekend in spring, when the wildflowers are beginning to appear.
Time Required:	This is a half-day's outing from Olancha, a full day if you go on to explore Black Rock Canyon and search for petroglyphs.
Distance Involved:	The total distance from Olancha to the road's end at Centennial Spring is 23 miles.
Degree of Difficulty:	Usually open all year, the roads described in this outing are generally no more difficult than Class II.

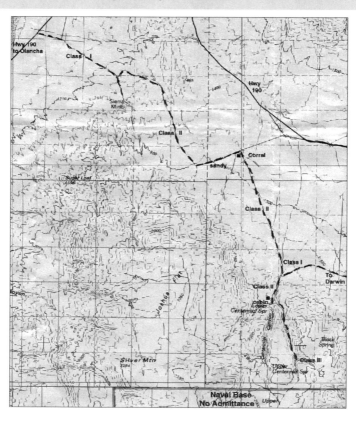

Centennial Canyon is a north-south trending gash at the north end of the Coso Range. From Olancha, take State Route 190 east as if you were going to Death Valley. Note your odometer reading as you leave Olancha. At a point 9.8 miles east of Highway 395, look for a large earthen berm on the right side of the road. Turn right here, onto the Class II road on the west side of this berm. (If you come to milepost 20.00 you have gone about one hundred yards too far.) This was once a wide graded road used daily by heavily laden ore trucks; however, since the mine closed, the road has deteriorated to Class II. It is now BLM Road SE9.

Follow the road up the alluvial fan for 2.5 miles. Here a side road goes off to the left. This is the way to Centennial Canyon, however you may wish to continue straight ahead for another half mile to take a look at was once the Calearth Mine. Some maps show this as the Sierra Talc Mine, but this is incorrect. While it is true that in the late 1940s and early 1950s, the Sierra Talc and Clay Company leased the mine, the commodity produced here was not talc, but "Fullers Earth". And just what is Fullers Earth you ask? It is special kind of clay very useful for filtration and decolorization purposes.

Lying beneath a layer of basalt lava is a clay bed sixteen feet thick, which contained the desired clay. The deposit was reached by way of a 900-foot long tunnel. Large chambers were created when the clay was removed by the use of large pneumatic clay digging tools. The roofs of these rooms were supported by 30 and 40-foot pillars of unremoved material. The ore was trucked to Olancha, where it was shipped by rail to Los Angeles for grinding and further processing. Shortly before the mine closed, the supporting pillars themselves were removed, a very dangerous job! **It is equally dangerous to enter any old mine. Stay out of all underground workings!**

When you have had your fill of the Calearth Mine, return to the side road which was passed 2.5 miles in from Highway 190. Reset your trip odometer to zero here, or otherwise note your mileage. You will now leave the Calearth Mine Road by turning eastward onto the BLM Class II Road SE9. It passes through a gap in the hills and turns more to the south, as it gradually climbs up the bajada. At a point four miles from the Calearth Mine Road, it suddenly makes a sharp turn to the left. An area of soft sand is encountered. **Maintain forward momentum by keeping your speed up.** You should be able to get through without the need to engage your four-wheel drive.

A mile and a quarter beyond the sharp turn, a corral is reached. Here several roads go off to the right. Choose the road that goes straight through the gates on either side of the corral. The road forks a tenth of a mile beyond the corral, with both forks heading to the southeast. The left fork eventually goes to Black Rock Canyon; for Centennial Canyon go to the right.

Still Class II, the road crosses Lower Centennial Flat as it slowly climbs the bajada to the south. Soon there is a scattering of Joshua trees, and as you climb higher they become more numerous. The Joshua tree is considered to be an *indicator plant* of the Mojave Desert.

The lonely road across Lower Centennial Flat

If you come this way in the spring, you should be treated to a wide variety of wildflowers, from the tall and stately Prince's plume, to the lowly phlox hugging the sandy ground. If you catch the time just right, the attractive yellow blossoms of the Gold cholla invite photography. About four miles south of the corral, some prospecting pits can be seen on the right. The commodity being sought here was industrial quality clay.

The geology of the Coso Range is varied and in places, quite complex. This range does not have the great sections of Paleozoic sediments as does its neighbor the Inyo Range just to the north. At the core of the Cosos are igneous rocks whose ages are both intermediate as well as recent. Centennial Canyon is a good place to see them both. The mountains to the west are igneous crystalline rocks like granite. They are probably related to the Sierra Nevada plutonic rocks pushed up from the depths of the earth in Cretaceous times. The dark rocks to the south are also igneous, but they were formed in relatively recent times and are volcanic in origin. The two contrasting rock types come together near the mouth of Centennial Canyon just ahead.

A quarter of a mile more, just before entering Centennial Canyon, a Class I road comes in from the left rear. Remember this intersection; we will be coming back here. For the moment however, continue south entering Centennial Canyon. You are in the canyon no more than a quarter of a mile when the road forks.

At one time the left fork went through this fork of the canyon to Upper Centennial Flat, where it connected with a high standard road built by the Navy during World War II as a part of their Naval Ordinance Test Station (NOTS). The road has long ago washed out, and the base, now called the Naval Air Weapons Station (NAWS), generally remains off limits to the public. The Class II and III road up this left fork now comes to a dead-end in 2½ miles.

The right fork is more interesting. It continues on 0.6 miles, where it too abruptly ends above the wash. Below is Lower Centennial Spring, a small but reliable source of water that quail and other local wildlife depend on. On the bench, above the wash, sits an old cabin of questionable parentage. It is reasonably weather tight, so if you are camping, the weather is nasty, and you don't mind the pitter-patter of little feet during the night, you might consider moving in. The small cabin will provide shelter from the elements. It is interesting to read some of the entries in the visitor log, some of which go back a number of years. If you do choose to stay here, leave the place a little cleaner than you found it, and if you use any of the cached food, leave more to replace it.

Two room cabin at Lower Centennial Spring

Upon leaving Lower Centennial Springs, backtrack the road you came in on for nearly a mile and then take the right fork. (There are actually two right forks at this intersection: a Class I road that goes northeast straight across the valley, and a Class II road that goes in a more easterly direction. It is the latter one that we will follow. After 1.5 miles a "T" intersection is reached. The road to the right goes only to a clay pit; go left. After a tenth of a mile, stay right at the fork. In another tenth of a mile, go straight ahead through the crossroads. In yet another 0.3 miles BLM Road SE4 comes in from the left rear; turn right onto SE4. After following it only 0.2 miles however, a side road right goes south 1.4 miles into Black Rock Canyon where it abruptly ends. Just up the canyon is Black Springs, a series of year-around seeps that are often fouled by range cattle.

If you choose not to see Black Rock Canyon, continue traveling to the southeast on SE4. After 1½ miles, take the road which goes east through a gap in the hills. Eventually you will come out in Darwin, where a paved road takes you back to the north to rejoin Highway 190.

Darwin has seen better days.

40

The Santa Rosa Mine

Primary Attraction:	An old lead mine, in a most unlikely place, where rock hounds can scour the tailings dumps for various minerals.
Time Required:	This is a half-day's outing from Olancha, is usually open throughout the year.
Distance Involved:	The total distance from Olancha to the road's end at the Santa Rosa Mine is 34 miles.
Degree of Difficulty:	In January 1998, El Niño rains washed the road out in many places, making the last four miles Class III. By June, the road was back to Class I again. Since then it has deteriorated again, but it should be no worse than Class II.

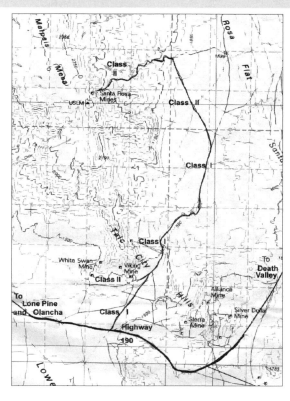

A lava-covered mesa is about the last place that one would expect to find precious metals, for lava flows of basalt seldom contain mineral wealth. Perhaps this explains why, during the rich strikes at Darwin just a dozen miles to the south, prospectors walked right on by Malpais Mesa at the southern tip of the Inyo Mountains. It would not be until 35 years later that someone would walk up to the base of the mesa to discover that under the lava there was a totally different stratum, which, from a distance, looked identical to the basalt covering it. These hidden layers of limestone would ultimately yield millions of dollars in various metals.

To find the Santa Rosa Mine from Olancha, go east on State Route 190 for 25 miles. Here, on Lower Centennial Flat, you will find a once-paved county road going off to the left in a northerly direction. Turn left here noting your odometer reading as you do so.

After slightly more than a mile, a Class II side road left goes over to the abandoned buildings of the Viking Mine Camp, less than a mile to the northwest. The White Swan Talc Mine is another mile around the hill to the west. Both of these mines tapped into small deposits of steatite grade talc and were first developed between the two World Wars. At the Viking Mine, talc was extracted from a one hundred-foot deep shaft that went to a shear zone between the Eureka quartzite and the Ely Springs dolomite; both are of Ordovician age. Shallow shafts at the White Swan Mine produced five hundred to seven hundred tons from the same geologic formation.

White Swan Talc Mine Camp in 1998.

Continue north on the county road winding through a shallow canyon to come out onto the broad expanse of Santa Rosa Flat, with its forest of scattered Joshua trees. At a point 5.8 miles from State Route 190, look for a once oiled road going off to the west; turn left here. After two and a half miles the road enters a canyon eroded out of the black basalt lava, and makes a sharp turn to the left. The Class II road continues climbing to the west another 2.3 miles, where it ends in a basin beneath Malpais Mesa.

In 1910 Ignacio Ruiz, a part time prospector from Lone Pine, wandered up this canyon to discover that the base of this mountain was dolomite, not lava, a fact that could not be determined by looking from afar. Although he did not know it at the time, this stratum was the Owens Valley Formation, deposited in the bottom of a Permian sea. Millions of years after these beds were formed, hot mineral-bearing solutions from deep within the earth squeezed upward to invade the limestone. As a part of this process, the limestone was changed to dolomite.

Ignacio could not believe his eyes. Before him, the talus, which had rolled off the hillside above, contained masses of heavy dark minerals. Specimens that he took back to nearby Darwin to be assayed revealed lead with traces of silver and zinc. In the following forty years the location Ignacio discovered would turn out to be the Santa Rosa Mine. The mine developed several different vein systems: the Sanger, the Jack Gunn, and the Hesson. Production from those veins would ultimately make the Santa Rosa Mine the eighth largest producer of lead in the State of California. The raw ore was transported to Darwin for milling and smelting.

In the 1950s there were still three tramways that brought ore down from the upper workings to ore bunkers at the base of the mountain. At that time there were eight buildings at the mine camp. Alas, none of these structures remains today.

During its heyday in the 1940s and early 1950s, the mine's 4,000 feet of tunnels turned out twelve million pounds of lead, nearly a half a million pounds of both copper and silver, some zinc, and even 478 ounces of gold. A 1953 state report on the mine suggests that the outlook for future mining was good. That optimism may have been overstated, as mining operations ceased in 1955.

For those who wish to explore, a Class III road goes steeply up a side canyon to the right to the Upper Sanger shaft. Rock hounds may wish to check out the lowest of the several tailings dumps. Here can be found specimens of a whole suite of copper minerals, including the very pretty malachite and azurite. Iron pyrite, with its brassy appearance and square crystals, can also be found. **Warning: Stay out of the underground workings. They are no longer safe to enter!**

The Santa Rosa Mine as it looked in the 1930s. The site was
so photogenic, that Hollywood filmed a motion picture here.
(County of Inyo, Eastern California Museum photo)

Appendix A

A Glossary of Geologic and Mining
Terms Used in the Text

Adit: a horizontal tunnel.

Alluvial Fan: the cone-shaped deposit of sand and gravel washed out of a canyon.

Andesite: a brown, reddish, or gray volcanic rock with a mineral composition equivalent to granite.

Arkostic: having a significant amount of feldspar.

Ash: very fine rock particles thrown out by explosive volcanic eruptions.

Auriferous: gold bearing, such as sand or gravel containing gold.

Bajada: the slope of sand and gravel where two or more alluvial fans have coalesced.

Basalt: a hard black volcanic rock, sometimes containing gas bubble holes.

Batholith: a large mass of igneous rocks still deep within the earth.

Bedrock: solid rock exposed at the surface of the ground.

Bunker: a hopper-like structure in which ore is stored while awaiting transport or processing.

Caldera: a large circular volcanic crater with the diameter much greater than the depth.

Chert: a rock or mineral composed largely of fine grained silica.

Cinder Cone: the accumulated pile of ash and cinder at the mouth of a volcano.

Collar: the rim surrounding the top of a shaft.

Conglomerate: a sedimentary formation of various rocks having a wide variety of particle size and shape.

Cyanide Process: a gold ore-milling process, wherein cyanide chemically bonds with gold.

Dike: an intrusion of molten igneous rock into a crack or joint.

Dolomite: a metamorphic form of limestone, containing magnesium carbonate and calcium carbonate.

Drilling Mud: a wet mixture of heavy barite injected down a drill hole to help float drilling waste out of the hole.

Epoch: a unit of geologic time within a "period" (example: the Pleistocene epoch of the Quaternary period of the Cenozoic era).

Era: the largest subdivision of geologic time (example: Mesozoic era).

Fanglomerate: conglomerate deposited and cemented together, as in an alluvial fan.

Fault: a crack in the earth's surface with one side moving in relation to the other side.

Feldspar: a very common rock-forming mineral containing silica and aluminum oxides.

Float: pieces of minerals which have naturally weathered out of a vein.

Flotation Process: a milling process where a foam of various chemicals physically attaches to metallic ores making them easy to recover.

Galena: lead sulfide, a common ore of lead.

Garnetized: the garnets are produced as part of the metamorphic process.

Glaciation: the formation and movement of ice masses.

Glory hole: a pocket of very rich ore.

Gneiss: a very hard, often banded metamorphic rock.

Granite: a coarse-grained igneous rock containing quartz, feldspar and mica as the principal minerals.

Granodiorite: an igneous rock of similar composition as granite, except it contains more plagioclase feldspar than granite.

Headframe: the structure over a shaft, which supports a pulley, used to hoist ore buckets.

Hornfels: a dense metamorphic rock, often formed when slate (another metamorphic rock) has come in contact with hot igneous rocks such as granite.

Ice Age: a long period of cold climate, where snowfalls on the land accumulated vast areas of ice because precipitation exceeded melting. Ice ages have occurred as early as the Precambrian and as recently as the Holocene epochs.

Igneous rock: molten rocks formed deep within the earth that have been forced to the surface.

Lava: magma that comes to the earth's surface by volcanic action.

Lens: an orebody which is thick in the middle and thin at the edges.

Limestone: sedimentary rock of calcium carbonate formed in the sea bottom by the accumulation of shells and other organisms.

Lode: a vein or deposit of valuable minerals in solid rock.

Magma: deep-seated molten rock.

Marine Terrace: a flattened natural terrace on a hillside originally formed by wave action on the shoreline.

Metamorphism: the alteration of older igneous or sedimentary rocks by great heat, pressure, or chemical changes, resulting in the changing of the original rock into something different.

Metasediments: sedimentary rocks that have been subjected to great heat and pressure causing them to become metamorphic rocks. Their original sedimentary composition may no longer be recognized.

Mine: a place where a mineral commodity has been extracted and processed for its economic value.

Mining claim: The mining law of 1872 permits a person who finds valuable minerals on Federal land to claim the right to mine it. Each lode claim measures 1500 feet long by 600 feet wide. Each placer claim covers twenty acres. Multiple claims are permitted. Improvements must be performed annually. In recent years more restrictions have been imposed on the staking of mining claims.

Monzonite: a granite-like igneous rock rich in both plagioclase and orthoclase feldspar and ferro-magnesium minerals, but having little quartz.

Mudstone: a sedimentary rock made up of layers of compacted mud.

Obsidian: a black volcanic glass that has formed by very rapid cooling of volcanic lava.

Orebody: a sufficient concentration of valuable minerals to warrant the expense of mining.

Patented Claim: a mining claim of sufficient value that a legal process has been gone through which gives the owner not only mineral rights, but ownership of the land with all rights of use.

Period: a unit of geologic time within an era (example: Jurassic period of the Mesozoic era).

Placer: sand or gravel deposits containing gold or other valuable minerals.

Playa: a flat dry lakebed in an enclosed desert basin.

Pluvial: caused by the action of heavy rains.

Pluton: a mass of deep-seated igneous rock that intrudes the crust of the earth and slowly cools.

Prospect: a place where an economically valuable mineral has been found, and explored for; however, no mining has (yet) taken place.

Pumice: a light-colored, lightweight frothy volcanic rock, often having enough air holes in it to permit it to float.

Pyroclastic: rock fragments formed by a volcanic explosion.

Quartz: a common rock-forming mineral of silicon dioxide often found in a crystalline state.

Quartzite: a metamorphic form of sandstone.

Quartz monzonite: a granite-like rock, except it is rich in quartz as well as the feldspars.

Raise: a mine shaft driven upward from within a tunnel.

Rhyolite: a volcanic rock similar in mineral composition to granite.

Richter scale: a system for measuring the intensity of earthquakes. It is a log-rhythmic scale, meaning each numerical increase represents a tenfold increase of intensity.

Sandstone: a sedimentary rock made up of layers of compacted and cemented sand.

Schist: a metamorphic rock, rich in mica that easily splits into plates or flakes.

Sedimentary rock: rocks formed by the accumulation of rock or organic material in the sea bottom or on top of the ground.

Shaft: an excavation of limited area compared to its depth, dug to access an orebody.

Shale: layers of silt or clay which have compacted into rock.

Shear zone: a place of massive rock moment where the rocks are fractured and crushed.

Siltsone: a very fine grained sedimentary rock derived from layers of compacted silt.

Stope: an underground opening above a tunnel from which ore is extracted.

Sulfide: the presence of sulfur, chemically bonded with other (metallic) minerals.

Tactite: a contact metamorphosed calcareous rock.

Tailings: A pile of waste rock at a mine, tunnel, or shaft. May also be finely ground ore left over after the milling process has extracted the valuable minerals.

Talc: a very soft, white mineral found in zones of some metamorphic rock.

Trilobite: a primitive and long extinct marine animal that lived on the bottom of Paleozoic seas.

Tufa: a chemical sedimentary rock of calcium or silica minerals deposited from solution in a lake.

Tuff: a rock formed from compacted volcanic ash.

Vein: any mineral deposit that has filled a fissure or fracture. A relatively few contain valuable minerals, but most do not.

Volcanic ash: fine rock material ejected from a volcano.

Wave cut bench: see Marine Terrace.

Winze: a shaft driven within a mine tunnel to connect one level with a lower level.

Appendix B

Geologic Time Chart

Era	Period	Epoch	Million years ago
Cenozoic	Quaternary	Holocene Pleistocene	2-3
			12
	Tertiary	Pliocene Miocene Oligocene Eocene Paleocene	26 37-38 53-54
			65
Mesozoic	Cretaceous		136
	Jurassic		190-195
	Triassic		
			225
Paleozoic	Permian		280
	Pennsylvanian		310
	Mississippian		345
	Devonian		395
	Silurian		435
	Ordovician		500
	Cambrian		570
Proterozoic	Keweenawan		
	Huronian		1,000
Archeozoic	Timiskaming		
	Keewatin		1,800

Appendix C

Collecting and Using Piñon Nuts

Piñon nuts are very nutritious. They were a dietary staple of the Paiute as well as other Native American cultures throughout the Southwest. The Indians ate them both raw and roasted, and they often mixed ground piñon nuts with animal fat to make a calorie rich pemmican that was nourishing and easy to carry on long trips.

There are a dozen different species of piñon pine, but only four of them are found in North America north of the U.S.-Mexico border, and of those only one, the single leaf piñon, *Pinus monophylla,* is found in California. Identifying a piñon pine should be no problem to most people. It is the only pine tree in the Sierra Nevada that has a single needle attached to each branchlet. The other pines have their needles in two, threes, or fives.

Like wild berries, the cones from the piñon pine can be collected in our national forests without any permit, or other bureaucratic red tape, provided they are for home consumption and are not sold commercially.

September is the month to go "nutting", although in years of abundant cones October may be good, too. If you start in early September, the cones may not have opened yet, but do not let that deter you. Simply pick the cones off the tree and place them in a bag to take home. A long stick or pole with a hook on the end may help you pick cones from the higher branches that are beyond reach. If the cones are still green, they take more force to twist them off the branches than cones that have ripened and opened. If the cones have already opened, pick the cone apart and let the nuts drop into a pail or pot. It is also OK to pick the fresh dark brown seeds off the ground. If you don't get them, the rodents and Piñon Jays will.

The cones are sticky with pitch, and soon your hands and fingers will be also. I have found that most brands of mechanic's waterless hand soap quickly and easily cut the pitch.

Once you bring your hoard home, the real work begins. If the cones are green and have not yet opened, bring them indoors, spread them out on a tarp, and let them dry out. Depending on the room temperature, the cones will open in a week or two. Then shake the seeds out of the cones onto an opened newspaper. If stored in a dry, well-ventilated environment, the seeds can be stored for a year or more. Do not store them in a sealed container.

The next step is a bit of a bore, cracking the seed shell to get to the meaty nut inside. One method is to spread a light layer over a dishtowel or paper towel, put another towel over them, and then lightly roll a rolling pin over the top towel. Use just enough pressure to crack the shells without crushing the seeds inside. Another more tedious method is to use Vise Grips with the setting adjusted to the size that will just crack the shell.

Once you have the actual nuts separated from the shells, the next step is to roast them. We use a large cast iron skillet over our wood stove, but any a low heat source will do. They can also be put on a large cookie sheet and placed in the oven on low heat. Roasting time and temperature will depend on the residual moisture content of the nuts. If you are using an oven, try one hour at 200-225 degrees, but check them every twenty minutes. Once roasted, the nuts can be stored for months in sealed containers.

Now that you have your nuts, what to do with them? Unfortunately, the writers of most cookbooks would not know a pine nut if one suddenly appeared on their plate. Your imagination is likely to be more useful than most cookbooks. Here are some ideas:

Baked Goods: Add roasted piñon nuts to any variety of breads, cakes, and cookies, just as you might use walnuts. They are also yummy in fudge.

Beverages: I found a café in Albuquerque that adds finely ground piñon nuts to their coffee. I tried it at home and achieved the same "woodsy" flavor.

Cereals: Granola, museli, and any number of other breakfast cereals can benefit from a light sprinkling of piñon nuts.

Fish Dishes: Lightly sprinkle piñon nuts over fish. They particularly enhance the flavor of baked bass and fried trout.

Meat Dishes: Do you like pepper steak? Try lightly broken piñon nuts rather than peppercorns, or add them to meatloaf. Piñon nuts are also good on roasts.

Pasta: The Italians use Piñon nuts (Pignolata) mixed with basil leaves, garlic cloves and Parmesan cheese to make a tasty pesto.

Pilaf: Simply add your roasted piñon nuts to the rice.

Salads: Sprinkle the roasted nuts over a green salad in the same way that you might use sunflower seeds. In a Waldorf salad, use them in place of walnuts.

Appendix D

Equipment Checklist for Backcountry Vehicles

Documents

Current vehicle registration (required by State law)
Proof of current liability insurance (required by State law)
Campfire permit (free, obtain one annually)
Map of the specific area you are in, the more detailed the better.
Shop manual for vehicle involved

Personal Safety & Comfort Items

First Aid Kit (the bigger the better)
Extra medications used by anyone present
Water, 2 gallons per person
Pot, cooking, small
Canteens, with carrying case, 2 minimum
Lightweight day or fanny pack
Extra food (sealed MREs are good for emergencies)
Warm clothing, jacket & hat for all
Compact disposable space blanket, 1 per person
Work gloves, 1 pair minimum
Flashlights, 2 minimum, with fresh or extra batteries
Citizens Band radio, or better yet, 2 meter radio transceiver
Compass
Swiss Army knife or equivalent (with can opener)
Fire extinguisher
Plastic tube tent
Matches (in waterproof container)
Whistle, shrill, emergency signaling
Toilet paper roll
Female sanitary pads, 2 each (can double as trauma dressings)
Notebook, small, with lead pencil
Highway flares, 2 minimum
Sun screen
Insect repellent
Poncho, 1 minimum
Tarp, plastic, small or medium size
Bucket, canvas, collapsible, (a required item in some National Forests)

Extrication Equipment

Shovel, folding GI type, or preferably long handle   (required item in some
    National Forests)
Nylon tow strap
Hi-Lift jack
Hydraulic jack, 4 ton
Come-along, 4 ton rating (minimum)
Tire chains (may be a seasonal item)
Hatchet, or preferably, full size ax
Saw, small

Automotive Tools

Socket set, SAE & metric, recommended
Spark plug socket for above
Open end wrench set, SAE & metric
Crescent wrench set, 3 sizes recommended
Screwdriver set, slot and Phillips
Pliers assortment
Wire cutters
Hammer
Battery post & terminal cleaner
Battery jumper cables
Hack saw with extra blades
Lug wrench
Mini-air compressor
Small funnel
Tire pressure gauge

Spare Automotive Parts

Spark plugs, 2 minimum
Spark plug wire material
Coil
Points set with condenser
Brake fluid, 1 pint
Power steering fluid, 1 pint
Motor Oil, 2 quarts minimum
ATF Fluid, 1 quart

Oil filter
Fuse assortment
Fan belts of appropriate sizes
Tire boot & inner tube
Hose bandage tape

Field Expedient Supplies

Duct tape, 1 roll
Electrical tape, 1 roll
Bailing wire, 1 roll
Electrical wire, 1 small roll, 16 gauge
Sealant, radiator (Stop Leak)
Gasket sealant
Tube, siphon, 5' minimum
Cord, nylon, 50' minimum
Hand Cleaner (waterless)
Paper towel roll
Plastic trash sack

Optional Non-Essential Items which are nice to have along

Camera with film
Binoculars
Glass cleaner
Bar soap, small
Plastic bags, small, resealable
NOAA Weather radio receiver
GPS receiver
Spare fuel container with spout
Cellular telephone
Family radio service transceivers, one pair

Appendix E
Some Useful Addresses and Telephone Numbers

California Highway Conditions: 1-800-427-ROAD
Nevada Highway Conditions: (775) 793-1313

Trails Out of Bridgeport

Bridgeport Ranger Station
Humboldt-Toiyabe National Forest
HCR-1, Box 1000 (just south of town on Hwy 395)
Bridgeport CA 93517
(760) 932-7070

Bridgeport Chamber of Commerce
P.O. Box 541
Bridgeport CA 93517
(760) 932-7500

Bodie State Historic Park
P. O. Box 515
Bridgeport, CA 93517
(760) 647-6445

Trails Out of Lee Vining

Mono Basin Visitor Center
Inyo National Forest
Highway 395 North
Lee Vining CA 93541
(760) 647-3044

Mono Basin Historical Society
(Schoolhouse Museum)
1st Street at Mattly Ave
P.O. Box 31
Lee Vining CA 93541
(760) 647-6461

Trails Out of Lee Vining continued

Mono Lake Committee
Highway 395 at 3rd Street
Lee Vining CA 93541
(760) 647-6595

Trails Out of Mammoth Lakes

Inyo National Forest
Mammoth Ranger Station and Visitor Center
State Route 203
P.O. Box 148
Mammoth Lakes CA 93546
(760) 924-5500

Trails Out of Bishop

White Mountain Ranger Station
Inyo National Forest
798 No. Main Street
Bishop CA 93514
(760) 873-2500

Bishop Field Office
Bureau of Land Management
785 No. Main Street, Suite "E"
Bishop CA 93514
(760) 872-4881

Laws Railroad Museum
Silver Canyon Road east of Hwy 6
P.O. Box 363
Bishop CA 93514
(760) 873-5950

Bishop Area Chamber of Commerce
690 No. Main Street
Bishop CA 93514
(760) 873-8405

Trails Out of Big Pine

Big Pine Chamber of Commerce
126 So. Main Street
Big Pine CA 93513
(760) 938-2114

Trails Out of Independence

Eastern California Museum
155 Grant Street
Independence CA 93526
(760) 878-0258

Independence Chamber of Commerce
P.O. Box 397
Independence CA 93526
(760) 878-0084

Trails Out of Lone Pine and Olancha

Lone Pine Ranger Station
Inyo National Forest
501 So. Main Street
P.O. Box 8
Lone Pine CA 93545
(760) 876-6200

Inter Agency Visitor Center
Highway 395 and State Route 136
P.O. Drawer "R"
Lone Pine CA 93545
(760) 876-6222

Bureau of Land Management
Ridgecrest Field Office
300 So. Richmond Road
Ridgecrest, CA 93555
(760) 384-5400

Lone Pine Chamber of Commerce
126 So. Main Street
P.O. Box 749
Lone Pine CA 93545
(760) 876-4444 or (877) 253-8981

276

References

Anon, "Geologic Map of California", *Death Valley Sheet*, San Francisco CA: California Division of Mines, 1958.

_____,"Geologic Map of California", *Mariposa Sheet*, Sacramento CA: California Division of Mines and Geology, 1967.

_____,*Romantic Heritage of Inyo-Mono*, California Interstate Telephone Company, 1966.

_____, "California Fossil Discovery Reveals New Species of Camel", *California Geology*, Sacramento CA: California Division of Mines and Geology, January and February 2000.

_____,*Prevent Hantavirus Pulmonary Syndrome*, Atlanta GA: Center For Disease Control, U.S. Dept. of Health and Human Services, 1994.

Alt, David, Donald W. Hyndman, *Roadside Geology of Northern and Central California*, Missoula MT: Mountain Press Publishing Co., 2000.

Antevs, Ernst, *Rainfall and Tree Growth in the Great Basin*, New York NY: American Geographical Society Special Publication No. 21, published jointly with the Carnegie Institution of Washington DC, 1938.

Bagley, Mark, and Daniel Pritchett, *Summer 1998 Botanical Survey for the Proposed Combined University Array Upper Harkless Flat Project, Inyo County CA*, Bishop CA: Team Engineering & Management Consultants, May 1999.

Bailey, Edgar H., Editor, *Geology of Northern California*, San Francisco CA: California Division of Mines and Geology Bulletin 190, 1996.

Bailey, Roy A., *Geologic Map of the Long Valley Caldera, Mono-Inyo Craters Volcanic Chain and Vicinity, Eastern California*, Washington DC: U.S. Geological Survey Map I-1933, 1989.

Bateman, Paul C., *Economic Geology of the Bishop Tungsten District*, San Francisco CA: California Division of Mines and Geology, 1956.

Billeb, Emil W., *Mining Camp Days*, Berkeley CA: Howell-North Books, 1968.

Blanc, Robert P. and George B. Cleveland, "Pleistocene Lakes of Southern California" (Parts I & II) *Mineral Information Service*, San Francisco CA: California Division of Mines, April and May 1961.

Cain, Ella M., *The Story of Early Mono County*, San Francisco CA: Fearon Publishers, 1961.

Carlson, Helen S., *Nevada Place Names*, Reno NV: University of Nevada Press, 1974.

Chalfant, W.A., *The Story of Inyo*, Bishop CA: Pinon Book Store, 1933.

_____, *Gold, Guns, & Ghost Towns*, Stanford CA: Stanford University Press, 1947.

Chartkoff, Joseph L. and Kerry Kona Chartkoff, *The Archaeology of California*, Stanford CA: Stanford University Press, 1984.

Clark, Lew and Ginny, *High Mountains and Deep Valleys,* San Luis Obispo CA: Western Trails Publications, 1978.

Clark, William B., *Gold Districts of California,* San Francisco CA: California Division of Mines and Geology Bulletin 193, 1970.

Clarke, Charlotte Bringle, *Edible and Useful Plants of California,* Berkeley, London, Los Angeles: University of California Press, 1977.

Curry, Robert R., "California's Deadman Pass Glacial Till is Also Nearly 3,000,000 Years Old", *Mineral Information Service*, San Francisco CA: California Division of Mines, October 1968.

Dedecker, Mary, *Mines of the High Sierra*, Glendale CA: La Siesta Press, 1966.

_____, *White Smith's Fabulous Salt Tram,* Death Valley CA: Death Valley 49ers Keepsake No. 33, 1993.

Diggles, Michael F., "Geology and Mineral Resource Potential of the White Mountains, Inyo and Mono Counties, California and Nevada", *Geology and Mineral Wealth of the Owen Region California,* Santa Ana CA: South Coast Geological Society, 1987.

Dodge, Natt N., *Flowers of the Southwest Deserts*, Globe AZ: Southwestern Monuments Association, 4th edition, 1958.

Donahoe, James L., and Edwin H. McKee, *Mineral Resource Potential Map of the Benton Rang Roadless Area,* Washington DC: U.S. Geological Survey Map MF 1317-C, 1983.

Downs, Theodore, *Fossil Vertebrates of Southern California*, Berkeley and Los Angeles CA: University of California Press, 1968.

Elias, Scott A., *The Ice-Age History of Southwestern National Parks,* Washington and London: Smithsonian Institution Press, 1997.

Egan, Ferol, *Fremont, Explorer for a Restless Nation,* Garden City NJ: Doubleday & Co., 1977.

Ekman, A, et al, *Old Mines and Ghost Camps of California*, Fort Davis TX: Frontier Book Company, 1970.

Farquhar, Francis P., *History of the Sierra Nevada*, Berkeley and Los Angeles CA: University of California Press, 1966.

Fischer, Pierre C., *70 Common Cacti of the Southwest,* Tucson AZ: Southwest Parks and monuments Association, 1989.

Fremont, John Charles, *Report of the Exploring Expedition to the Rocky Mountains in the year 1842, and to Oregon and north California in the years 1843-44,* Washington DC: U.S. 28th Congress, 2nd session House Ex. Doc. Np. 166, 1845.

Gamett, James, and Stanley Paher, *Nevada Post Offices, an Illustrated History,* Las Vegas NV: Nevada Publications, 1983.

Gath, Eldon, "Quarternary Lakes of the Owens River System", *Geology and Mineral Wealth of the Owens Valley Region California,* Santa Ana CA: South Coast Geologic Society, 1987.

Goodwin, J. Grant, *Lead and Zinc in California,* San Francisco CA: California Division of Mines, Volume 53, 1957.

Glass, Al and Mary, *Western Nevada,* Reno NV: Nevada Historical Society Guide Book Series (undated).

Grant, Cambell, James W. Baird, J. Kenneth Pringle, *Rock Drawings of the Coso Range,* China Lake CA: Maturango Museum Publication #4, 1968.

Grayson, Donald K., *The Deserts Past, A Prehistory of the Great Basin,* Washington DC: Smithsonian Institution Press, 1993.

Gore, Wilma Willis, "Ghost of a Skeleton Revisited", *The Album, Vol. V No. 4,* Bishop CA: Chalfant Press, August 1992.

Gudde, Erwin G., *1000 California Place Names,* Los Angeles, Berkeley CA: University of California Press, Second Revised edition, 1959.

_____, *California Gold Camps,* Berkeley, Los Angeles CA: University of California Press, 1975.

Hall, Clarence A., *Natural History Of The White-Inyo Range Eastern California,* Berkeley, Los Angeles, Oxford: University of California Press, 1991.

Hall, Wayne E., with E.M. MacKevett, *Economic Geology of the Darwin Quadrangle, Inyo County, California,* San Francisco CA: Special Report 51, California Division of Mines, 1958.

Harper, Kimball T., with Larry L. St. Clair, Kayne H. Thorne and Wilford M. Hess, editors, *Natural History of the Colorado Plateau and Great Basin,* Niwot CO: University of Colorado Press, 1994.

Harris, Stephen L., *Fire Mountains of the West,* Missoula MT: Mountain Press Publishing, 1988.

Hart, John, *Hiking The Great Basin,* San Francisco CA: Sierra Club Books, 1991.

Heizer, Robert F., and Martin Baumhoff, *Prehistoric Rock Art of Nevada and Eastern California,* Berkeley and Los Angeles CA: University of California Press, 1962.

Henry, Donald J., *California Gem Trails,* Long Beach CA: Lowell R. Gordon, 1957.

Hickman, James C., editor, *The Jepsom Manual,* Berkeley, Los Angeles, and London: University of California Press, 1996.

Hill, Mary, *Geology of the Sierra Nevada,* Berkeley, Los Angeles, and London: University of California Press, 1975.

Houghton, John G., Clarence M. Sakamoto, Richard O. Gifford, "Nevada's Weather and Climate", *Special Publication 2 Nevada Bureau of Mines and Geology,* Reno NV: University of Nevada, 1975.

Houghton, Samuel G, *A Trace of Desert Waters,* Reno NV: University of Nevada Press,, reprint of second edition, 1994.

Jaeger, Edmund C., *The California Deserts,* Stanford CA: Stanford University Press, Revised Edition, 1938.

_____, *The North American Deserts,* Stanford CA: Stanford University Press, 1957.

Jahns, Richard H., Editor, *Geology of Southern California*, San Francisco CA: California Division of Mines Bulletin 170, 1954.

Jeffrey, Joseph A., "The Sillimanite Group of Minerals", *California Journal of Mines and Geology Vol. 39, No. 3*, San Francisco CA: California State Division of Mines, July 1943.

Johnson, Russ and Anne, editors, *The Ancient Bristlecone Pine Forest,* Bishop CA: Chalfant Press, 1966.

Kelsey, Bill and Louise, "The Champion Spark Plug Mine", *The Album Vol. V, No. 4*, Bishop CA: Chalfant Press, October 1992.

Krauskopf, K.B., *Geologic Map of the Mt. Barcroft Quadrangle, California-Nevada*, Washington DC: U.S. Geological Survey Map GQ-960, 1971.

Langenheim, Virginia A.M., James L. Donahoe, and Edwin McKee, *Geologic Map of the Andrews Mountain, Mazourka, and Paiute Roadless Areas,* Washington DC: U.S. Geologic Survey Map MF-1492-A, 1982.

Lanner, Ronald M., *The Piñon Pine,* Reno NV: University of Nevada Press, 1981.

Leigh, Rufus Wood, *Nevada Place Names,* Salt Lake City UT: Deseret News Press, 1964.

Lewis, Ernest Allen, *The Fremont Cannon, High Up and Far Back,* Penn Valley CA: Western Trails Press, Revised Edition 1981.

Likes, Robert C., "Mono Mills to Bodie", *Desert Magazine*, Palm Desert CA: Desert Magazine, December 1971.

Lillard, Richard G., *Desert Challenge,* Lincoln NB: University of Nebraska Press, 1942.

Likes, Robert C. and Glenn R. Day, *From This Mountain - Cerro Gordo,* Bishop CA: Chalfant Press, 1975.

Lofnick, Swell "Pop", *Mojave Desert Ramblings*, China Lake CA: Maturango Museum, Publication 2, November 1966.

MacKevett, Edward M., *Geology of the Santa Rosa Lead Mine, Inyo County California,* San Francisco CA: California Division of Mines Special Report 34, 1953.

Merriam, Charles W., and Wayne E. Hall, *Pennsylvanian and Permian Rocks of the Southern Inyo Mountains, California,* Washington, DC: U.S. Geological Survey Bulletin 1061-A, Government Printing Office, 1957.

_____, *Geology of the Cerro Gordo Mining District, Inyo County California,* Washington DC: U.S. Geological Survey Professional Paper 408, Government Printing Office, 1963.

Mifflin, M.D. and M.M. Wheat, *Pluvial Lakes and Estimated Pluvial Climates of Nevada,* Reno NV: Nevada Bureau of Mines and Geology, Bulletin 94, Mackay School of Mines, University of Nevada, 1979.

Miller, C. Dan, *Potential Hazards from Future Volcanic Eruptions in California,* Washington DC: U.S. Geological Survey Bulletin 1847, Government Printing Office, 1989.

Mitchell, Roger, "Saga of Cerro Gordo", *Four Wheeler Magazine,* Tarzana CA: September 1965.

_____, *Inyo-Mono Jeep Trails,* Glendale CA: La Siesta Press, 1969.

_____, *Death Valley Jeep Trails,* Glendale CA: La Siesta Press, 1969, revised edition 1975.

_____, "Avalanche on Copper Mountain", *Desert Magazine,* Palm Desert CA: Desert Magazine, November 1975.

Munz, Phillip A., *California Desert Wildflowers,* Berkeley and Los Angeles CA: University of California Press, 1962.

Murdoch, Joseph, and Robert Wallace Webb, *Minerals of California,* San Francisco CA: California Division of Mines and Geology Bulletin 189, 1966.

Myrick, David F., *Railroads of Nevada, Volumes I & II,* Berkeley CA: Howell-North Books, 1962.

Nadeau, Remi, *City Makers,* Los Angeles CA: Trans-Anglo Books, 1965.

_____, *Ghost Towns and Mining Camps of California,* Los Angeles CA: Ward Ritchie Press, 1965.

_____, *The Silver Seekers,* Santa Barbara CA: Crest Publishers, 1999.

Norman, L.A. & Richard M. Stewart, *Mines and Mineral Resources of Inyo County,* San Francisco CA: California Division of Mines, January 1951.

Page, Ben M., *Talc Deposits of Steatite Grade, Inyo County California,* San Francisco CA: California Division of Mines Special Report 8, 1951.

Patraw, Pauline M., *Flowers of the Southwest Mesas,* Globe AZ: Southwest Parks and Monuments Association, 6th edition, 1977.

Peattie, Donald Culross, *A Natural History Of Western Trees,* Boston MA: Houghton Mifflin Co., 1953.

Preus, Charles, translated & edited by Erwin G. & Elizabeth K. Gudde, *Exploring With Fremont,* Norman OK: University of Oklahoma Press, 1958.

Ransome, Alfred L., "General Geology and Ores of the Blind Spring Hill Mining District, Mono County, California", *California Journal of Mines and Geology, Vol. 36, No. 2*, San Francisco CA: California Division of Mines, April 1940.

Rinehart, C. Dean, and Donald C. Ross, *Economic Geology of the Casa Diablo Mountain Quadrangle California*, San Francisco CA: California Division of Mines Special Report 48, 1956.

_____, and Donald Ross, *Geology and Mineral Deposits of the Mount Morrison Quadrangle Sierra Nevada, California,* Washington DC: U.S. Geological Survey Professional Paper 385, Government Printing Office, 1964.

Ross, Donald C., *Geology of the Independence Quadrangle, Inyo County, California*, Washington DC: U.S. Geological Survey Bulletin 1181-O, Government Printing Office, 1965.

Sampson, R.J., "Mineral Resources of Mono County", *California Journal of Mines and Geology, Vol. 36, No. 2*, San Francisco CA: California Division of Mines, April 1940.

Schumacher, Genny, with Dean Rinehart, Eden Vestal, and Bettie Willard, *Mammoth Lakes Sierra*, San Francisco CA: Sierra Club, 1959.

_____, editor, *Deepest Valley*, San Francisco CA: Sierra Club, 1962.

Sharp, Robert P., *Geology, Field Guide to Southern California*, Dubuque IA: Wm. C. Brown Company, 1972.

_____, and Allen F. Glazner, *Geology Underfoot in Death Valley and Owens Valley,* Missoula MT: Mountain Press Publishing Co., 1997.

Slemmons, David B., *Cenozoic Volcanism of the Central Sierra Nevada, California,* San Francisco CA: California Division of Mines and Geology Bulletin 190, 1966,

Smith, Jenny, editor, *Sierra East, Edge of the Great Basin,* Berkeley CA: University of California Press, 2000.

Snyder, C.T., George Hardman, and F.F. Zdenek, *Pleistocene Lakes In The Great Basin,* Washington DC: U.S. Geological Survey Misc. Geologic Investigations Map I-416, 1964.

Stone, Irving, *Men to Match My Mountains,* Garden City NJ: Doubleday & Co., 1956.

Stone, Paul, with Calvin H. Stevens, and Michael J. Orchard, *Stratigraphy of the Lower and Middle Triassic Union Wash Formation, East-Central California,* Washington DC: U.S. Geological Survey Bulletin 1928, Government Printing Office, 1991.

Storer, Tracy and Robert Unsinger, *Sierra Nevada Natural History,* Berkeley and Los Angeles CA: University of California Press, 1968.

Stinson, Melvin C., *Geology of the Keeler 15' Quadrangle, Inyo County, California,* San Francisco CA: California Division of Mines and Geology Map Sheet 38, 1977.

Strong, Mary Francis, "Inyo's Crystal Ridge", *Desert Magazine,* Palm Desert CA: Desert Magazine, July 1972.

_____, *Desert Gem Trails,* Mentone CA: Gem Books, 1996.

Townley, John M., *The Lost Fremont Cannon Guidebook,* Reno NV: The Jamison Station Press, 1984.

Tucker, W.B. and R.J. Sampson, "Recent Developments In The Tungsten Resources of California", *State Mineralogist's Report XXXVII, Vol. 37, No. 4,* San Francisco CA: California Division of Mines, April 1941.

Voge, Hervey, editor, *A Climber's Guide to the High Sierra,* San Francisco CA: Sierra Club, 1954.

Von Huene, Roland, *Fossil Mammals of the Indian Wells Valley Region and How to Collect Them,* China Lake CA: Maturango Museum Publication 5, 1971.

Ward, Grace B. and Onas M., *Colorful Desert Wildflowers,* Palm Desert CA: Best-West Publications, (undated).

Wedertz, Frank S., *Bodie 1859-1900,* Bishop CA: Chalfant Press, 1969.

_____, *Mono Diggins,* Bishop CA: Chalfant Press, 1978.

Weight, Lucile, "White Mountain Circle Tour", *Desert Magazine,* Palm Desert CA: Desert Magazine, October 1960.

Welsh, Liz and Peter Welsh, *Rock Art of the Southwest,* Berkeley CA: Wilderness Press, 2000.

Whitney, Stephen, *The Sierra Club Naturalist's Guide, Sierra Nevada,* San Francisco CA: The Sierra Club, 1979.

Wright, David A., "Sparks on the Mountain", *The Album, Vol. VI, No.1,* Bishop CA: Chalfant Press, Feb. 1993.

Index

Index

Index

Index

Index

Index